T3-BEE-737

ENGLISH MEN OF LETTERS

BEN JONSON

MACMILLAN AND CO., Limited
LONDON · BOMBAY · CALCUTTA · MADRAS
MELBOURNE

THE MACMILLAN COMPANY
NEW YORK · BOSTON · CHICAGO
DALLAS · SAN FRANCISCO

THE MACMILLAN CO. OF CANADA, Ltd.
TORONTO

ENGLISH *MEN* OF *LETTERS*

BEN JONSON

BY

G. GREGORY SMITH

GEN. THEO. SEMINARY
LIBRARY
NEW YORK

LONDON: MACMILLAN & CO., LIMITED
NINETEEN HUNDRED AND NINETEEN

92
J738

71418

COPYRIGHT

GEN. THEO. SEMINARY
LIBRARY
NEW YORK

CONTENTS

CHAPTER I

BEN JONSON

CHAPTER I

EARLY LIFE

WE know more of Jonson than of any of the greater writers of his age. There are no mysteries, or at least great mysteries, in his literary career, and the biographer is not driven, with the Shakespearians, to conjectural reconstruction from the shards of record and anecdote. Even his personality stands forth fresh and convincing beside the blurred portrait of Marlowe, or Shakespeare, or Fletcher. For this fuller knowledge we are indebted to Jonson himself. Hard fighters have few secrets, and he of all men was least willing to shirk open encounter. He has received poor thanks for thus revealing himself; and posterity, always willing to forgive the sins of youth and sack, has turned rather coldly from his virtues of honesty and self-reliance to his faults of harshness, pugnacity, and egotism; as, too, in its estimate of his art, it has chosen to forget altogether the poet of the Witches' Dimble in the academic and antiquary of Humours.

Ben claimed that he came of Annandale stock, presumably from one of the families of the turbulent Johnstones of that countryside.[1] The kinship may help to explain, if blood counts for anything, that vigour of self-assertion which he shows in all his actions, even from earliest youth. His grandfather, a "gentleman," had gone, so Jonson thought, from the Scottish border to Carlisle, and had been in the service of Henry VIII. His father had been forfeited in the reign of Mary, and after his enlargement had "turned minister," and so remained till his death in 1572 or 1573. Benjamin was a posthumous child, born, probably in Westminster, "a month after his father's decease." The exact date cannot be determined, and his mother's name is unknown. She, it appears, soon thereafter chose a bricklayer for her second husband, and young Ben removed with her to Hartshorne Lane, Charing Cross, where he began an apprenticeship to the hod. There is no evidence that he fared badly in his new home. Examination of the story of his unhappiness, at best a confused borrowing from Aubrey, Fuller, Walton, and Jonson himself, discloses no stepfatherly tyranny, and we know from a later episode recorded by the dramatist that he had not lost his mother's affection. He was educated at a school within the church of St. Martin's-in-the-Fields, and at Westminster. We may believe the anecdote that as he helped

[1] Jonson bore "the three spindles or rhombi" of the Johnstone blazon (*Conversations*, xvii.). There is ample evidence, from title-pages, official documents, and the works of contemporaries, that his surname was written in the usual English way, Johnson, though he deliberately dropped the "h" at times, perhaps under the influence of the Latin form. The shorter spelling is now universally accepted, partly, it may be, to avoid confusion with his namesake the Doctor.

his stepfather, perhaps after school-hours at St. Martin's, he attracted the notice of a passer-by, by his repeating of Latin verses, and was by his influence admitted to Westminster School. Tradition has identified this good fairy as the learned Camden, then second-master, and the episode as the beginning of Jonson's lifelong attachment to that

> most reverend head, to whom I owe
> All that I am in arts, all that I know,[1]

and of the senior's respect for one whom he was to describe in after years as a "most pregnant wit" and worthy of the admiration of "succeeding ages."[2]

Whether this Westminster relief from bricklaying was followed immediately, or at all, by residence at one of the Universities cannot be determined. The gossips Aubrey and Fuller state that he went to Cambridge— the one says to Trinity, the other to St. John's—and the former gives another and less likely version of the Westminster story, in which a bencher, happening to hear the boy reciting Homer as he worked on the garden-wall of Lincoln's Inn, offered him "some exhibition to maintain him at Trinity." Jonson's later remark to the poet Drummond, that "he was master of Arts in both Universities, by their favour, not his study," does not exclude the possibility of his having made plans for a University course, or of his having been for a short time in residence. The Cambridge records are silent;[3] and when we next hear of him, he is back at the craft "which

---

[1] *Epigrams*, XIV.   [2] *Remaines*, 1605.
[3] The Oxford association may date from Ben's rollickings with Corbet at Christ Church.

he could not endure." [1] Thus thwarted of his "wonted studies," he resolved to leave London and soon set out to seek his fortune with the English troops in the Low Countries. There was little to do there, but much to learn in rough camp-life with the Hungrys and Bobadils. On one occasion he had opportunity of showing his prowess in single combat " before both armies"; and in after years he was slow to forget how well he had proved himself by the killing of his man, and the taking of "*opima spolia* from him." Once again, in less honourable circumstance, he slew an opponent in a duel, and then had less reason to congratulate himself on the event; and we may believe that he could argue well with the cudgel and had trounced others besides the unfortunate Marston. In this habit of encounter we seem to read the secret of his literary quarrels in later life, when he fought and spoiled the poetasters and base fellows of the stage.

Between this military adventure abroad [2] and the beginning of his London career as a playwright, five or six years may have passed. It is certain that before the appearance of *Every Man in his Humour* in 1598 he had had some experience of the stage. Dryden tells us that he had made the venture "very unsuccessfully";

---

[1] Whether it was then or during his earlier spells of bricklaying that he snubbed a city madam in lines still familiar, may be left to the curious in Jest-book literature. See Aubrey, *Lives*, ed. Clark, ii. 16 n. Jonson, it may be noted, was the victim of two Jest-book ventures: *Penkethman's Jests* and *Ben Johnson's Jests*, both reprinted several times.

[2] Fleay has suggested that the author of *Wily Beguiled* (? Peele) c. 1596, drew Jonson in Fortunatus, "wafted safe from Mars his bloody fields."

and there was a persistent tradition that, like Shakespeare, he had some apprenticeship as an actor, at Paris
Garden and other "obscure playhouses." Henslowe
refers to him in his *Diary* both as a maker of plots and
as a player. Dekker's gibes in *Satiromastix*, even if taken
with some words of Jonson himself in *The Alchemist*,[1]
hardly prove, as some have thought, that one of his
parts was Hieronimo in Kyd's popular *Spanish Tragedy*,
unless the small stature of the marshal in *The First
Part of Jeronimo* had passed as a stage tradition. His
tall lank figure [2] and his plain features and pimpled skin [3]
were odds against his success in any but exceptional
rôles. Aubrey compares him with Shakespeare and
says "he was never a good actor, but an excellent
instructor." Sir Thomas Overbury had his *Wife* read to
the Countess of Rutland by Ben, who performed his
task "with an excellent grace";[4] and the Duchess of
Newcastle records the opinion of her husband "that
he never heard any man read well but Ben Jonson, and
yet he hath heard many in his time." Dekker, on the
other hand, makes one of his characters say, "It's cake
and pudding to me to see his face make faces when
he reads his songs and sonnets."[5]

We first learn of his association with the stage from

[1] IV. iv.

[2] "Horace was a goodly corpulent gentleman, and not so lean a
hollow-cheekt scrag as thou art" (*Satiromastix*, l. 2570). See *infra*,
p. 35, note. We learn from the same book (ll. 1517-1527) that
Ben played in Nash's *Isle of Dogs*.

[3] "Like a rotten russet apple when 'tis bruised," *ib.* l. 1894.
Aubrey says "he was (or rather had been) of a clear and fair skin."
The "dark pale face" of the "Apologetical Dialogue" is not offered
by Ben as a historical statement.

[4] *Convers.* xii.   [5] *Satiromastix*, l. 1899.

an acknowledgement by Henslowe, of the Rose Theatre, on 20th July 1597, of three shillings and ninepence "received of Bengemene Johnsone's share," and, on the same day, of an advance of four pounds. On 3rd December 1597, Ben made proposals for a new play, and, having undertaken to complete it by Christmas, got a further advance of twenty shillings from the same hand. A later payment of five shillings is recorded in the *Diary* on 5th January 1598. On 18th August 1598 he is named with Chettle and Porter as joint-author of a comedy, *Hot Anger soon Cold*, for the Admiral's Company —the earliest clue to his literary work, unless we accept the suggestion that he had a share, in 1597, as author as well as actor, in Nash's "imperfit embrion of his idle hours," the lost *Isle of Dogs*; and two months later (23rd October) we hear of Chapman's being paid for writing two acts for an unfinished tragedy, perhaps the very play promised by Jonson ten months before. These apparently trivial entries find their place in this brief memoir because of their bearing upon a crisis in the affairs of the Rose and of Ben himself in the autumn of 1598. They throw light on a dark place in the story ; and if they do not excuse the felony which nearly brought Jonson to the gallows, they help us to take a more generous view of his conduct.

It is clear that Jonson's slaughter of a fellow-actor, Gabriel Spenser, was in self-defence, and that his protest in later life that his honour was untouched was honest. His relations with Henslowe and the Admiral's men had been weakening since the mysterious cross-transactions on the 20th of July, and he had shown no desire to hasten on the work for which the manager clamoured.

Later facts compel the conclusion that he had resolved
to break with his colleagues, and to try his fortune with
the rival company of the Lord Chamberlain. We are
told that he offered a play, which he must have written
during the summer of 1598, to the manager of the
Curtain, and that the good offices of Shakespeare, then
a member of the company, secured its acceptance. We
cannot test this story of Shakespeare's part, but it is
now certain, thanks to a gossipy letter of one Tobie
Matthew, that the first performance of *Every Man in his
Humour* had taken place before the 20th of September.
This success at the Curtain boded ill for Henslowe and
his actors at the Rose. One of these, Gabriel Spenser,
who two years before had killed a man in a barber's
shop, chanced to meet Ben in the fields at Shoreditch.
What passed at this encounter on the 22nd of September,
who made the first taunt about traitors and robbers of
honest men's pockets, how Ben's soldierly arm and
three-shilling rapier came to give a mortal six-inch
wound in Gabriel's right side, need not now be matter
of speculation. For the law there was only one course;
and Jonson was committed and arraigned in October at
the Old Bailey for manslaughter. Henslowe's comment
is significant. Four days after the brawl, he craves
counsel of Edward Alleyn over the loss of one of his
company ("which hurteth me greatly"), slain "by the
hands of Benge[men] Johnson, *bricklayer*." [1] The designa-
tion measures very prettily the commercial man's sense
of disaster—two actors and one author lost, and the
rival Curtain the richer by one playwright and the

---

[1] Jonson's enemies were slow to forget the bricks. Dekker makes
persistent fun of the "mortar-treader."

bricklayer's *Every Man in his Humour*. But hard words
are less deadly than three-shilling rapiers, and these
were to be forgotten when the Rose again secured the
dramatist's favour.

Jonson escaped the gallows. He claimed benefit of
clergy, and was enlarged with no further penalty than
loss of goods and a Tyburn "T" on his left thumb.
We hear nothing later of the branding, and have reason
to think that, as no mark was found at his death,
the complaisant gaoler had applied a cold iron, not
the "hissing T." His defiant attitude to the judges,
for he would answer nothing "but Ay and No,"
delayed his freedom, and gave him some trouble with
"two damned villains" who spied upon him in prison.
There was suspicion of a Catholic plot, and his curt
replies had disturbed the Queen's agents. Later, he
confessed to Drummond that when he was in prison he
took his religion "on trust" from a priest who visited
him, and that for twelve years he was a recusant.

An early marriage, after his return from the Low
Countries, had not added to his happiness. He describes
his wife, whose name we do not know, as a shrew,
"though honest," and he told Drummond that for five
years (?1602–?1607) he lived apart from her in the
household of Lord Albany. In 1602 he found a
friend in "one Townsend," but it is not clear whether
this person, of whom we hear from Manningham, the
diarist, was the John Townsend who figures in certain
bonds to Henslowe, or, more probably, his friend
Aurelian, the poet, and whether "lives upon" means
that he was supported by him or lived with him. It
has been assumed that Ben was reunited to his wife,

after Albany's marriage in 1607, when we find him in a house in Blackfriars, where he wrote the dedication to *Volpone*. Aubrey records, on the authority of one who knew him, that "in King James's time" he lived without Temple Bar, at a comb-maker's shop, in the neighbourhood of the Elephant and Castle.[1] We have no further particulars of Jonson's wife, and it is mere conjecture on the part of Payne Collier that the record of a marriage in 1623 in St. Giles's, Cripplegate, between a Ben Jonson and a Hester Hopkins shows that Ben made a second matrimonial venture. We hear of three of his children—a daughter Mary, who died in infancy, a son, who succumbed in his seventh year to the plague which raged in 1603, and another son, who predeceased his father by two years. His affection for the first boy, "thou child of my right hand," is shown in his tale to Camden, and later to Drummond, of the appearance of his wraith at the hour of death, when he was in the country, at Connington House, the seat of the antiquary Cotton ; and in his lines of farewell.[2] There is no proof that other children, whose father is named Benjamin Jonson in contemporary registers, were the dramatist's offspring, legitimate or illegitimate.

Jonson's rough outsetting could not undo his self-confidence. "Fortune could never break him, or make him less"[3]—at least for some time to come. The threat of Tyburn passed as a bad dream, and, once more a free man, he was on terms again with managers and public, as if nothing had happened. Indeed, nothing had happened to mar his professional reputation, and Henslowe, pricked by his tradesman conscience, was

---

[1] *Lives*, ii. 12.   [2] *Epigr.* XLV.   [3] *Cynthia's Revels*, II. iii.

willing to forgive and be forgiven. There is some
show of fact that within two months of Jonson's
release the Children of the Chapel performed his play
The Case is Altered in their newly acquired theatre
in Blackfriars, and that an earlier version of that
comedy, as yet unseasoned with satire of Anthony
Munday, had been presented by them during the
summer of 1598, doubtless to the great annoyance of
Henslowe. The success of *Every Man in his Humour*
with the Chamberlain's Company and the reappearance
of *The Case is Altered*, towards the close of 1598,
darkened the prospects of the Rose, but Henslowe's
commercial instinct saved the situation. By August
1599 the "bricklayer" was again at work for his old
theatre, collaborating with Dekker in a tragedy, *Page
of Plymouth*, a bit of dramatic journalism on a recent
murder, and one of a series of plays of the type pur-
veyed at this date by Henslowe and his rival the Lord
Chamberlain; and in September of the same year he
was commissioned, with Dekker, Chettle, and others, to
furbish up another piece, *Robert II., King of Scots*.
Both plays, with some others written or botched at this
time, for bread and sack, if not for fame, have perished.
To this oblivion he probably gave no indifferent consent;
and their exclusion from the collected edition must be
interpreted as the older Jonson's judgement on early
hackwork and collaboration.

With the appearance, in 1599, of *Every Man out of
his Humour*, Jonson's literary career enters on another
phase. We do not pause to defend this separation of
the two like-named comedies, in seeming contradiction
of what we shall say later about the second as an

elaboration of the first, or in ignorance that in Jonson
of all men continuity of purpose is almost a fault.
The division here is not arbitrary, if we take the view
that in *Every Man in his Humour* the dramatist discovers
the purpose which he hints at in his part as Valentine
in *The Case is Altered*[1] about the same time, and that
in its successor he starts afresh with certain axioms and
begins his body of proof that the New Comedy can
justify its protest. This fuller development was, however, interrupted for a time; and it is in *Every Man
out of his Humour* that we read the first evidence, on
Jonson's side, of the disturbing forces.

The playwrights' quarrel of 1599–1602 is not a mere
"matter of antiquarism." It remains, by reason of its
vigour, its complicated character, and its range of action
and effect, one of the most memorable in the records of
literary seismology. It shook the citadel of letters so
intimately and at so many points that in any study
of Ben Jonson, however small the scale, it must have
some place. It was, in a very real sense, his quarrel.
His claim to pass censure on his neighbours for literary
and personal faults, and the frankness with which he
expressed himself in judgement were provocation direct.
The tone of his later conversations with Drummond
shows, with full allowance for exaggeration or error on
the part of his reporter, that Jonson laid about him
with a strange freedom in his encounter with the poor
poets and "miserable fellows." The reiteration of his
attacks and his persistency in the characterization of his
victims in the quarrel-plays, above all his sensitiveness
to the criticism which his opponents urged in their

[1] II. iv.

defence, supplied the conditions for tumult in any
Bohemia less quick-witted than theirs.

This Bohemia was in no mood to decline Jonson's
challenge. Never before, and rarely since, were the
ambitions and energies of literary youth so fretful of
restraint as in this London of the pontifical Ben. Text-
book commonplaces about wit-combats and shake-scene
jealousies have made us familiar with some of the more
spectacular aspects of this restlessness. Less frequently,
if at all, has attention been drawn to the general trans-
formation of literary habit, of which the give-and-take
at the Mermaid and St. Dunstan's was but a partial
expression. Literature had become, almost suddenly,
and at every turn, the plaything of the satirist. In
earlier periods in England, as in Greece and Rome, the
man with the scourge or the cynic with his laughter
had been a solitary; now the voices of the market-place
of letters had grown raucous, and every greater and
lesser Hall made free of his neighbour's character. In
this "dissension of poets among themselves," Francis
Meres saw something "very profitable," for "that ship
is endangered where all lean to one side." Profit or no
profit, there was certainty of no little "dissension" in
the fact that Jonson's chief opponent John Marston
was a satirist before he became a playwright, and had
in 1598 made some stir with his *Pigmalion's Image* and
Scourge of Villainy. Another cause of the general
disorder was the angry feeling engendered by the
sudden popularity of the "little eyases" of the Chapel.
This was, at first, a business quarrel, of the older actors
and of the playwrights who wrote for their houses, but
it contributed directly to the general hubbub among the

theatres. The natural alliance of the players with
Jonson's opponents made him a partisan of the Children.
The position of the latter was improved by his support,
and they in turn vexed his victims doubly hard by
piping the heavy satire of *Cynthia's Revels* and *The
Poetaster*. But the insolence of boy-actors could be
more easily forgiven than masterful Ben's assault on
vested interests.

The progress of this quarrel cannot be set out
here, except in the barest outline. Jonson, we have
seen, showed his hand in *Every Man out of His Humour*,
and the reference in the "Apologetical Dialogue" to
his having been worried for three years by the "petulant
styles" of the poetasters dates the origin of the trouble
about 1598. The beginnings of the feud are obscure.
There seems to have been some friction with Munday,
perhaps through his giving of offence in a play now lost.
Jonson does not appear to have retorted at once, and
the author of *Histriomastix* (in its recast form, probably
of 1599) avenged the insult in the character of Posthaste.
In the same play Ben is drawn, with no unfriendly
hand, in the character of Chrysogonus (Crysoganus). If
Marston was the author or reviser of this play, we may
assume that he was then on reasonably good terms with
Jonson. There had been no unkind reference to him
in the *Satires* of 1598, or in the stronger *Scourge of
Villainy* of the same year, for the Torquatus of the
latter is, on recent showing, Gabriel Harvey rather than
Jonson. But the intimacy of the sketch in *Histriomastix*,
however innocently intended, may have roused the
hypersensitive Ben, rather inclined, as Drummond tells
us, to interpret "best sayings and deeds often to the

worst." [1]   Jonson confided to Drummond that the
beginning of his quarrel with Marston was "that he
represented him in the stage," [2] but whether as
Chrysogonus or in another part in a lost play is left
to conjecture. [3] It is hard to believe that this joke in
Histriomastix was the only excuse for the thunders called
forth upon his old friend and on Munday, or that
Jonson was so touchy that he saw in Chrysogonus an
insolent identification with the rascal whom Cicero rated
in his defence of Roscius Amerinus.

Late in 1599, Jonson developed his attack in *Every
Man out of his Humour*, dedicated to the Gentlemen of the
Inns of Court, and performed by the Lord Chamberlain's
Company at the Globe. The interest of this "comical
satire," as it was called, is mainly as a contribution to
Jonson's theory of comedy, and as a general protest,
with small pretence to dramatic action, against contemporary methods. But, in addition, it discloses an
intimate satirical purpose. We have lost the clues to
the dramatist's originals, if they were ever clear; and
we must remember that he often protested that he
was not to be charged with direct representation of his
neighbours. Of two, however, we are allowed to be
certain. Asper of the Induction, "an ingenious and free
spirit, eager and constant in reproof, without fear
controlling the world's abuses—one whom no servile
hope of gain or frosty apprehension of danger can

---

[1] *Convers*. xix.   [2] *Ib*. xiii.

[3] Drummond's text may be faulty in punctuation—"represented
him in the stage, in his youth given to venerie." A full stop after
"stage" would extenuate Marston and refer the charge of
"venerie" to the pertinent matter which follows in Drummond's
gossip.

make to be a parasite, either to time, place, or opinion,"
is, with Macilente in the same play, Jonson himself, and
one of a series of portraits beginning with Valentine in
The Case is Altered and continued in Crites of *Cynthia's
Revels* and Horace of *The Poetaster*?[1] As yet Asper is
unwilling to break with Marston for his poor compliment
of Chrysogonus, but he cannot resist a thrust, to test
whether his friend has that "dead unfeeling sense"
which he will not acknowledge for himself.   His Carlo
Buffone is called a "Grand Scourge, or Second Untruss
of the Time,"[2] by the vain-glorious Puntarvolo; and his
Clove says: "Prithee, let's talk fustian a little and gull
them; make them believe we are great scholars,"[3] and,
to that end, borrows pedantries from the *Scourge of
Villainy* and *Histriomastix*.   Thus provoked, Marston
ventured on a second study of Jonson in Brabant Senior[4]
in *Jack Drum's Entertainment* (September 1600), where
he is pilloried among

> bombast wits,
> That are puft up with arrogant conceit
> Of their own worth; as if omnipotence
> Had horsed them to such unequalled height
> That they surveyed our spirits with an eye
> Only create to censure from above."[5]

Jonson prepared a second and heavier blow.   In
Cynthia's Revels, or the Fountain of Self-Love, which was
acted by the Children of the Chapel at the Blackfriars
in 1600 and printed in 1601, Marston is dragged
into the open, under the ugly name of Anaides or
"Impudence itself."   The author is disguised as

---

[1] So too in Dekker's *Satiromastix*: "You must be called Asper,
and Criticus, and Horace."   [2] II. i.   [3] III. i.
[4] Fleay doubts this (*Chron. of Eng. Drama*, ii. 74).
[5] IV. 316-320.

Crites ; [1] and it may be that Daniel, who had suffered as
Matthew in *Every Man in his Humour*, appears as Hedon
(Pleasure), Lodge as Asotus (Prodigal), and Munday as
Amorphus (Deformed), though Gabriel Harvey seems, in
the first act, to have the honour of model for the last
character. Mercury's description of Crites might well
be a jest in hyperbole were the author another than
Jonson. He is "a creature of a most perfect and divine
temper, one in whom the humours and elements are
peaceably met, without emulation of precedency . . .
in sum he hath a most ingenuous and sweet spirit." [2]
Let us say for excuse of Jonson that, being so concerned
with his general protest against the bad taste of the
age, or against fashions he would ascribe to others,
he sought to enhance his doctrine by exaggerated
eulogy of himself. *Cynthia's Revels* is a critical argument
rather than play, a "comical satire" making good the
lack of episode and movement with the spice of
personality. In it Jonson is angry as well as magisterial. Marston replied at once (? April 1601) in his
"slight-writ play" *What You Will*, where, in the Induction, but chiefly in the character of Lampatho Doria,
he touched Ben to the quick. In this encounter
Marston has the advantage in the art of attack, and
shows he is less minded to punish Jonson than to
provoke him to bad temper. When Doricus dreads
the censure of the author by auditors Snuff, Mew,
and Blirt, Philomuse, thinking haughtily of Jonson's
prologue quarrels with his public, asks them to
believe that

---

[1] Criticus is the form in the Quarto of 1601.   [2] II. i.

> his spirit
> Is higher blooded than to quake and pant
> At the report of Scoff's artillery.
> Shall be crestfallen, if some looser brain
> In flux of wit uncivilly befilth
> His slight composures ? [1]

Though Quadratus, Marston's proxy in the play, describes Lampatho as a "fusty cask, devote to mouldy custom," and the "snaffle to freer spirits" [2] he does not rely only on the battery of epithet. He retorts by parodying the lines of Crites, more often by referring ironically to Ben's arrogance. "He is very nectar; if you but sip of his love, you were immortal." [3] So again, when Lampatho cries revenge upon him for wronging his muse, the retort is, "How prithee? In a play. Come, come be sociable." And when he cries out, "Why, you Don Kynsader! [4]—a merry hit at his own Satires — he nimbly scores a point against Crites, who had no knowledge of such tricks of self-criticism.

The summer or early autumn of 1601 saw the crisis of the quarrel—Jonson's third and heaviest onslaught in The Poetaster and Dekker's first and last in his Satiromastix. Ben spent only fifteen weeks on his "Arraignment" [5] of the "base detractors and illiterate apes." The opening lines of Envy, followed by a prologue in armour, are frank confession of resentment of the insults from Marston and his friends. He arms his prologue with no hint of whimsical purpose, but to show "in allegory" that a "well-erected confidence"

---

[1] Induct. ll. 25-30.   [2] II. i.
[3] IV. i.   [4] II. i.
[5] The full title is Poetaster, or His Arraignment.

can fight the pride of his gainsayers. We see how
the satire of *What You Will* had gone home, when his
accoutred eyas requests the house not to believe him
arrogant, however much the "common spawn of
ignorance" may "beslime" his fame.   He offers
no quarter to Democritus (Dekker) and Crispinus
(Marston); he represents himself in the character of
Horace (more shadowy than his Crites), and calls in
Virgil as judge. It is hard to believe that this Virgil
is a mask for Shakespeare; less hard that it is the
friendly Chapman; perhaps easiest that there is no
personal clue, and that Jonson invokes the spirit of
Classicism to act as arbiter in his cause against the
ribald poetasters. Yet it is significant that at this
stage of the 'Poetomachia' Shakespeare is associated
with Jonson in some way. We have the statement in
the *Return from Parnassus* of this year, that "our fellow
Shakespeare" had given a "purge" to the "pestilent"
Horace for his treatment of his fellow-poets; the quip
in *Troilus and Cressida* (probably of the same year) about
an armed prologue; Shakespeare's connexion with the
Chamberlain's Company; and some remarks by Ben,
especially on *Julius Cæsar*, also of 1601.[1]   Perhaps
this hitting and parrying was the public's instalment
of the Mermaid 'wit-combats'; perhaps the making
of the tradition of these more or less legendary
encounters. It may be that the reference in the
Return from Parnassus expresses a contemporary conviction that Shakespeare had already come between
Ben and popular success; that he had outstripped

[1] See the list of passages in *Notes and Queries*, 9th Ser. ix. p.
282.

him, even on his own ground; that Falstaff had ousted Bobadil; that Ben's early ambitions in tragedy had suffered eclipse. Considerations of this kind appear to have some force when we speculate on the lull in Jonson's activity after his onslaught on the poetasters.

The counter-plot of the Chamberlain's men came to a head in Dekker's *Satiromastix, or the Untrussing of the Humorous Poet*, which was produced in the autumn (? Sept.) of 1601. "Horace," says the Prologue ('To the World'), in the print of 1602, "haled his Poetasters to the Bar; the Poetasters untrussed Horace: how worthily either, or how wrongfully, leave it to the Jury. Horace, questionless, made himself believe that his Burgonian wit might desperately challenge all comers, and that none durst take up the foils against him. It's likely, if he had not so believed, he had not been so deceived, for he was answered at his own weapon." The answer, notwithstanding its harshness, is on the whole fair, against Ben's abiding fault of arrogance, his libels on soldiers, courtiers, actors, good burgesses and their wives, his satire in Lupus on the administration of the law, and the indecent fun of his "Arraignment" at the expense of Marston and Dekker. Jonson, out-matched, not so much by harsh satire as by a more effective appeal to public opinion, covered his retreat with an "Apologetical Dialogue" (" only once spoken on the stage," but inserted in the Folio of 1616), in which he protested that in his *Poetaster* he was never "more innocent or empty of offence," that he had chidden vices not persons, and certainly not true soldiers, and that the only fault which his enemies found in his play was that it was his. But the close of

the "Dialogue" shows that Jonson is done with defiance
and debate—for a time.

> I leave the monsters
> To their own fate.   And, since the Comic Muse
> Hath proved so ominous to me, I will try
> If Tragedy have a more kind aspect.
> Her favours in my next I will pursue.

So ended the stage-quarrel. Its importance as a
biographical key will become clear to the reader who
will examine the evidence more closely than is possible
in this memoir. Few controversies in the satirical vein
appear to yield so much that may be accepted as fact,
or to bring conviction by the reiteration of details.
Peace came with the complete exhaustion of the fighters.
Marston had said nothing since his attack in *What You
Will*, and was to be silent for nearly three years ; Dekker
had spent himself, though to some purpose, in his
Satiromastix ; and Jonson, who had opened the artillery
of *The Poetaster* of set purpose to secure his authority
once and for ever, found himself a refugee from his
kingdom for four years. When the fatigue of encounter
is over and Jonson and Marston next write for the stage,
they appear as authors metamorphosed. Marston's and
Dekker's wand had turned the propagandist of the
Comedy of Humours into a botcher of tragedies for
Henslowe, then into a confessed votary of the serious
Muse ; Jonson's had transformed Marston's art to the
fashion for which he had fought so strenuously. It was
a critics' battle.

The immediate effect on Ben Jonson was that he
returned to tragedy, on which his reputation, when
Meres wrote in 1598, had solely rested. He set to

work again in his old way as a maker of "additions."
We are told that he had some share in a lost play,
Richard Crookback, and also in the refurbishing of Kyd's
Spanish Tragedy, for which he received ten pounds from
Henslowe; and there is reason to believe that it was
his success in editing the latter which stimulated
Shakespeare to the *rifacimento* of Kyd's *Hamlet*.   There
followed in 1603 the more deliberate study of *Sejanus,
his Fall*, in which Jonson, in collaboration with another,
made the first official declaration of his views on tragedy.
The piece was performed at the Globe, with Shakespeare in the cast.   When the play was printed in 1605,
Jonson replaced the passages by the "second pen,"
which are more likely to have been Chapman's than
Shakespeare's, with others of his own, "no doubt less
pleasing." [1]   His plea that he would not "defraud so
happy a genius of his right" by "loathed usurpation"
may be taken at its face-value.   Collaboration could
never have been a comfortable arrangement for Ben,
and he had then reached the point of declaring against
it once and for all.   Some reason of this kind must be
found for his strict suppression of all his earlier work,
and for his revision of *Sejanus* when he had determined
to make it the first exposition of his purpose in tragedy.
On the other hand, though he was careful to eliminate
all that was not exclusively his own from the authorized
edition of his *Works*, it is by no means improbable
that in the hard circumstances of his later life he was
sometimes glad to help a manager or an author with an
"addition."   Two plays are said to disclose his hand
in places—*The Bloody Brother, or Rollo, Duke of Normandy*,

[1] *Infra*, p. 197.

mainly by Fletcher, and written before 1637, and *The Widow*, the "lewd play" of Evelyn's note in 1662, which is generally allowed to be Middleton's. But all is conjecture, and though Jonson's alleged eking of other men's work be provocation to the antiquaries, it is to others an excuse for the compliment of silence.

CHAPTER II

THE fortune of the stage-war, not his own liking, had driven Jonson to tragedy. But it was a short refuge, for though he turned to it once again, in *Catiline*, in 1611, he soon regained his public place as the playwright of the Humours, and discovered a fresh literary opportunity in the entertainment of the Court. The accession of James I. marks the turning-point in his development. Though James was attracted by Jonson's erudition, it is hard to believe that the latter, with his theory of divine right in letters and his record of controversy, could accept the risks of a career as Court poet on the ordinary conditions. Yet it happened that by his own vigour rather than by any courtierly adaptability he achieved success greater than any contemporary poet. He did little or nothing to conciliate antagonisms, and as age and ill-health came upon him showed that he had no courtier's reserve of amiable cunning to counter his opponents. He was certainly never again tempted to the extravagance of the cancelled lines in honour of the Queen at the close of *Every Man out of his Humour*, which "many seemed not to relish" but which were, for his own stubborn sake rather than in devotion to "the Blessed, Divine, Unblemisht, Sacred, Pure" Eliza, printed with "reasons" in the Quarto. He was more truly "in his humour" when he expressed the wish that he had been a "churchman," to "make one sermon to the King," and promised himself that "he would not flatter, though he saw death";[1] or when on another occasion he protested that "he never esteemed of a man for the name of a lord."[2] Enemies like Dekker suggested that he was glad "to write out of the courtier element," only when his plays were misliked at Court.[3]

Jonson's first chance came at Lord Spencer's house at Althorpe, where Queen Anne and Prince Henry, resting on their way to London, heard his Entertainment of *The Satyr* (25th June 1603), a fantasy of Mab and her elves, in strange contrast with the pranks of his Knowells and Tuccas or the rhetoric of his Romans. This introduction to the new Court did not however secure for him the honour of writing the first masque. In January 1604, his rival Daniel, a "good honest man" but "no poet," produced his *Vision of the Twelve Goddesses*. In *Every Man in his Humour* he had been pilloried as a plagiary;[4] and when his *Defence of Rhyme* appeared in reply to Campion's tract (1602), Jonson wrote, as he told Drummond, an answer to both, but with special point against Daniel. Jonson was in no mood to enjoy the *Vision of the Twelve Goddesses*. He was present at the performance in the company of his friend Sir John Roe, but for some reason, of which no hint is given in their record of the episode, he was "ushered

---

[1] *Convers.* xiii.   [2] *Ib.* xiv.
[3] *Satiromastix*, l. 2633.   [4] V. i.

from" the hall (Sir John says "thrust out") by the
Chamberlain, Lord Suffolk. We may guess that Jonson
was too free in censure, in the unkind way of which
Daniel makes general complaint in his introduction;
perhaps too hilarious with his friend, who, as he tells
us, was "an infinite spender" and apparently a good
fellow.[1]

> God threatens Kings, Kings Lords, as Lords do us,

says Roe in amused recollection. This *contretemps* had
however no lasting effect, for, nine months later, Jonson
shared with his old antagonist Dekker the honours of
The King's Entertainment in passing to his Coronation,
which doubtless pleased James by its learning and its
compliments to his pose as The Peacemaker; and a few
days afterwards (19th March 1604) he saluted James
in a *Panegyre* on his going to his first Parliament.
Other pieces in this kind followed, and in January 1605
he began his remarkable series of Masques at Court.
The grudge against Daniel remained, and found expression perhaps in the passage on Italian taste in *Volpone*,[2]
certainly in the prefatory account of the masque
Hymenæi and elsewhere.

Meanwhile, Jonson had renewed his relationship with
the popular stage. Ill-luck met him at his first venture.
He had joined his old friend Chapman and Marston,
the latter of whom had declared his complete reconciliation in the dedication and epilogue of *The Malcontent*
(1604), in writing a comedy of city-life, entitled *Eastward Ho*, which was performed with success by the

---

[1] Later, Roe " died in his arms, of the pest," and Ben advanced
£20 for expenses (*Convers.* xii.).

[2] III. ii.

Queen's Revels Children before Christmas 1604. The play was witty, and on the whole harmless, but in one place a northern courtier found a covert attack on Scotland, and, by easy reasoning, on the King. Seagull's gibe about the Scots' liking for England,[1] and the first gentleman's mockery of the royal accent [2]—both already stale subjects for southern jesting—were treated by the King as the informer Sir James Murray had hoped, and the writers were thrown into prison. Jonson chivalrously declined to be excused his share of punishment, though his part in the collaboration had been small, and he was not the author of the offending words. He escaped sentence of mutilation, and on his enlargement, about Christmas 1604, made a feast for his friends, including Selden and his old patron Camden. Jonson's mother, of whom we know so little, drank to her son, and showed him a paper " which she had (if the sentence had taken execution) to have mixed in the prison among his drink, which was full of lusty strong poison, and that she was no churl, she told she minded first to have drunk of it herself." [3] There is perhaps a touch of melodrama in the tale ; but it is helpful family evidence to our understanding of Ben's character. Jonson, however, cannot have been in serious danger, for he had been commanded to write the Queen's Masque for 6th January 1605, and the Court could ill afford to lose its frolic at this late date, however indiscreet he or his friends had been.

This misfortune was not the only one of the kind which befell Jonson about this time. He told Drummond that he had been summoned before the

---

[1] III. iii.   [2] IV. i.   [3] *Convers.* xiii.

Council, at the instance of Lord Northampton (one of
whose retainers he had drubbed on St. George's Day,
1605), for his *Sejanus*, and had been accused by him of
popery and treason.   There is no evidence that he was
incarcerated on this charge ; but in a remarkable letter
to the Earl of Salisbury he makes complaint that he
had been committed to a "vile prison" with Chapman,
"unexamined and unheard," on account of some un-
named play.   Some arguments have been advanced to
show that the cause of offence was *Sir Giles Goosecap*,[1]
now ascribed to Chapman, and, as his first effort for the
Children of the Chapel, likely to have had Jonson's
revision ; and the reference to his "first error," in the
same letter, has been ingeniously interpreted as an
allusion to Nash's *Isle of Dogs*,[2] not to *Eastward Ho*.   In
the restless public mood of the early years of the new
reign it was hard for any man, much less Ben, to escape
giving offence or being credited with malpractices.   Yet,
unfortunate as he was, he had more than an ordinary
share of good-luck in recovering himself.   He had lived
in charmed security against the severest penalties for
manslaughter, libel, and nonconformity, had quarrelled
with and beaten old friends and won them again, had
lost caste with the managers of theatres and been coaxed
once more for plays, had scuffled in Bohemia and been
the flattered poet at country - houses and in Court
festivity.   Only once and most gallingly had his reserve
force, his belief in himself and in his literary ideals,
failed him ; but the humiliation had been brief.

[1] A full discussion will be found in M. Castelain's *Ben Jonson*,
Paris, 1907 (Appendix C).   The letter is endorsed ' 1605.'
[2] See M'Kerrow, *Works of Thomas Nashe*, v. 30.

During this time, when, as has been noted, he fell thrice into the clutches of the law, he wrote, in May 1604, an *Entertainment of the King and Queen* (sometimes styled *Penates*[1]), for Sir William Cornwallis's House at Highgate; and for the Court, on Twelfth Night, 1605, a masque of *Blackness*, the first of his "Queen's Masques." Evidence of his revived confidence comes later, in 1605, in the production at the Globe of *Volpone, or The Fox*, a re-exposition, but with greater breadth of human interest, of the theory of comedy which he had enunciated in *Every Man in his Humour*. It is the old Ben who protests in the prologue against

> some, whose throats their envy failing,
> Cry hoarsely, all he writes is railing,

and reminds us of the proud and angry leave-taking in the "Apologetical Dialogue." Like a restored prince he wipes out the years of exile from his calendar. When he dedicates the play to the "Two Famous Universities," in 1607, he rates, once more, the miserable traffic of the poetasters, and, in denouncing their "petulant styles" (the very words of the "Dialogue"), says: " I choose rather to live graved in obscurity, than share with them in so preposterous a fame "; and, "if my Muses be true to me, I shall raise the despised head of Poetry again, and, stripping her out of those rotten and base rags wherewith the times have adulterated her form, restore her to her primitive habit, feature, and majesty, and render her worthy to be embraced and kist of all the great and master-spirits of our world." Marston and Dekker had chidden in vain. The chastened author of *The Malcontent* had made his peace and commended

[1] The title was given by Gifford.

Sejanus in verse; but Jonson yielded nothing. Marston was the first to cry out, in his note ("To the General Reader") introducing his *Wonder of Women, or the Tragedy of Sophonisba*, in 1606, where he declares that "to transcribe authors, quote authorities, and translate Latin prose orations into English blank verse hath, in this subject, been the least aim of my studies." With this plain countercheck to his praise of *Sejanus* the disillusioned Scourger declines further controversy and forsakes the theatre for the calm of a country living.

At the close of the year we find Jonson involved in some obscure business in connexion with the investigations into the Gunpowder Plot. He tells us, in a letter to Lord Salisbury,[1] that he had been commissioned by the Council to get what evidence he could from priests, under promise of safety, but that, notwithstanding promise of help from the chaplain to the Venetian ambassador, he had failed of his purpose. "All so enweaved in it," he says, "as it will make 500 gent. less of the Religion within this week, if they carry their understanding about them"; and he adds, "For myself, if I had been a priest, I would have put on wings on such an occasion, and have thought it no adventure, where I might have done, besides His Majesty and my country, all Christianity so good service." There is no suspicion of dishonour in the transaction, and it is not likely that he had any intimate knowledge of the ramifications of the plot. It is not necessary to hint that his Catholic sympathies thwarted the hopes of the

[1] *State Papers* (*Domestic*), James I., xvi. No. 30, quoted from the MS. by M. Castelain, and printed in précis in the *Calendar* of 1603–1610, p. 245. The date is 8th Nov. 1605.

Court; or reasonable, in the light of our knowledge of his character, to charge him with double-dealing. The main biographical interest of the episode is that he, a known recusant, who had, during his first imprisonment, defied the Council and their emissaries, was now in their confidence and above fear of reprisal when he confessed his inability to find an informer. It may be that his recusancy was already weakening, although a few years were yet to elapse before he was reconciled to the Church of England.[1]

Between this date and the early years of Charles's reign lies the period of Jonson's fullest activity and success. The favours of the Court and "Great Ones" distracted him for a time from following up the popular triumph of *Volpone*. He was, as his enemies often reminded him, a slow writer; and the claims of his patrons occupied his energies for nearly four years in producing such spectacular pieces as the marriage masques of *Hymenæi* (1606) and *The Hue and Cry after Cupid* (1608), the second of the Queen's Masques, *Beauty* (1608), and the masque of *Queens* (1609). But in 1609 he returned to the stage with *Epicœne, or the Silent Woman*, "that pattern of a perfect play," as Dryden chose to call it; and in 1610 he added *The Alchemist*, in which by good situation and ridicule of the tribe of imposters he may be said to have achieved his masterpiece in satirical comedy. He wrote no more in this kind for other four years, but in the interval he produced *The Speeches at Prince Henry's Barriers* (1611),

---

[1] *Convers.* xiii. If Jonson's 'twelve years' (*supra*, p. 8) is an accurate statement, he would appear to have abjured his recusancy about 1610.

the masques of *Oberon* (1611), *Love freed from Ignorance and Folly*, and *Love Restored* (? 1611), *A Challenge at Tilt* and the *Irish Masque* (1613), with *Catiline* (1611), his last acknowledged attempt in tragedy (if we exclude the mere fragment of *Mortimer, his Fall*) and a first book of *Epigrams*, licensed in 1612 but published in 1616.

This literary record is interrupted by an episode which brings us once again into direct personal touch. Sir Walter Raleigh, then a prisoner in the Tower, had sought aid from "the best wits in England" in the preparation of his *History of the World*, and Jonson, according to Drummond's report, gave him some material for his chapter on the Punic War.[1] We know, too, that the verses, "The Mind of the Frontispiece to a Book,"[2] which introduced the volume in 1614, are from Jonson's pen. The Mermaid, in Bread Street, where Raleigh had brought together the wits and antiquaries of London, had established an intimacy between the two men; and Jonson happened for a short time to be a fellow-prisoner in the Tower, together with their common friend, the witty John Hoskyns. Early in 1613, Sir Walter employed the poet as governor to his eldest son Walter during a visit to France, an arrangement happily timed for Jonson, as all plans for the writing or presentation of masques at Court had been interrupted by the death of Prince Henry in November 1612. The same event had deprived Inigo Jones of his surveyorship to

[1] This is discredited by a writer in the *Camb. Hist. of Eng. Lit.* (iv. 59) as a Jonsonian boast made "over his cups"; but Mr. C. H. Firth has shown (*Proceedings of the British Academy*, viii., 30th October 1918) that the claim may not be thus easily dismissed.

[2] "The Mind of the Frontispiece" is not a *sonnet*, as stated in the *Camb. Hist. of Eng. Lit.* (*u.s.* p. 63).

the Prince and had induced him to return to Italy for
further professional study. The young Raleigh was
"knavishly inclined," and among other frolics caused
the poet one merry day to be "dead drunk, so that he
knew not where he was." Thereafter, in Drummond's
version, his pupil "laid him on a car, which he made to
be drawn by pioneers through the streets, at every corner
showing his governor stretched out, and telling them
that was a more lively image of the Crucifix than any
they had." This frank story is supplemented by the
remark that the youth's mother "delighted much, saying
his father young was so inclined, though the father
abhorred it." The Parisian escapade corroborates the
testimony from many quarters of Ben's festive habits.
Drummond, perhaps scandalized by his guest's conduct
at Hawthornden or vexed at the draining of his cellar,
makes the unfriendly remark that drink was "one of
the elements in which he liveth"; and Aubrey passes on
gossip that need not be disputed, to the effect that "he
would many times exceed in drink (canary was his
beloved liquor), then he would tumble home to bed,
and, when he had thoroughly perspired, then to study."
There must have been more sack than could be "perspired" on that night when he lay "looking to his great
toe, about which he hath seen Tartars and Turks,
Romans and Carthaginians, fight in his imagination." [1]
The only other detail recorded of the visit to Paris
is that he informed the Cardinal du Perron that his
translations of Virgil "were naught." What the Cardinal
said, or thought afterwards, of the opiniative Englishman
and his views of paraphrase, the *Perroniana* has not

[1] *Convers.* xiii.

preserved. Before Jonson's return the Court had laid
aside its mourning for the Prince, in preparation for the
marriage of the Princess Elizabeth. Campion had his
opportunity, as Chapman and Francis Beaumont had
theirs, of writing a masque for the festivities; and
again, in December 1613, for the Somerset - Essex
marriage. Jonson was back in time to contribute his
Challenge at Tilt in honour of the latter; and, two days
later, his *Irish Masque* was performed.

Jonson's next comedy, *Bartholomew Fair*, was produced by the Princess Elizabeth's Company at the Hope,
in the Bankside, on 31st October 1614, and, on its
repetition at Court next day, was ushered in by a short
Prologue to the King. It is slighter in construction
than its predecessors, more deliberate as a transcript
from life, and more directly contemporary in its satire.
In its extravagance Jonson seems to seek relief from the
austerities of his unsuccessful *Catiline*. He is conscious
of the *volte-face*, and in the Epilogue to the King asks
whether he has wandered beyond the "scope of writers."
The play is an amazing picture of London low-life, showing how well Jonson knew every corner and habit of
sloppy Smithfield, and how much more than a critic-
pedant he was who created Ursula and her bedraggled
company. The motive of *The Alchemist* is re-expressed
about this time—perhaps as a result of its success on the
stage — in a masque, entitled *Mercury Vindicated from
the Alchemists*.

The Devil is an Ass, which was acted by the
King's Company at the Blackfriars in 1616, completes
the group of Jonson's Jacobean comedies. He wrote
no more for the popular stage till 1625, but devoted

himself to the making of masques. Their titles form a
long list. Beginning with *The Golden Age Restored* and
Christmas his Masque (1616), he added between 1617
and 1619 *The Vision of Delight, Lovers made Men, Pleasure
reconciled to Virtue*, and the supplementary antimasque
For the Honour of Wales; then, after his return from
Scotland, *News from the New World discovered in the
Moon* and *The Metamorphosed Gipsies* (1621), *The Augurs*
(1622), *Time Vindicated to Himself and to his Honours*
(1623), *Neptune's Triumph* (1624), *Pan's Anniversary*
(? 1624), and *The Fortunate Isles* (1625). In 1616, too,
Jonson saw through the press the first volume of his *Works*,
on which he would appear to have been engaged during
1612—a manifesto, endorsed by laudatory verse from
the pens of Selden, Chapman, Francis Beaumont, and
others, that whatever more he might hope to do, he had
now a place which posterity would acknowledge. This
Folio contains all the plays before *Catiline* (excluding
The Case is Altered) together with the earlier Entertainments and the Masques down to January 1616, the
Epigrams, and a miscellany of verses known as the
Forest, which was to have a sequel in the *Underwoods*
of the second volume. Perhaps the publication of this
volume was not unconnected with James's expression of
his appreciation of the poet in the grant of a pension of
one hundred marks (3rd Feb. 1617). Between 1618 and
1621 Jonson was silent, but of his movements during
this interval we have some information, especially of
his journey to Scotland and his visit to Oxford.

The descent of King James and his northern Court
on London in 1603 had not put Englishmen in good
humour with things Scottish, but the hearty welcome

to the King and his English retinue during the visit in
1617, the elaborate arrangements for the royal progress
(witness the endless fuss in the records of the Scottish
Privy Council), and the reports circulated when all were
safely back in the South, had aroused some curiosity in
the sister kingdom. Jonson may have had some of that
"salmonlike instinct to revisit his native waters," which
had compelled James northward, some desire to see the
haunts of his Border kin. Other travellers, such as
the Water Poet, who, as Ben averred, followed him "to
scorn him,"[1] were merely curious persons, stricken with
the itch of pilgrimage and book-making. Jonson's verse-
story of his "Adventures," which was lost when his
library was burned, could not have been mere wayfaring
gossip, in the manner of Coryat or Lithgow. It was to
have borne the significant title of "A Discoverie," and,
as Drummond hoped, to have established the fame of
the Scottish scenery, so highly praised by the wanderer.
Towards the end of June, Ben set out on foot—no small
enterprise for that "mountain belly," of which he often
made jocular plaint.[2] Bacon, hitting at his heavy gait
and at the absence of a proper equipage for the master-
poet's tour, remarked facetiously that "he loved not to

[1] The Water Poet protested that he had not gone to Scotland
"either in malice or mockage of Master Benjamin Jonson"
(*Penniless Pilgrimage*, Address to Reader).
[2] Cf. *The Staple of News* (Induct.), *The Magnetic Lady*, I. i.,
III. iv., *Expost. with I. Jones, Underwoods*, VII. LXXI. LXXIII.
LXXV. He had become corpulent about his fortieth year. Macilente
(Jonson) in *Every Man out of his Humour* is described by Carlo
as a "raw-boned anatomy" who "walks up and down like a
charged musket" (IV. iv.). This is not the later Jonson, the
Seignior Multicarni of Suckling's *Sad One* (1659), who weighed
20 stones less 2 lb. (*Underwoods, u.s.*).

see Poesy go on other feet than poetical dactylus and spondaeus." Jonson tramped on and reached Edinburgh early in August 1618, before his friend the Sculler. They did not meet till September, in the house of a Leith worthy, Master John Stuart, when Jonson gave the Water Poet, then on his way south, a piece of gold to drink his health in England : diplomatically done, if there was risk of tales of Poesy's convivialities in the North or of unkind censures in the *Penniless Pilgrimage.* "So with a friendly farewell," says the Water Poet, "I left him as well as I hope never to see him in a worse state ; for he is amongst noblemen and gentlemen that know his true worth." Jonson may have gone to Annandale; he seems to have been in the lower West Highlands, near Loch Lomond; but most of his time was spent in the capital and its neighbourhood. The burgesses of Edinburgh gave him the freedom of the city, and everybody vied to do him honour. His chief hosts were the poet William Drummond and his friends, of whom Ben speaks kindly in his correspondence. From about Christmas till the middle of January he spent his time at Drummond's seat at Hawthornden, seven miles south of Edinburgh. Legends have grown up regarding this memorable visit, but there is no evidence that Ben undertook the journey by invitation or was acquainted with Drummond before; and when the modern tourist is shown the tree under which the two poets discoursed, he is not asked to picture to himself the rigours of a northern winter. We get into closer touch with Ben and his host in a corner in the University Library at Edinburgh, where the volumes which once filled the shelves of Hawthornden are now preserved. To the book-loving Ben these had been familiars and doubtless prompters (good Leith canary aiding) of many of the censures of the poets and reminiscences of London life handed down in the *Conversations*. Jonson played the grand seignior to this little northern coterie, and was perhaps not a little tried by his admiring hosts. It may be that he would have toned down some of his 'censures' and left others unsaid had he suspected there was a chiel taking notes of all the off-hand hyperboles of conversation; and it may be that Drummond showed, as some have thought, an unfriendly delight in repeating these and Ben's confessions about himself, or, as Coleridge cruelly hints, an inability to distinguish between jest and earnest. We have to reckon too with the failing of all note-takers that they jot down only the things that are most vigorous or unexpected. What they give us is but a fragment, as unsatisfactory to us when we try to recover the total effect of a man's conversation as it would appear to those who heard him talk. We are reminded by M. Jusserand[1] of Taine's remark on the Goncourts' record of literary gossip: "Yes, maybe all this was said, but if this only had been said, more than one among us would never have gone again." The visit was a severe pleasure to Drummond; and it has ever been the right of a good host to sigh relief when the entertaining of greatness is well over. "Ben," says Drummond, "was a great lover and praiser of himself, a contemner and scorner of others"; and the laird was at times tempted to forget his guest's virtues (though these he has put handsomely on record) when Ben ruled

[1] *A Literary History of the English People*, iii. 375.

his house during a whole winter-month. They parted good friends, and their later correspondence about *impresas* and other antiquarian curiosities gives proof of their mutual respect. Jonson started southward from Leith on 25th January 1619, again on foot, in an old pair of shoes which had brought him from Darnton (? Darlington)—poor comfort on the heavy roads, for "they were appearing like Coryat's," and "for the first two days he was all *excoriate.*" He had written little or nothing, except some rough drafts on subjects suggested by his visit, which he had directed to be sent to Drummond if he died by the way. Drummond, on his part, fulfilled an undertaking to forward descriptions of Edinburgh, Loch Lomond, and other places. The line

> The heart of Scotland, Britain's other eye

is all that remains of a poem on Edinburgh; and a "fisher or pastoral play," with Loch Lomond as the setting, appears to have been interrupted, or to have been lost at the burning of his library, with the poem on his Scottish adventures already mentioned, and notes on Pinkie, the 'government of Edinburgh,' the curricula at the Universities of Edinburgh and St. Andrews, and other things, drawn from material put at his disposal by Drummond.

Jonson was back in London early in May 1619. His ten months' holiday had made him, for a time at least, restless and in no mood for serious literary effort. So that summer he went to Oxford, for regale with his roguish friend, Richard Corbet, senior student of Christ Church, later Dean there, and afterwards Bishop of

Norwich. It was not Ben's first visit or likely to be his last, for Corbet was still the merry versemaker and wit, the lover of sack and hater of Puritans, he had been when Ben caroused with him in London taverns in younger days. The festivities in the North had whetted Ben's appetite for easy gossip and good cheer. With Corbet the best was to be had, and with no risk of posterity's being invited to listen, though posterity may be sorry that they kept their 'conversations' to themselves. Jonson, however, could not forget that he had broken with his old habit of work. In the masque which he wrote for production in January 1621, the short but witty *News from the New World discovered in the Moon*, the dialogue between a printer and a herald makes confession that "one of our greatest poets (I know not how good a one) went to Edinburgh on foot, and came back: marry, he has been restive, they say, ever since; for we have had nothing from him; he has set out nothing, I am sure."

During his visit to Corbet he received the degree of Master of Arts, on 19th July. The University of Oxford had offered it before he set out on his northern journey, in gratitude for the dedication of *Volpone*, which had been played before both Universities in 1606. Whether Cambridge did likewise, we do not know. Jonson was still in roving mood, and the production of his masque of *The Metamorphosed Gipsies*, the only piece 'set out' in 1621, took him to Burleigh, to Belvoir, and, in August, to Windsor. On this there followed, before the close of the year, the royal gift of the reversion of the Office of Master of the Revels, which he did not live to enjoy, and an increase of his pension, which does not, however, appear to have been paid.

During the remaining years of James's reign his literary work was confined to the writing of masques [1] and to the translation, by the King's request, of Barclay's *Argenis*.[2] There are hints in *Time Vindicated* that some tongues were beginning to wag enviously of the "now flourishing Jonson," as Wither had written in the preface to his *Abuses Stript and Whipt*. Ben felt it necessary to put this Scourger in his proper place, especially as he had been honoured by schoolmaster Gill, in his popular *Logonomia Anglica* (1619), as a model with Spenser and Daniel; and he administered punishment with studied, and unusual, politeness in the character of Chronomastix.

The loss of his library by fire about this time, perhaps in the winter of 1623–4, was greater vexation than the threats of enemies "now militant amongst us." He had always been a lover of books. As a *helluo librorum* he had few rivals among writers of his day, and perhaps few, other than Selden and Camden, among antiquaries and collectors. Selden speaks of his friend's "well furnished library" and of its use to him. Ben received, each New Year's Day, from Lord Pembroke, twenty pounds for fresh purchases,

---

[1] See Chapter V.

[2] This is not extant. It is entered in the Registers of the Stationers' Company on 2nd October 1623. Six years later, when Jonson was an invalid, Robert le Grys's translation appeared, with the verse rendered by Ben's friend Thomas May. It too was issued by royal command (that of Charles I.). A third translation of this popular book, by Kingsmill Long, was in its second edition in 1636.

and many gifts from other friends — all the more
welcome, as he confesses that he frequently changed
the contents of his shelves, being compelled to
"devour," that is part with, some in times of
necessity.[1] In this fire, too, there perished some
unpublished material of his own—the 'preface' or
essay supplementary to his version of the *Ars Poetica*,[2]
which he had read to Drummond at Hawthornden, and
the commentary in dialogue; the *English Grammar*,
completed from the notes of which we have only a
portion;[3] the poem on his Scottish journey; three
'books' of the *Sicilian Maid*; a history of Henry V.,
nearly finished; stores of "twice twelve years" on
humanity and divinity, apparently gathered together
in the manner of *Discoveries*; perhaps the prosodic
thesis which he told Drummond had been inspired by
the Campion-Daniel dispute of 1603; perhaps, also, the

[1] Many of these and of his later acquisitions have been preserved.
See R. W. Ramsey, *Books from the Library of Ben Jonson*, in the
Transactions of the Royal Society of Literature, 2nd ser. xxvii.
pt. iii.

[2] See Ben's reference to this translation of Horace in the Preface
('To the Readers') to *Sejanus*; also *Convers.* v. and xvi. "The
old book that goes about, *The Art of English Poesie*, was done
20 years since and kept long in write as a secret."

[3] There is little to be added to Wotton's remarks on this book.
"Jonson was the first man that I know of that did anything considerable in it [English grammar], but Lilly's *Grammar* was his
pattern; and from want of reflecting upon the grounds of a
language which he understood as well as any man of his age, he
drew it by violence to a dead language that was of a quite different
make, and so left his work imperfect" (*Reflections on Ancient and
Modern Learning*, 1694, chap. v.). There is evidence that Jonson
had made some comparative study and had collected a number of
volumes for his task. It may be noted that Gower is quoted in his
illustrations oftener than any other author.

intended *Heroologia* ; and some "parcels of a play."
The sarcastic egotism of his long *Execration upon Vulcan*
shows how hard he had been hit. A second alarm, in
1629, prompted his friend Howell to urge that he "look
better hereafter" to his "charcoal fire and chimney,"
and avoid the god's revenge—"it may be because you
have spoken ill of his wife, and been too busy with
his horns." [1]

Jonson owed much of the prosperity of these years
to the sympathy of the King. In the ease secured by
the royal favour he had few hard words for anybody
but Vulcan ; and enemies never to be reconciled, and
more bitter in purpose than Wither and his friends,
had not dared to rouse him. With the death of James
in March 1625 there came a change. Charles was
unconcerned in staying the outbreak of old animosities.
The odds were not in Ben's favour, even if Charles
had been as sympathetic as his father. For against
poverty, palsy, the bitterness of declining powers, and
jealousies, no man, even with crowds of friends, may
keep heart—least of all, one with such pride of intellect
as Jonson, when what had been earned as praise and
reward had to be accepted as a grace to his necessity.

In the first year of the new reign Jonson found
himself in difficulties. His money was spent. He had
written little, and what he had received for his "Entertainments" at noble houses was, if it brought him
more than merry company and good fare, poor return
for the outlays in junketings to and from Scotland
and in Oxford. He told Drummond that "of all his
plays he never gained two hundred pounds," and that

[1] *Familiar Letters*, ed. Jacobs, p. 267.

Poetry had beggared him;[1] and he glanced, rather enviously, at those who, having but saluted the Muse "on the by," had been advanced in their professions. We read his circumstances and temper in the *Epistle to the Earl of Dorset*,[2] and in his epigram to King Charles, in which, with pained wit, he pleads to be touched for "the *poet's-evil*, poverty."[3] Necessity turned him again to the public stage, with his satirical comedy of *The Staple of News*. We do not know the date, but as the King's servants who produced it were idle from 12th May to 24th November 1625 (there being more than forty deaths daily in the City from plague) and were not likely to have been engaged during the earlier months when the Court was in mourning, we cannot place it before the close of the year. In October, as if to recall the ill-luck of younger days, he was placed under arrest, on the charge of being the author of a verse eulogy of Felton, the assassin. He was, however, released immediately, and the official error was admitted. If he found some entertainment in reflecting on his being suspected of sympathies which brought the son of his enemy Gill to disgrace, he was not likely to miss the hint which the 'accident' conveyed. *The Staple of News* did little for his reputation, and the masques and plays which followed showed the failing of his powers. After the appearance, in 1626, of the monologue of *Owls*, incorrectly described as a masque, there is a complete break in his record of literary work till the production of the ill-starred play *The New Inn*, in January 1629. For this three years' silence there is the explanation that

---

[1] *Convers.* xvii. xviii.   [2] *Underwoods*, xxx.

[3] *Ib.* LXXX.

early in the interval he was stricken with paralysis
and cheated of convalescence by gout and dropsy, and
was again stricken in 1628, or was still suffering from
the effects of the first attack. His letters to Lord
Newcastle about this time give a sad picture of his
condition. More than once he says "his needs are such,
and so urging," but he will not borrow, for he has
neither fortune to pay nor security to engage.[1] He did
not ask in vain, and the City offered in 1628 some
additional cheer by appointing him Chronologer, in
succession to Middleton. This "chanderly pension"
of £33 : 6 : 8 did him little good, for in 1631 the
Aldermen, in true counting-house spirit, ordered the
stoppage of Jonson's salary "until he shall have presented unto this court some fruits of his labours in that
his place." He gives, that year, a sorry account of
himself in an "Epistle Mendicant" to the Treasurer.[2]
A partial answer came exactly three years later
(September 1634), when the King compelled the
Aldermen to restore their pittance.

About this time, certainly not later than 1630,
Jonson interested himself in preparing for the press
a second volume of his *Works*. It appeared in
instalments and was not completed till after his death,
in 1640 (1641), under the care of his friend Sir Kenelm
Digby.[3] Three plays were issued in 1631, *Bartholomew
Fair, The Staple of News*, and *The Devil is an Ass*. He was
worried by his "lewd printer" Benson, who had the
work in hand for the well-known 'editor' Robert Allot,

---

[1] See the apologue of the speaking fox in the letter to Newcastle, referred to *infra*, p. 50.

[2] *Underwoods*, XC.

[3] See 'H. M.'s.' Preface to Suckling's *Sad One* (1659).

and he told Lord Newcastle, when sending him the last-named play, that "before he will perfect the rest I fear he will come himself to be a part under the title of The Absolute Knave, which he hath played with me." The texts show that Jonson had good reason to curse the printer.   In these volumes he gives us the first collected edition issued by an English author under personal supervision ; and he would appear to be the first who published a play with a preface or dedication, who indulged the luxury of prolegomena and annotation (in some of the Quartos and more fully in the Folio), and, generally, who attended to the make-up and scholarly equipment of his own writings. This concern in his *Works* was of course a standing matter for contemporary ridicule, perhaps as much for its novelty as for its implied vanity. "It never was any great ambition in me to be in this kind voluminously read," said Thomas Heywood in pointed reference ;[1] Marston was even troubled with the thought "that scenes, invented merely to be spoken, should be enforcively published to be read,"[2] not to mention their being edited and collected ; and others were more amazed and unkind.

Jonson had turned again to the stage, only to receive the heaviest blow of his whole career. His *New Inn, or the Light Heart* (the irony of it !) was hissed off before the actors reached the epilogue. It was some kindness to the expelled poet that the confidences of the epilogue had not been mocked by the house ; for there he pleads—

> If you expect more than you had to-night,
> The maker is sick and sad,

---

[1] *English Traveller* (To the Reader,) 1633.
[2] *The Malcontent*, Preface.

and, if the play has miscarried—

> All that his faint and faltering tongue doth crave
> Is that you not impute it to his brain,
> That's yet unhurt, although, set round with pain,
> It cannot long hold out.

Charles, touched by the words that

> had he lived the care of king and queen,
> His art in something more yet had been seen,

made him a gift that year (1629) of one hundred pounds,
which the poet acknowledged in his *Underwoods*.[1] On
his remorseless public he threw himself as a death-sick
lion on its hunters. The ferocity of hate and pride
which shakes every line of the *Ode to Himself* shows how
much of the old fight was left in him; but the pathos
is deepened, and the situation becomes painful when
the author of *The Resolves* burlesques the angry lines,
in an Ode beginning—

> Come leave this saucy way
> Of baiting those that pay
> Dear for the sight of your declining wit,[2]

and when Randolph, Carew, and Cleveland rush in to
defend the brave rage of their 'Father.' In another
Ode to Himself[3] the poet defies the neglect of the age,
and vows to

> sing high and aloof,
> Safe from the wolf's black jaw and the dull ass's hoof.

Charles's gift encouraged Jonson, still necessitous,
to crave soon after, in verses "half-facetious, half-angry
with his detractors," the conversion of the hundred

---

[1] LXXX.

[2] Felltham made some amends by contributing to *Jonsonus
Virbius* in 1638.

[3] *Underwoods*, XLI.

marks of James's pension into one hundred pounds.[1]
Charles would not, or could not, refuse the petition,
and he added an annual tierce of Ben's favourite canary,
direct from the Whitehall cellars, which, it would appear,
the Household was, after its way, slow in sending.[2]
This supplementary gift has acquired an exaggerated
interest as evidence in support of the legend, still
lively, that Ben enjoyed the *office* of Poet Laureate, and
had held it since the grant of his first pension in 1616.[3]
The royal letters-patent give no authority for the title,
and the very explicit document of 1630 merely states
that the pension was "especially to encourage him to
proceed in those services of his wit and pen, which We
have enjoined unto him, and which We expect from
him." Jonson himself may share responsibility for the
technical ascription, by his request to Selden [4] to gather
the information which the latter printed in his *Titles of
Honour*, in a chapter "On the Custom of giving Crowns
of Laurel to Poets," and by his sanction of the wreathed
effigy drawn by Robert Vaughan for the Folio of 1616.

[1] . . . Please your Majesty to make
Of your grace, for goodness' sake,
Those your Father's marks your pounds. . . .

Underwoods, XCV.

[2] *Underwoods*, LXXXVI.

[3] In *Underwoods*, LXXVI. Jonson appeals through John Burgess
to Sir Robert Pye, Remembrancer of the Exchequer, for the arrears
of his pension. Sir Robert was a direct ancestor of 'Laureate
Pye,' in whose time the tierce of canary was commuted for a
cash allowance.

[4] Jonson liked to consult his learned friend on knotty points
requiring research. Cf. the correspondence on the taking of women's
parts in plays (in special reference to *Bartholomew Fair*) and on
the interpretation of Deut. xxii. 5, in Selden, *Opera* 1726, ii., coll.
1690, *et seqq.*, and *Table Talk*, CV.

Perhaps Ben meant no more than Falkland intended
in the poetic compliment, that he was

> worthiest to receive
> The garland which the Muses' hands did weave,[1]

and only claimed the bays, in familiar continental
fashion, as a craft-symbol or badge, just as later poets
and their artists have claimed the "awful turban" or the
book and pen. But though Jonson's position was not
legally described as Dryden's was in 1670, it had
higher 'official' credit than that of any of the self-styled
and University 'laureates,' before and after Skelton.
With him it marks a stage in the disjunction of the
literary from the other business of the Master of the
Chapel—a disjunction which his reputation, and the
exceptional opportunities he had in the writing of
masques and in other ways, made possible and definite.
The public mind easily transformed 'poet laureate' into
'the Poet Laureate'; and it was not more difficult to
give technical validity to an 'office' which had already
set forth its functions. The fuss over the succession to
Jonson—Thomas May "stood candidate for the laurel" is
Aubrey's phrase[2]—argues an impression that the post was
considered to be definitely constituted and attainable.
The annuity and canary encouraged the belief; but even
in D'Avenant's time, though he too is often spoken of as
Laureate, the Crown had not formally granted the style.

The literary share in the production of masques had
become more and more subservient to the spectacular;
the 'inventor' who made machines, built the wonderful
scenery, and designed the luxurious dresses usurped the
place of honour. It was Ben's ill-luck to collaborate

---

[1] *Jonsonus Virbius*, i.   [2] *Lives*, ii. 55.

with one who to reasonable pride in his craftsmanship added a masterfulness which more than matched
Jonson in his own methods. Van Dyck's portrait of
Inigo Jones is testimony enough to the dangers which
threatened this partnership of the Talents. There was
some ruffling over first place for title-page honours, and
Jonson had cause to resent his rival's selfish use of the
opportunity which his illness had given. Before his
Scottish visit he had remarked to Prince Charles that
when he wanted words to express the greatest villain in
the world he would call him an Inigo.[1] Jones had
returned in 1615 from his second visit to Italy a
declared disciple of Palladio, and had succeeded to the
post of Surveyor of the King's Works. It was not
likely, when he was engaged once more in supervising
the staging and dressing of the Court masques, that his
eagerness to show his Italian experience and to vaunt
his increased official importance would make collaboration less difficult than it had been in the past. The
enforced reduction of outlays on these shows and
Jonson's attempt to strengthen their dramatic character
could not fail to cause bickerings between the inventors,
rivals by nature and in their tasks. Small surprise,
therefore, that when the crisis came in 1631 Jonson
wrote the surly verses of "expostulation" with the
Master-Surveyor "Inigo Marquis Would-be." Ben was
slow to forget his humiliation; indeed, it was not till
1635 that Howell persuaded him to withdraw his ill-
tempered satire. It is difficult for us to pass judgement
on this miserable quarrel and unprofitable to make the

---

[1] *Convers.* xvii. ; perhaps insinuating 'Iniquo.' Cf. *infra*, p. 52
and Chapter V. *passim.*

E

attempt. Jonson's references to Jones, years before the
open quarrel, are doubtful support of Gifford's view that
Ben was once happy in his association. When Ben tells
the audience of the masque of *Queens* that the "device
of [the] attire was Master Jones's, with the invention and
architecture of the whole scene and machine," and, later,
in a note, says, "all which I willingly acknowledge
for him," he is not without suspicion of merely putting
the carpenter in proper perspective. So, too, the
declaration in *Love's Triumph through Callipolis*, that
the argument was resolved on "after some debate of
cogitation with ourselves," is by no means free from a
sinister interpretation, especially when it comes so near
to the time of open rupture. We need not blame Jonson,
but we need not excuse him overmuch. And we must
not forget that he, in contrast with the successful
Surveyor, was in the poorest circumstances, in health
and pocket; uncertain, in his Westminster lodging, of
his "Castalian liquor," perhaps even of the "good
philosophical diet, beans and buttermilk," of early days.[1]
A begging letter to the Earl of Newcastle in December
1631 [2] thinly veils his desperate condition in an amusing
apologue of his pet fox and a mole-catcher and their
views on the penury of the poet's house. Jones's victory
was secured in the magnificent masques of 1634, in
Shirley's *Triumph of Peace*, presented by the four Inns
of Court, and in Carew's *Coelum Britannicum*. But
these were solemn confessions that the true triumph
had been Jonson's, and that without his art the hope of
the genre was passing.

---

[1] See *Every Man out of his Humour*, Induction.
[2] *Shakespeare Society's Papers*, i. pp. 8-9.

When Jones had usurped the place of masque-maker
to the Court—so securely, that Aurelian Townsend, one
of Ben's 'sons,' was commissioned to find the words
for his 'inventions' of *Albion's Triumph* and *Tempe
Restored*—Ben turned once again to the "loathed stage"
to which he had twice said farewell. *The Magnetic Lady,
or Humours Reconciled* (1632) has a testamentary interest.
Master Damplay asking, in the Induction, "Why
Humours Reconciled?" is answered by a 'boy of the house'
thus: "My conceit is not ripe yet; I'll tell you that
anon. The author beginning his studies of this kind
with *Every Man in his Humour*, and, after, *Every Man
out of his Humour*, and since continuing in all his plays,
especially those of the comic thread, whereof *The New
Inn* was the last, some recent humours still, or manners
of men, that went along with the times; finding himself
now near the close, or shutting up of his circle, hath
fancied to himself in idea this Magnetic Mistress, a lady,
a brave bountiful housekeeper, and a virtuous widow,
who having a young niece ripe for a man and marriage-
able, he makes that his centre attractive, to draw thither
a diversity of guests, all persons of different humours,
to make up his perimeter. And this he hath called
Humours Reconciled." This retrospective appeal, which
provides further proof of the pertinacity of Jonson's
artistic purpose, was favourably received at the Blackfriars
in October 1632, and some of the bitterness which *The
New Inn* had brought into his life was forgotten. But
the old man could not hope for respite from attack.
The actors were haled before the High Commission Court
to answer for the oaths freely used in their parts, and
they meanly laid upon the poet, then confined to his

chamber, the responsibility for what they afterwards admitted was their own gag. More direct assault came from Jones and his friends. One Gill, the younger, who had nursed a feud with Jonson since the latter's criticism of the elder Gill's praise of Wither,[1] made cruel mock of the poet and "this child" of his "bedridden wit," and added a spiteful reminder of Ben's bricklayer youth—

> Thou better knows a groundsell how to lay
> Than lay the plot or groundwork of a play ;
> And better canst direct to cap a chimney
> Than to converse with Clio or Polyhymny.[2]

But young Master Gill was asked to remember that he was "a rogue by statute," and was ignominiously dismissed in an epigram.

Prompted by this partial reconciliation with his old public, Jonson produced within the short space of seven months what was to be his last comedy. His Squire Tub of Totten-Court, Medlay the cooper, Audrey Turfe, and the bucolic brethren of *A Tale of a Tub* (1633) lead us from the old haunt of Alsatia to a new setting in the cotes of clowns, in which he pokes heavy fun at Jones, first as Vitruvius Hoop, and, when Court influence ordered this part to be excised, in the burlesque of In-and-In Medlay, cooper and headborough. The play was "misliked" when it was acted before the King and Queen on 14th January 1634, but whether because it attacked Jones, or because its bucolic manner was too much of a novelty in high places, we are left to guess. Jonson himself may not have rated it highly, if there is

---

[1] *Supra,* p. 40.

[2] Printed from the Ashmole MS. by Gifford, in a note to *The Magnetic Lady.*

no false modesty in his choice of the motto from Catullus, *Inficeto est inficetior rure*; but in the rebuff he, of course, saw the hand of his enemy. He again made mock of Vitruvius when his Entertainment of *Love's Welcome*, performed at Welbeck in 1633, was re-edited for the fêtes at Bolsover in July 1634. There were risks in continuing the quarrel. He had been warned, as we have seen, by his friend Howell that the King was not well pleased with this continual scuffling with the architect; but the royal favour was not withdrawn, for it was at this time (September 1634) that command was given to the City Aldermen to restore the poet's pension as City Chronologer.[1]   On New Year's Day and on the King's Birthday, 1635, the poet 'sang' his loyalty and gratitude to Charles, for the last time.[2] In the same year (20th November) he lost his last surviving son, for whom he had procured the reversion of his Mastership of the Revels, when he despaired of outliving Sir John Astley.

Jonson was now near "the shutting up of his circle." So many farewells had been taken—to the theatre, to the Court, to country - house revels, to children and friends, to enemies unreconciled. Even his lifelong ally Chapman, "who was loved of him," had left as his dying gift an *Invective written against Ben Jonson*.[3] Of personal history in the next two years we know little or nothing, and we might conclude that the door of his sick-room had been closed against a gossiping world, had not Howell told us that on 4th April 1636 Ben gave a "solemn supper" with "good company, excellent

---

[1] *Supra*, p. 44.   [2] *Underwoods*, XCVIII. XCIX.
[3] Preserved in part in a commonplace-book in the Ashmole MSS.

cheer, choice wines, and jovial welcome." He "began to vapour extremely of himself, and, by vilifying others, to magnify his own Muse." This almost spoiled the "relish" of the evening, but Howell is content to excuse the poet, "now that time hath snowed upon his pericranium." George Morley,[1] when Bishop of Winchester, told Isaac Walton that he often visited Ben in his "long retirement and sickness" in his lodging near Westminster Abbey, that his pensions ("so much as came in") were given to a woman "that governed him," that "neither he nor she took much care for next week, and would be sure not to want wine, of which he usually took too much before he went to bed, if not oftener and sooner." [2] But the public had so lost touch with him that even as early as September 1632 the alert John Pory could express surprise at the announcement of *The Magnetic Lady*, by saying that he thought Jonson "had been dead." [3] It is hard to believe that during these months of retirement Jonson had surrendered all his old ambitions, or, though bedridden or confined, was altogether stricken in his powers. The memories of the Mermaid and of his rule at the Apollo and the devotion of generous youth, soon to prove its piety,[4] must have brought solace and forbidden him to lose his confidence in himself. Then, as if in recompense for this undaunted spirit, fate permitted the decrepit poet to give us what was perhaps his greatest work. The *Sad Shepherd*, fragment though it is, reveals a new Jonson, unlike the satirist and realist of other days. It

---

[1] See *infra*, p. 280.　　　　　　[2] Aubrey, *Lives*, ii. 15.
[3] Ellis, *Orig. Letters*, 2nd ser. iii. 270.
[4] See *infra*, Chapter IX.

comes upon us as a miracle, and seems to compel us, of a sudden, to recast our general estimate of its maker's literary place.   Yet we have hints, growing more and more certain as we approach the period of his *Tale of a Tub* and his *New Year's Gift to King Charles*, how the spell of pastoral had touched his imagination.   And earlier, perhaps as far back as 1613, he had in the lost poem of the *May Lord* shown this shepherd liking,[1] as he did again in his masque of *Pan's Anniversary*.   For this fragmentary idyll of Æglamour and Earine, rich in the music and tints of English woodlands, not a few would give much or all of what goes for Jonson's best, even Bobadil or Tucca, all that is most characteristic in his art, most striven for or best achieved.   And perhaps Jonson himself would have chosen thus.   So let us think he had his blessing of the Muse.

The end came on 6th August 1637.   Three days later he was buried in the nave of Westminster Abbey.   Later, as every one knows, a visitor, Sir John Young, gave a few pence to an Abbey mason for the carving of these words [2] on the slab which covered the grave,

"O Rare Ben Jonson."

[1] See *infra*, pp. 208-212.

[2] This epiphonema was, as Gifford reminds us, first applied to Jonson after the production of his *Bartholomew Fair*.   It was also inscribed over the door of the Apollo Room.   It threatened to become a lapidary fashion when "O Rare Sir William Davenant" was carved on another slab in a neighbouring aisle.

CHAPTER III

LITERARY CONSCIENCE

IF Jonson fell out with his age because, like his Asper, he claimed to be "a free spirit" and would not be compelled by any "frosty apprehension of danger" to be a "parasite to time, place, or opinion," posterity has inclined to fall out with him because in his art he has laboured overmuch for doctrine. Bohemian though he was, he indulged a tyrannical conscience. His solicitude for the critical proprieties has alienated the modern reader, however willing to find compensation in the sheer vigour of his intellect, and has provoked comparison with the broader humanity and impersonal range of so many of his contemporaries. He remains one of the hardest to enjoy, even by those who have learned the difficult art of reading a play as a book, or are not distracted by the riddles of forgotten quip and allusion. We are not permitted nowadays to applaud the stage-craft of his masterpieces as were the seventeenth-century Londoners, and Mr. Pepys in particular. This denial must always tell against a dramatist's later reputation, Shakespeare's alone in English excepted; and in Jonson's case the movement of the theatre is most needed to vitalize learning, theory, and homily, and to give his talent for realism its full effect. Abel Drugger was probably a greater part in Garrick's hands or Brainworm in Munden's than either can ever be on the printed page ; whereas the best-played Falstaff or Jaques will never put us out of conceit with them as the best of armchair friends. Had Jonson been more generous to his neighbours and to his art, his later honour might have been greater.

> And he told them plainly he deserved the bays,
> For his were called works, where others were but plays.
> And
> Bid them remember how he had purged the stage
> Of errors, that had lasted many an age.

Thus does Suckling's gentle malice tell us why, great as Jonson is, he has failed to win that upper place in popular regard which is not denied even to scholars and critics. But if Ben falls short with the general, because there is no mystery either in his craft or in his personality, or because he lacks the insinuating gentleness which not a few propagandists have possessed, he must remain, as long as character counts for anything, one of the master-spirits of English letters. In estimating that character it is not enough to acknowledge the mere persistency of his purpose in every department of literary activity, that long show of fight and staying power which, even in a career so varied and full as his, might be no more than prize-ring valour. It were better to ask whether character had not as great a part in the framing of his ideal as in the struggle for its attainment.

In all Jonson's work the pressure of his literary conscience is clear, but it is in drama that its working

is most deliberately disclosed. Drama is his fighting
engine, his laboratory, his confessional ; in other genres
he stores his materials for this preparation, or states
his final convictions. To a writer of his temper and
intellect conflict with existing conditions was unavoid-
able ; and in estimating his work nowadays, when the
passions of the fighters are long spent, we must not
neglect the historical setting. Jonson cannot be taken
in the detached way in which we have accustomed ourselves, not without risk, to take Shakespeare ; and if
this be kept in mind, we shall be in a better position to
revise some of the commonplaces in the contrast of the
two poets.

The earlier English drama, even down to the "face-
tiously-quick and unparalleled" John Lyly, yields only
haphazard evidence of the qualities which are characteristic of the drama of the Great Age. It is a miscellany
of sketches in episode and character drawn on traditional
lines, interesting enough to the student in spite of its
reiteration, but, with rare exceptions, inert or clumsy
in movement. The incoming of classical models did
much to moderate this disorder, if often, in the severe
discipline of Seneca and Roman comedy, at the expense
of native vigour. Not till we reach Kyd do we find any
hint that the playwright can show, or the audience can
appreciate, an advance in dramatic action, even if that
advance be no more than the better ordering of the
familiar story. To this promise of development Marlowe
and Lyly added another. They first gave the drama
the touch of literature and transformed the home-
spun to the finer web of poetry. Lyly, though by no
means lacking in constructive talent, is remembered for

that strategy of style and that handling of metaphor and phrase from which Shakespeare drew fresh courage in the shaping forth of his masterpieces. Marlowe, with scarcely the prentice's cunning in the weaving of a plot, discovered to an age, as yet untroubled by pedantries about 'rant,' that drama was a concern of the Muse, and that it could compass great things greatly. In other words, Marlowe and Lyly, with one or two minors, invited the English mind to treat the drama, tragic and comic, as a literary problem; and Shakespeare, profiting by the lesson, confirmed the claim in his greater and more complex achievement.

Jonson confirmed this too, but with a difference. He was at one with his contemporaries in the purpose of regenerating the drama, or, what is not quite the same thing, of turning its powers to fuller account; but, whereas they approached the task with more or less of the unconsidered confidence of the artist, he made deliberate survey of the conditions and as deliberately sought an escape. The others are, apart from occasional satire on popular taste, more or less indifferent to the goodness or badness of that taste and to their own accomplishment. Jonson, like the Aschams and Chekes of an earlier generation or the Harveys of his own, turned with a critic's instinct to analyse his discontent and to find relief in terms of that analysis. To him the dramatists of the workaday sort are, like the poets, a "rakehelly rout," following at random outworn and foolish patterns; their art is weak, because it has lost its touch with life, and is only superficially or partially bettered as drama by the poetic gifts of Marlowe and Lyly; and it lacks that higher purpose which should accompany the entertainment it tries to provide. The playwrights of greater account, who had transformed this commoner material by the aid of romance, and of not a little rhetoric, stood to his critical eye condemned in their methods for the attainment of a more just, more national, and more permanent drama. So it is that Jonson starts on his career in protest against the dramatic practice of his age, against its crudeness, its unreality, and its helplessness. His misfortune was that, being more than an Ascham or a Harvey, he so often allowed himself to gratify this ardour of intellect at the expense of his imagination.

The most patent of Jonson's protests, his criticism of existing method, was not in itself dangerous to his art. Many writers since his day have made similar dissent, and even justified their practice by a formal aesthetic, without serious hurt to their creative energies or their reputation. But to a man of Jonson's temper the risks were greater. Having convinced himself of the justice of his censure, he allowed it to assume an exaggerated importance, to involve him in debate, long-drawn and angry, and sometimes to tempt him to make his own work the mere antithesis of what he condemned. This he shows in his second protest, in which his insistence on a more realistic method in comedy is intended as flat contradiction to romantic licence. Having thus encouraged himself to the performance of a public duty rather of the schoolmasterly kind, he could not deny himself the further gratification of discoursing on the general purpose of art and of explaining his own efforts, in part academic and traditional and in part suggested by controversy with vulgarians and disorderly playwrights.

It is by keeping this pedagogic habit in view that the familiar but risky contrast of Jonson with Shakespeare is most strictly adjusted. When Dryden called Shakespeare the Homer or "father of our dramatic poets," and Ben the Virgil, "the pattern of elaborate writing," he seemed to be hinting not only at the artifice in Ben's style but at his claim to be a model and even to impose his views. Often, at least in the work of his prime, he gives the impression that he is addressing a pupil-audience; whereas with Shakespeare we feel that the subject is left to take care of itself, or is allowed a freer development, and that by its self-revealing it wins its convincing completeness. Jonson's care to interpret and teach compels him to isolate his material. He selects phases, episodes, conditions, and works them up to 'dramatic' completeness, as he understands the term, by a free use of detail, differing in kind or shown in a variety of ways. By his devotion to this realism in his doctrine of the Humours he weakens the sense of *ensemble* and allows himself little or no process in characterization. Each case is taken on its own merits; each 'humour' stands apart strongly individualized; and the purpose of the play is confined somewhat rigidly to the illustration of each. When he desires a fuller plan of comedy, he must have a fuller list of explanatory personages and occasions. In Shakespeare a character does not end as he begins. In Jonson the single whim or temper persists, and when the scheme is to be enlarged, fresh characters are added, it may be partly like the others, but plainly preserving their individuality throughout. In his synthesis of many elements he is driven by an imperturbable logic to expect certain results : he makes small allowance, in theory at least, for the accidents of combination which are the true discovery of the romantic spirit. He never feels, except in the rarer moods which inspired work like *The Sad Shepherd*, the stirring of the literary knight-errantry of his age. He knows too well why and how he shall journey, and he goes forth with ceremony and in brave order. He has the provoking confidence of the Oracle, and none better than contemporaries could smoke the satirist's jest in presenting him as the keeper of the Trophonian Den.[1] Yet he lacks the perfect self-possession of the Oracle, the silence only to be broken, and in measured terms, when the curious or needy choose to crave its aid. Hence to contemporaries, as to us, he shows a rather schoolmasterly habit. Though he has great pride and is doubtless sincere when he adapts from Horace, as a motto for his *Alchemist* and again for his Folio—

> Neque, me ut miretur turba, laboro :
> Contentus paucis lectoribus,

or tells his bookseller to let his book

> lie upon thy stall till it be sought,
> Not offered, as it made suit to be bought,[2]

he is by no means indifferent to reputation with the crowd. He will not beg their attention ; he will compel it. Sometimes, too often, he does this by lessons of the class-room kind, sometimes by quarrel unbecoming a great talent that should win its way by its own momentum.

This difference lies, too, behind the traditional

---

[1] *The Great Assizes holden in Parnassus*, 1645.

[2] *Epigr.* III.

description of Jonson's art as 'classical,' though a cheaper criticism would confine that description, as it would in Milton's case, to his profound scholarship. It is the possession of the qualities expressed by the epithet taken in its fuller sense which has given Jonson his importance in our literary perspective, and at the same time, and notwithstanding that to it much of the permanent value of his work as art is directly due, has reduced his claims to higher individual honour.   For it is the Nemesis of the classical habit that, though by the best of theories it should attain finality in expression or a fair approximation thereto, and in its exercise does offer to literature not merely a wholesome discipline but the only competent aid to the understanding of its own mysteries, it often secures these with loss of that vitality by which alone the best things are sustained. When a writer plays the schoolmaster, not only to himself but to his public, he runs many risks from which talent less orderly and reasoned may escape.   If the play or poem, though it have a hundred excellences, does not speak for itself to the general mind, as distinguished from the critical and curious, how must it fare when he who is both its creator and expositor has passed away and public taste has changed?   Jonson insists overmuch, and denies himself that freedom of movement which even the classicist, however studious in selecting and ordering, can enjoy.   His devotion to the theory of the Humours blunts his interest, perhaps his powers, in the self-development of his characters; his views on plot and arrangement deprives his work, even when at its best, of its full range, and of a convincing liveliness of action; and, above all, his care to keep the

spaniels of imagination and emotion on the leash
tells heavily against him. For in general he is unre-
ceptive of sensations as Shakespeare is in their fulness
and variety. He is critical of his intellectual fervours,
and if he give rein to himself in an apostrophe to Poesy,
he will on revision condemn his own extravagance.
His love of rules has played havoc with his claim to be
our master-realist; and his narrow realism has damned
the larger hope of his art. No one in that ingenious
age was happier in the self-criticism of his *impresa* or
emblem—a compass with one foot in the centre and
the other broken, with these words for motto, *Deest
quod duceret orbem*.[1] Yet when he fails, he fails
greatly, and the limitations of his genius can neither
annul his right to be remembered for his moments
of highest power, nor be judged, even at their worst,
as the folly of the doctrinaire or ineffective writer.
Jonson invites us to analyse his work and to apply
an intellectual test. Under that he becomes self-
explanatory, and takes his place, if not as one of the
greatest of creative artists in English, at least one, and
assuredly the first, of those who have shown that gust
of literature which, with learning less than his, has
gone to the making of our best critics and men of
letters. On rare occasions, and almost at the close, he
breaks with this professional habit, and challenges the
knights of romanticism on their own ground. We may
like him the better for this, for art's sake, and as an
amiable acknowledgement of contemporary ideals. We
may, in grateful relief from the pedantries and severity
of the critic, be tempted to say that here is the true

---

[1] *Convers.* xvii.

Jonson. Such an inference would be more generous than just, if we are to judge him by his lifelong purpose. It may be the *best* Jonson, but posterity must take him as Fate and his own will shaped him; and conclude from the completed testimony of his ambitions and practice.

F

CHAPTER IV

THE COMEDIES

I

IT may seem strange that the critical habit which discloses itself at every turn in Jonson's work should be so vigorous in the comedies, where, by the nature of the medium, the intrusion of pedantry is least to be expected or tolerated. Yet it is not so strange; for comedy, unlike tragedy, is not based on emotion and does not demand a personal interest in the fortunes of its characters. Its function is to be a good spectator of the foibles and intrigues of life in its less unhappy moments, and, as a looker-on, to comment in a detached way on the fun or scandal provided. It never ceases to be critical. The laughter of the audience and the dramatist's purpose are each a criticism of follies; and if to the latter there be added the touch of satire, it is still more critical. Had Jonson been less noisy, or altogether silent, about the why and how of his venture in comedy, it would still be clear that neither by accident had he chosen that vein, nor by accident had achieved in it his best work. It is, of course, another question whether he has given, or was the man to give, the happiest presentment of the Comic Spirit.

A writer on Jonson's comedies is easily tempted to generalities. There is a strong family likeness in all. Differences are no more than a matter of degree, of strength variously sustained, of purpose freshly drawn, or decked, or posed. Even the 'dotages' explain themselves as mumblings of familiar things. Within the modest compass of this volume it is difficult to find a middle way between assuming much and marshalling the proofs. Nor is there space, had the writer so desired, to play the part of the old-fashioned cicerone and repeat the 'Here-we-haves' and 'There-we-haves,' as we pass from one piece to another in a descriptive round. There can be no excuse, merely because Jonson is not a familiar author like some of his companion 'Men of Letters,' for treating his text as a discovery.

Jonson found his purpose and manner early. We may believe that in his first attempts as a playwright he did no more than follow the fashion as a good learner would; that his tragedies, whether wholly planned by him or only reset or eked out by 'additions,' were dutiful handlings of the 'Revenge' stuff that pleased those days. They are lost, happily perhaps for Jonson's reputation, and apparently with his connivance, as things not merely poor or partly his own, but inconsistent with the profession of his manhood. For a like cause, doubtless, it came about that, as he told Drummond, "half of his comedies were not in print." Evidence of his apprentice manner has been found in *The Case is Altered*, perhaps his earliest comedy, and the only relic of a period of dramatic effort which he desired to forget.[1] It may be placed at the very close of that period, within a month or two of the appearance of *Every Man in his Humour*, rather than, as some would have it, between the 'Every Man' masterpieces.[2] What Jonson had found for himself, and, as he hoped, for comedy, in the first of these, was not likely to be surrendered by him on occasion or easily. But we are not compelled to put too fine a point on his exclusion of *The Case is Altered* and to treat it only as an expression of the earlier style from which he escaped. The bibliography of the matter gives us too small a margin of time for such a quick change, and the testimony of the text is against us. For, after all, the early manner of the *Case* is less striking than its hints of later habit. It is true that there are many things in it unlike, or inconsistent with, what we distinguish as Jonsonian. There is an unmistakable 'romantic' quality in the setting and characterization, most strongly shown in Rachel de Prie, a pleasant study of the Jessica kind, and Ben's only approach to Shakespeare's art in the portrayal of Woman; in the turning to 'nuptials' at the close; and in the co-ordination of the plots. On the other hand,

---

[1] Yet some would make the omission only a matter of copyright (cf. Pollard, *Shakespeare Folios*, 1909, p. 116).

[2] Onion's reference in I. i. to Meres's compliment to Anthony Munday—"You are in print already for the best plotter"—makes 1598 the earliest date possible for *The Case is Altered*. As Jonson is mentioned by Meres only as a 'tragic poet,' it is more likely that he was quoting from the *Palladis Tamia* soon after its publication than referring to it towards the close of his career, without a hint of how its record of his work must be supplemented. Jonson's attack on Munday in *Cynthia's Revels* (1600) suggests a near but anterior date for the hit in *The Case is Altered*.

there is more than enough to show that Jonson was already at variance with precedent, certainly enough to prove his authorship, had it been in doubt, by traits which are the hall-mark of his best known work. There is some significance in the remark by Jonson's butt, Antonio Balladino, that is Munday, at least in the early part of the play. "Why look you, sir, I write so plain, and keep that old *decorum*, that you must of necessity like it; marry, you shall have some now (as for example, in plays) that will have every day new tricks, and write you nothing but humours: indeed this pleases the gentlemen, but the common sort they care not for't; they know not what to make on't; they look for good matter, they, and are not edified with such toys":[1] a hint that Jonson was already attracted to the problem of humours, and had perhaps sketched in mind his later distinction between the 'good' and the 'bad.' There is, however, more than this critical thrust. Jaques de Prie is a character-sketch frankly suggestive of Jonson's familiar method; and if it fails by comparison with later studies, it cannot be denied kinship with them. Nor is there wanting that personal critical note which is so characteristic of Jonson, and comes so naturally to the Comedy of Humours. His long quarrel with contemporaries has already begun in his treatment of Munday in Antonio; he, as Valentine, makes his first gibe at the self-sufficiency of playgoers;[2] and in that Valentine he draws in the rough that picture of himself which we know so well in the Asper of *Every Man out of his Humour* and the Crites of *Cynthia's Revels*. Indeed, Asper's grumblings and tirades may be described as a

[1] I. i.   [2] II. iv.

recovery, but with fuller technique, of the mutterings in *The Case is Altered*. The chief interest of the play is, therefore, that it shows Jonson emerging from the 'romantic' manner of the stage of his youth and committed to a dramatic purpose which he would explain more fully. The play may be enjoyed for its own merits, of a second-rate kind, but it will be best understood if taken in connexion with the work of Jonson's prime, and after some acquaintanceship with that work.

Aubrey tells us that Jonson's "first good" play was *Every Man in his Humour*, and that in it, in contrast with what he had produced before, he "did hit it admirably well." Jonson appears to have concurred in this opinion when he jettisoned his earlier hack-work and began the folio edition of his *Works* with the comedy of the Knowells and Bobadil. In this play Jonson offers a carefully thought out example of his new method, and, by its title and by references throughout to the dramatic vogue of 'humours,' seeks to give warrant to the more critical of his audience that it is new. In *Every Man out of his Humour* he intrudes into the fabric of the piece definition and exposition of a more deliberate kind, and proceeds thereafter on a round of great comedies to illustrate by his stage-craft, with but free support of a critical or academic kind, what variations could be found within the limits he had chosen. With *The Magnetic Lady, or Humours Reconciled*, his effort ends, and in the Induction to it he makes retrospect contentedly of his long task. He had yielded himself to the tyranny of an idea and professed to be happy, chiefly because the bondage was of his own making.

What, then, was the novelty cried in *Every Man in his Humour*? The play has come down to us in two versions, the Quarto of 1601 and the Folio of 1616. The latter, the accepted text, is a thorough recast of the former in word and line, in the disposition of the scenes, in the change from Italy to England, and in the renaming of most of the characters. Both plays appear to have been acted in 1598. Why Jonson chose to publish the first text in 1601, when the revised piece had been before the public for some time, is difficult to explain on any other ground than resentment at being compelled to excise a few passages on Daniel in the last scene— some unnecessary changes in the speeches are almost proof of bad temper—and a stubborn resolve to take the reader into his confidence. He could afford in the Folio of 1616 to forget this minor quarrel and give his blessing to what by that time, if not long before, he knew to be the better version.

In the Prologue which is added to the Folio text he girds at the stage practice of the day in tragedy, history, and comedy. In the first two he deplores the neglect of the unities of place and time, the paltry and ludicrous settings, and the bombast of the writers; and in comedy the lack of reality and the confusion of its purpose with that of farce. Some of these charges are the "gross absurdities" which Sidney had exposed in his *Apology* a few years before and in almost identical words. Then the criticism was merely academic and, for the time at least, as ineffectual as other Elizabethan pleadings for classicism. Now it is not only restated with vigour; it is to invade the theatre and usurp the authority of Marlowe and Kyd, perhaps of Shakespeare.

The attack on the simple stagecraft of the day was natural and reasonable, and Jonson must have had many sympathizers even among those who went to the play only for pastime. Shakespeare in the first Prologue in *Henry V.*, produced in the same year, refers again and again to the "unworthy scaffold," its make-believe of the splendours of Agincourt, and its

> Turning the accomplishment of many years
> Into an hour-glass.

But Shakespeare admits this only to make an appeal [1] to the superior court of the imagination—

> Still be kind
> And eke out our performance with your mind

—an appeal which has never failed him, in whatever circumstance his plays have been produced, and least when that circumstance has been simple. Jonson, it must be admitted in fairness, offers no plea for elaboration. He does not condemn the three rusty swords because they are not three hundred and shining, and even in his earlier years he had as pronounced views as he had later on Inigo Jones and his carpentry. He treats the matter according to the rules of *decorum*; audience and reader must not be invited to excuse the impossible or be asked to collaborate with the dramatist in making good what his own art should have offered. It is not a foolish view; it is only different from Shakespeare's.

The points in Jonson's general attack that are the most directly pertinent to comedy are the pleas for 'real life' and for a clear issue between comedy and

---

[1] Prologue to Act III.

farce. To these he added others, which, though not
as yet formally set forth, are disclosed in the workmanship of his earliest plays. We may take them
together here in a preliminary exposition of what he
intended by the Comedy of Humours as differing from
the familiar forms which relied mainly on plot and
incident. It is better to do this before offering any
impressions of the success with which Jonson carried
out his own precepts. The critic is rightly bidden to
discover intention before passing judgement on accomplishment. Here the instruction is peremptory.

There is the plea for *real life*, for "deeds and
language, such as men do use." Jonson felt that
comedy, as distinguished from tragedy, in which the
remote or the ideal does not hinder and may even help
the dramatist's purpose, had lost its touch of life in
romantic extravagance. Reaction had already set in
against this, as, for example, in the work of his friend
Chapman, whose *Blind Beggar of Alexandria* (1596), with
its romantic setting and rough farce, yielded to *An
Humourous Day's Mirth*[1] (1597) and *All Fools* (1599),
where the continuity of the comic story is broken up
into a number of more or less separate studies of
characters or 'humours,' in some respects (as in the
parts of Dowsecer and Florilla, the Puritan wife) rather
suggestive of the Jonsonian personages than reminiscent
of the types in Plautus. Change was in the air, as is
shown in the contrast between the Middleton-Rowley *Old
Law* (1599) and later plays like Middleton's *Michaelmas
Term* and *Your Five Gallants*, and even in the stuff and
manner of tragedy, as in the contrast in Marston

---

[1] Probably the *Comedy of Umers*, wrongly ascribed to Jonson.

between the romantic mood of *Antonio and Mellida*
(? 1599) and the satirical directness of the *Malcontent* and
its successors. Jonson, if not the first to express this
change, was the first to define it, and, in his *Every Man
in his Humour*, to supply the canon. It may be that his
constitutional habit of satire compelled him to turn
readily to realism as the only medium in which he could
obtain the effects desired, but he was undoubtedly
helped by the scholar's despair over the waywardness
of the romantic drama. His classical training encouraged him on this path. He appreciated the "quick-
ness" of Latin comedy, but when he borrowed—on rare
occasion—he transformed all to contemporary purpose.
He recognized that the whole must be self-expressive to
Englishmen of their own London, and that though
literary habit might still hanker after Aspers or Puntar-
volos, one need not be out of sight of St. Paul's.
There is, therefore, some significance in the change
in the second version of his first great play from the
Lorenzos to the Knowells, Musco to Brainworm, Thorello
to Kitely, and the like, in the retention of Cob and Tib,
and in the setting of the scene in familiar streets; as
there is in placing the entire action of the fourth act of
The Staple of News in the Apollo Room of the Devil
Tavern, where, as a Temple Bar reality, not a stage
illusion, he and some of his audience would find themselves later in the day for discussion of the play. There
can be no doubt that this English quality, shown in his
free use of 'local colour' and in his more general
national sentiment, as expressed in his protests against
Italian and other foreign material and in his denial of
its aid in plot, gave his work a more generous and sus-

tained vogue throughout the century than it would have
had on its playhouse merits.   It cannot be said that this
plea for realism was a novelty, or that it helps us to a clear
definition of the differences between the Jonsonian and
the traditional English comedy.   We do not require to
search long in the latter, even in plays furthest removed
in their art from the *Gammer Gurton* kind, for evidence
of actuality, though we may admit that Jonson was the
first to explain the plea in critical terms and to insist on
its allowance as a professional necessity.   Its importance,
however, comes from its connexion with other elements
in his general theory of comedy.

Jonson's view is that the English theatre had misunderstood the functions of comedy, through its neglect
not only of the differences between comedy and tragedy
in their modes of presentation, but of the individual
rights of the latter as a literary genre.   The differences
had already been discussed by Sidney and others on the
traditional classical lines, but with little or no effect on
the acted drama.   Jonson, therefore, did no more than
translate a persistent and accepted doctrine of the study
to the practice of the theatre.   In this pioneer work he
deserves acknowledgement of the kind we offer to the
inventor who turns the researches of the laboratory to
ends useful or marketable.   But his true claim as an
innovator rests on his recognition of comedy as an
independent literary form, not to be treated in mere
contrast with tragedy, and on the methods he framed
for its fuller self-expression.

What is really new in the practice of the stage as set
forth in Jonson's Comedy of Humours is that it is based
on the likeness rather than on the contrasts of the two

great dramatic kinds. In other words, he worked ana-
logically from the definition of tragedy to the definition
of comedy. Both in criticism and in the writing of plays,
the relationship of the two kinds had hitherto been considered only from the point of view of their antithesis,
and especially in discussion of the propriety of tragi-
comedy. Jonson had come to see that the differentiation
had grown more and more artificial and that comedy
was being sacrificed in the interest of her stately sister.
It was the tradition in criticism to the time of Scaliger
to begin with the latter and often to consider her as the
only member of account in the dramatic circle. The
rights of comedy, such as they were, seemed to be
granted to her for no stronger reason than that they
could not be claimed by the other. She remained a
Cinderella, in free enjoyment of her kitchen delights,
uncared for, and forbidden, except on festive occasions,
the company of her betters. If English tragedy had,
in its romantic moods, too often gone astray, there
were rules enough for stricter minds to measure the
offence : to such a disordered thing as English comedy
no tests had been applied, for none had been seriously
sought. Jonson concluded he had found these, and he
made haste to use them. If he owed them to others
(and his debt to classical and Renaissance scholarship in
this as in other matters must not be overlooked),[1] there
is no disputing the fact that the English stage owed its
knowledge of them to him.

"The parts of a comedy," as Jonson translates from
Heinsius in his *Discoveries*,[2] "are the same with a
tragedy, and the end is partly the same. For they both

---

[1] See Chapter VIII.   [2] § 131.

delight and teach; the comics are called διδάσκαλοι,
of the Greeks, no less than the tragics." This
parallelism had been urged with increasing insistence in
later Renaissance criticism, and a definition of comedy
had been framed in some such terms as these : that its
purpose is to create laughter to the end that men's
lesser faults may be made to appear ridiculous and so
may be avoided.   As tragedy works out its morality
by the effects of pity and fear, so comedy achieves its
aim, which is also ethical, by mockery of baseness and
folly in their lesser degrees, by "sporting," as Jonson
puts it, "with follies, not with crimes." He tells the
Universities in the Dedication of *Volpone* that his "special
aim" is "to put the snaffle in their mouths that cry out,
we never punish vice in our interludes." In each the
process is cathartic and corrective, but the material
differs.   The one deals with things greater and rarer,
the other with the lesser matters, familiar in general
experience ; the one works with the emotions and with
incidents produced by their clashing with each other
and with Fate, the other with the contrasts in character
and with incidents or "intrigue"; but with this
difference in the latter that the 'action' is hardly, if at
all, external or controlling, but mainly an internal effect
of these contrasts set forth dramatically.   On this
analogy Jonson based his defence of comedy, and from it
sought his opportunity of reform.

Jonson's acceptance of this definition fixed his attention
on the cardinal fact that, however 'pleasant' Comedy
was in its aim and in its method, laughter was not its
chief end ; that the false importance given to what was
only an instrument had played havoc with the comic

stage. This doctrine, drawn from Heinsius, is restated again and again—perhaps most forcibly in the
Dedication of *Volpone*, where the ethical element is so
insisted on, that Jonson pronounces on "the impossi-
bility of any man's being the good poet, without first
being a good man." Later, when Jeremy Collier attacked
Dryden on this question, he used Jonson as his best
weapon. It matters not, for our present purpose,
whether Jonson in adopting this passage from Heinsius
has misunderstood Aristotle's meaning of τὸ γελοῖον.
The statement has its value as an expression of his
attitude. Here he touches on the dangers of exalting
laughter overmuch, and shows that, as Sidney had
pointed out, there may be "delight without laughter,"
and that comedy must not "stir laughter in sinful things,
which are rather execrable than ridiculous." Delight is
the first consideration, and laughter may be a means to it.
In the second place, there is the danger of exaggeration
in its use. When that which is but a medium is employed
as an end, not only is literary *decorum* violated but the
dramatic interest is destroyed. Exaggeration, he would
hold, is the undoer of comedy even more than it is of
tragedy. Exaggeration in situation is the mainspring
of farce, and farce is the lowest kind of drama. We
may not, in Hamlet's words to the players, "o'erstep
the modesty of nature ; for anything so overdone is from
the purpose of playing." So Jonson argued, though he
did not always escape the fault of excess in his drawing
of character.

This general position established, that comedy is, in
Sidney's phrase, an "excelling part of Poesy," but
deprived of honour through the ignorance of playwrights,

the problem remained how that honour was to be recovered from and made secure against "theatrical wit,
right stage-jesting, and relishing a playhouse, invented
for scorn and laughter."[1]   That Jonson took a more
intimate view of the matter than was to be expected of
a mere academic becomes clear in his method of applying his principles to the contemporary theatre.   It was
by this that he asked to be judged.   Here he is most
constructive, and throughout his career most consistent.
Briefly stated, his hope for comedy lay in realism and in
satire.   In his plea for the first, to which we have already
referred, he was undoubtedly guided by his scholarship.
He saw, for example, that the purpose of the Unities [2]
was to obtain verisimilitude.   One flew away from facts
when one took the wings of Ariel; and comedy had
to deal with facts, known and near.   But the discipline
suggested by scholarship must not become a tyranny.
Jonson lays himself open to some misconception when
in his verses for Brome's *Country Lass* he speaks

> . . . of those comic laws
> Which I, your master, first did teach the age.[3]

He neither makes a claim nor shows the confidence in
himself or his age which Dryden does in the opening
stanza of his Prologue to *Secret Love*.[4]   He would never

---

[1] *Discoveries*, § 131.

[2] The Comedies observe "time" with some strictness, from a few
hours in *The Silent Woman* to a day and a half in *Every Man out
of his Humour*; "place" best in *The Alchemist*.   For the tragedies
see p. 193, *infra*.

[3] *Underwoods*, XXVIII.

> [4] He who writ this, not without pains and thought,
> From French and English theatres has brought
> The exactest rules by which a play is wrought.

consent that English comedy should be a *pastiche* of
Roman : but a little more attention to methods which
happened to be known long before would reveal
London to herself more fully. Even the allegory of
the earlier English drama was not to be ruled out as
incompatible with the comedy of real life, though its use
was never without danger even to a dramatist as careful
and experienced as he was ; and one success in *The
Staple of News*, against many failures, might justify the
method. As for satire he was committed to it by his
conception of the purpose of comedy. The audience
must laugh to some end, and the play must deal with
some folly and cure it by its ridiculous presentation.
A comedy was a 'comical satire,' as he styled more than
one of his plays ; and, that he might enjoy the fuller rights
of the satirist, he chose in most of his plays the more
corrosive affectation of hypocrisy rather than the mere
'hatband' affectation of vanity.[1] To prove his theory
and to secure in practice his double purpose of realism
and satire he applied himself mainly in two directions,
to the development of the device of the Humours, and
to the treatment of the Plot. The first is the more
important and the most characteristic ; and the second
is corollary.

'Humour' was, as we have seen, already a catchword
in literature when Jonson began to write. It was used
carelessly, and its history was unknown. Dryden's
discussion of it, seventy years later, is the least satisfactory section of his brilliant essay. Jonson himself,
when protesting against the popular travesty of the
term and explaining its doctrine as the basis of his

[1] Cf. Fielding's 'Author's Preface' to *Joseph Andrews*.

dramatic reform, is silent on its history. Hence, probably,
students of English literature, even to our own day, have
treated the matter as Jonsonian in origin as well as in
achievement. The idea comes, as so many metaphors
do, from medieval medicine. In the older physiology
the four major humours, corresponding with the four
elements and possessing the qualities of moisture, dry-
ness, heat, and cold in different combinations, formed,
according to their proportionate allowance in each body,
the 'temperament,' or 'complexion,' or 'constitution'
of a man and declared his character.[1] Variations in
the relative strength of these humours disclosed the
individual differences. These differences might be great
or small, in respect of one or more of the contributing
humours. By simple arithmetic it was easy to show
that great odds were against any two men's having the
same 'formula' of temperament; and so the theory
fitted itself comfortably to experience. Thus far the
physiology of the matter. Our interest becomes patho-
logical when we suggest not that A has more of, say,
the 'sanguine' than B, but either that he has more
than is good for him or has at one time or another
more than his normal proportion. In other words, it is
a case of excess or plethora, or, in the Italian phrase, an
'overboiling' of the dominant humour,[2] and the procedure of the physician is clear. It will be noted that
the root idea in this medical tradition is that there is a

[1] The same idea of combination and normal balance, also
indicated by the etymology, appears in 'disposition,' but the
source is probably astrological, and not physiological.

[2] Pope's 'ruling passion' (*Moral Essays*, i.) has some family
likeness, but it is by no means to be identified, as has often been
done.

natural balance of the humours in the composition of each body and that the disturbance of the balance is dangerous and must be adjusted. Hence many purgings and bleedings and other painful 'reductions' to serve a crude diagnosis.

We can see how easily this popular view was transferred to the uses of literature, especially during the Renaissance. The Italian commentators were probably the first to play with the subject, but it soon took the fancy of others and was used in every branch of letters. Drama, in any of its kinds, could not escape the infection, and was indeed infected before Jonson interested himself in the matter. But the playwrights had been careless in its application, treating it as whim, as Shakespeare did, or as eccentricity, often of the most external and low-comedian kind; and it is not unlikely that Jonson was strongly attracted by it not so much because it gave him an opportunity for pedantic censure as because by its right use he could offer the theatre some relief from its romantic follies. There are so many references throughout his plays, and indeed the idea is so freely woven into the fabric of each, that we have small excuse for not understanding what he meant.[1]

The purpose of comedy is to note those elements in human character which are either naturally and permanently dominant in each man, or which, on occasion, in the hazard of life, overflow and exceed their limits at the expense of the other contributing elements; to note this in a number of characters differently 'humoured'; and, in the clash of contrasts, to point,

[1] Especially in the deliberately explanatory passage in the Induction to *Every Man out of his Humour*.

with pleasant laughter, the 'moral' of these disorders.
A man whom we call avaricious because avarice is to
us his most striking characteristic and to him his most
absorbing 'humour' may preserve the established proportion of this dominating quality in all his dealings,
or he may, as is likely, under stress of living with fools
and troublesome persons, be tempted to let it grow at
the expense of other qualities, perhaps good, perhaps
indifferent. In the one case he may be said to be
'in his humour,' in the other 'out' of it. Both are
opportunities for comedy, and the problem is one of
degree. The latter is the more tempting to the playwright, not merely because 'excess' gives him more
striking stage-effects, but because it serves his ethical
purpose better. Humours of the mind, like those of
the body—as the old leechcraft maintained, and modern
medicine may not refuse—are to be cured by their own
excess.

So far the theory is clear, but complications begin
when we try to decide what are the true humours in
which comedy may find its material. It was the
confusion of the true and false which Jonson claimed
as his excuse for the venture : and his admirers praised
him for his

> Plain Humour, shown with her whole various face,
> Not masked with any antic dress,
> Nor screwed in forced, ridiculous grimace
>   (The gaping rabble's dull delight,
> And more the actor's than the poet's wit).[1]

Yet Jonson by his attitude to the 'cable hatband' style
forgets that excess in humour may be affected or

[1] Oldham, *Ode upon the Works of Ben Jonson.*

artificial as well as real, and may be useful matter
for comedy. And here Shadwell, never bright as a
critic and often dull as a dramatist, speaks to the point,
when, after lamenting the "farce-fools" whose humour is
nothing more than "by-words" and "extravagant dress,"
adds, "but the artificial folly of those, who are not
coxcombs by nature, but with great art and industry
make themselves so, is a proper object of comedy."[1]
Further, since in a well-developed comedy there should
be variety of characters or humours—artistic combinations in different ways of different 'dominant'
and subsidiary humours—it is tempting, and even a
necessity, to the writer to put some emphasis on habits
and symbols, if only as a programme-aid to the audience.
Congreve has observed pertinently, and with the
character of Morose directly in view, first, that "excess"
is what qualifies the character for comedy, otherwise
the audience would condemn the author for exposing
a humour which was neither remarkable nor ridiculous,
and, secondly, that "the distance of the stage requires
the figure represented to be something larger than the
life."[2] This artifice is, of course, necessary to all
drama, and indeed to other forms of art, whether for
the placing of the whole in proper perspective, or, by
intentional exaggeration, for aiding suggestion or enforcing some special purpose. "And sure," continues
Congreve, "a picture may have features larger in proportion, and yet be very like the original"—a plain
reminder of the problem facing every artist. It was
Jonson's problem, and he had to strike the balance

---

[1] *The Humourists*, Epilogue.
[2] *Letter concerning Humour in Comedy.* To Dennis, 1695.

between the reasonable excess he used and the demand
for reality.   Because he claimed that excess was reasonable, neither overdone nor accidental nor external in its
fun, he was probably encouraged to lay the stress he
did on his countervailing plea for real life.   This consideration is of some value when we set ourselves to
test the commonplace charge of improbability which
is levelled against both Jonson's characters and plots.
The more humours paraded in the play, or the finer
the differences in the composition of each, the greater
became the temptation to extravagance.   Jonson was
justified in seeking protection against this by the special
terms of his plea for realism and by his denunciation
of the clowning in English comedy.   Though he does
not always follow his own counsel against these 'hatband' devices, he shows that he recognized at least one
of the dangers that lay in the path of dramatic reform.

If we say that Jonson was attracted to this theory
of comedy by his classical instinct, we must dissociate
ourselves from a popular misinterpretation.   There is
no denying the fact that Jonson has many things which
suggest the method of the Latin masters, though the
more closely we study him the more we seem to see
the differences between him and his predecessors.   But
it is a strange critical error that the Jonsonian conception of the dramatic humours is only an English
copying of the Plautine and Terentian types, that his
braggarts and misers and gulls were but Romans in
doublet and ruff, and that their disguises are not less
apparent because the action and setting were Jonson's
own and English.   Jonson was attracted, as his
Renaissance guides were, by the idea of balance, pre-

vailing in physical and medical science. To restrain enthusiasm or "cure excess" is the first article of duty to the classicist : and Jonson and others in following this dictate of the literary conscience are not classicists in a derivative sense. We may say with some, if we like, that these humours have their origin in the *decorum* preached by Ben's favourite Horace and Quintilian and discussed to weariness throughout the Renaissance. There is no contradiction in saying this, and no injustice to Jonson. His insistence, in his theory and in his practice, that comedy should be real, that English comedy should be 'living' and English, was in part a measure of defence for his 'reformed' comedy against the charge that it was a scholar's affair and literary in origin, and, for himself, against the charge of affectation.

There were, however, more serious difficulties, which Jonson had not measured or, it may be, recognized. Taken together, even singly, they explain to us much of the opposition of the age and the ultimate failure of the Comedy of Humours as he planned it. If it was almost a success in his hands, and can stand comparison with some of the best romantic work, it was so only because the task was his. When it was attempted by the Shadwells, greater and lesser, the theatre began to yawn and call for a change. Some of the more obvious difficulties may be named as they suggest themselves, even in Jonson's masterpieces. In the first place, the presentation of certain selected humours throughout a long play involves the playwright, as it does novelists like Dickens, in one of two risks, either of making the characters too rigid or uniform in habit, puppet-like after the fashion of the personages in the old Morality,

and dramatically unreal, or, in the consciousness of this
danger, of striving to escape from it by exaggeration.
Jonson was alert enough to see that the latter leads to
unreality, and for this reason he protested against over-
emphasis, especially of the 'accidents' and frillings, and
counselled a close attention to 'life' as a corrective of
artifice.   In the second place, and as a corollary to
what has just been said, characters thus fixed tend to
become too simple.   Even when the humour is not a
plain study of a single folly, but a complex impression
of several, with one only slightly overtopping the rest, it
is hard to sustain the combination throughout the action.
The audience will make its own selection, and see the
man who is not altogether 'subtle' or 'morose' as little
else.   This weakness reacts in a serious way by preventing any self-development in the characters; in
which respect the Comedy of Humours stands in most
striking contrast with Romantic Comedy, and Jonson
at his best with Shakespeare always.   Jonson catches
each of his 'persons' at a moment when they appear
most expressive for his purpose.   So caught, they
remain.   They do not grow up or change; and perhaps
they do not degenerate.   They never explain themselves
as Shakespeare's men and women do; and although
some variety is effected in their presentation by a device
which Jonson made his own, and to which we shall refer
immediately, they rarely permit the action to wrest from
them anything of which they do not stand confessed
at their first entrance.   In the third place, when we
compare Jonson with Shakespeare we must ask ourselves why so few, if any, of his characters are self-
sustained, that is, can exist or do exist apart from

their setting and are individual and lively to-day as so
many of Shakespeare's people are. Bobadil is perhaps
the single exception, and he is but poor cousin to
Falstaff. The explanation must be sought in the
method which Jonson ingeniously chose to compensate
for the loss of dramatic interest entailed by his choice
of fixed and simple characters. He makes his stock
humorists explain themselves by placing them in a
variety of situations, or rather he throws upon them, as
they pose (and being humours they pose rather than
move freely), changing lights and shadows. By this
artifice he gives life to his characters, and would make
us believe that the 'person' representing the miser, or
braggart, or gull, and so referred to throughout the
play and sometimes so described programme-wise, as
in the preliminaries of *Every Man out of his Humour*, is
a real miser, or braggart, or gull. He seeks his effects
by working from the outside, by picking out the contours
of character in the changing limelight of circumstance.
He intensifies the image by the contrast of other
humours, and makes the dialogue of the other characters
draw attention to points in the delineation that must
not be missed. In this last respect Jonson is using
something more than the device, common in Shakespeare and his contemporaries, of giving clues to an
audience who had none of the stage-advertisement of
the modern theatre. With Jonson it was used less as
a guide to the action than as a supplementary and often
necessary explanation of a character. It makes the
characters interdependent in the most intimate way and
beyond the mere requirements of the action ; and hence,
as already hinted, they cannot be so easily dissociated

from their setting. Also, their lack of individuality deprives the audience of any sentimental interest in them, even with the allowance that this interest is never high in comedy. Taken as a whole, it is spectacular art rather than dramatic; and it freely uses the subsidiary aids of allusion and the "business of buff-jerkins." Like Scott, but without Scott's saving grace of movement, Jonson allows himself to be imposed upon by his antiquarism, even to the choking of his Subtles in the fumes of their own pedantries. If he fails by comparison with Shakespeare, who stands aside benevolently and lets each character be its own philosopher and its independence its warrant to posterity, he fails because even with his art and doggedness of purpose the method stands self-condemned. What puppets do those 'humours' appear when Jonson does not hold the strings, and pieces 'in the Jonsonian vein,' like *Every Woman in her Humour*, are offered as reasonable play-making! In Jonson, alone, the characters have some expressive force of their own, notwithstanding the free use of these external aids. We suspect him of some self-satisfaction in having succeeded in a hard task in which others must fail. He overlooked that a solitary personal triumph in a style offered for the general use of the stage was condemnation of that style.

We get a clearer idea of Jonson's method of presenting his characters by noting another contrast with Shakespeare's. In the latter's greater characters, and more especially in those of his comedies, and most strikingly in Falstaff, there is a double personality, the one as the stage shows it, the other as we feel it to be fundamentally. The second is of course adumbrated in the theatrical personage, otherwise we could not understand it in its fuller and deeper sense. This fuller sympathy is not the immediate effect of the words or action, but is subtly conveyed by the dramatist's art. Maurice Morgann first drew attention to this quality in Shakespeare's work, in his remarkable and unduly forgotten essay on the *Dramatic Character of Falstaff* (1777), in which he showed why we like Jack though we abuse him for his many faults, and how his stage cowardice is consistent with natural courage. In other words, the Falstaff of the average actor and reader (and no blame to their worships) is not the whole Falstaff or the true Falstaff; and, as a corollary, the comedy of the one is but superficial or partial when compared with the comedy of the other. This subtle expressiveness may be Shakespeare's own, for it is hard to think of any other dramatist who shows this power. It is certainly not possessed by Jonson, and it is referred to here to give emphasis to the fact already noted from another side, that his characters have only what may be called a stage-significance. We take them as they are, as they are 'built up' in the progress of the drama, or, to repeat our metaphor, displayed in the changing lights and shadows. They are rigid, as Jonson makes them. There is small risk of his public differing in their interpretation, as that public may in the case of Shakespeare's people, who are bodied forth by impressions outside the actual record of the stage and text and as various as the minds to be impressed.

Jonson's second concern was the plot. This may appear to be a matter of less importance in comedy, which concerns itself with humours and manners at the

expense of action and incident. Yet he lets slip no
occasion to repeat the protest of the Prologue to *Every
Man in his Humour*, as in the Prologue to *Volpone* and
in *Bartholomew Fair*,[1] where he burlesques the ancient-
modern "confusions of the playwrights." What Jonson
appears to have had in mind is shown towards the end
of his *Discoveries*, when, translating from Heinsius, *De
Tragoediae Constitutione*, Book IV., he lays down two
principles. The first deals with the 'bound' or 'extent'
of a play. It should not exceed the compass of one
day, but there should be "place left for digression and
art." "For," he adds, "the episodes and digressions
in a fable are the same that household stuff and other
furniture are in a house." The second is concerned with
the complexity of the plot. "It should be one and
entire. One is considerable two ways: either as it
is only separate and by itself, or as being composed of
many parts, it begins to be one, as those parts grow or
are wrought together. That it should be one the first
way alone, and by itself, *no man that hath tasted letters
ever would say, especially having required before a just
magnitude and equall proportion of the parts in themselves.*
Neither of which can possibly be, if the action be
single and separate, not composed of parts, which laid
together in themselves, with an equal and fitting proportion tend to the same end; *which thing out of antiquity
itself hath deceived many; and more this day it doth deceive.*"
Jonson's emphasis (here indicated by our italics) has
not saved his theory from being misunderstood, and
Dryden's pointed commendation has been passed by
or forgotten.[2] It is true and it is not true that

---

[1] V. iii.   [2] *Essay of Dramatic Poesy.*

Jonson, as the text-books persist in stating, "will have no double plot"; true, only if a second (or, for that matter, a third or tenth) plot is not, in Dryden's words, "subservient to the great one"—what "our language expresses in the name of under-plot."[1] Jonson's criticism and his own practice were inspired by the more extreme examples of romantic comedy which sinned chiefly, not because they co-ordinated different plots, but because they failed to show a just relationship between each. He would not have condemned the triple plot of *The Merchant of Venice*; and in his own comedies he has allowed a reasonable amount of the "household stuff" of second plot for the embellishment of his action. It is conceivable that he would allow a second plot of equal "magnitude" with his first, as a relief to his first and for its enhancement, but as a rule there must be a dominant action, as there is generally a dominant humour. And just as a dominant humour may fall to excess or be unwholesomely reduced in its proportion to the other contributing humours, so, in rough analogy, may a major action be varied in combination with other actions. The disposition of the humours constitute the subject of comedy and the disposition of the action its method. In both the essential facts are that there is combination, and that in the combination the effect is of a whole rather than of a series of parts, of a complete and individual character and a complete and single action. The complexity of the plot is not in itself a fault, but its handling is difficult; and Jonson, however convincingly he framed his theory, found it convenient in practice not to venture beyond the simplest

[1] *Essay of Dramatic Poesy.*

of actions. He was more concerned with the delineation
of character; and his method of displaying it, by what
we have called 'lighting,' made a stirring action less
necessary. That method will perhaps explain why in
some of his plays there is hardly any plot, just as in
those of his successors in the Comedy of Manners at
the close of the century there is little or none—a
'neglect' which has been made the occasion of some
ill-judged criticism. His manner of introducing minor
episodes and illustrations freely, with the set purpose
of rounding off each character, sometimes obscures the
action. Hence probably the modern reader rushes
to the conclusion that his plots are not really simple.
Though this eking out cannot always be defended as
Broker and his friends defend themselves in *The Staple
of News*—

> We know our places here, we mingle not
> One in another's sphere, but all move orderly
> In our own orbs; yet we are all concentrics;[1]

and though its effect upon us, who must take the text
without the aids of the theatre, is to make it hard to
unravel some of the plots (notably of *The Alchemist* and
Epicœne), we must allow that Jonson holds to his
principle of simplicity. It is beside the point to say
that *his* method fails in its impression on *us*, or that it
stands condemned by its excess; and it is no proof of a
mixed plot (some would like to say 'confused') that he
elaborates overmuch or makes his plays too long. In
Bartholomew Fair, the most crowded of all his comedies,
the reader's difficulty in keeping the action in hand is
not due to any neglect on Jonson's part to hold the

[1] II. i.

various episodes and characters in proper control. True, the play is dramatically weak. But it is realistically strong and effective; and it was Jonson's primary purpose to convey the impression of a fair with its bustling confused humanity.

Jonson cannot therefore be charged with imposing harder classical discipline on the Comedy of Humours in the making of its plots. When once comedy was allowed one or more underplots, and humours were to be shown off from different standpoints—with the elastic proviso that the unity of the play must be clear—there was not much risk of its becoming, in competent hands, a slave to classical *decorum*. Perhaps it was some fear of this, especially as a possible censure of his own efforts, that made him proclaim that the plot must be, above all things, original. He boasted that he "acknowledged no man master." In this he was but making a virtue of necessity, for his dramatic method being what it was, in contrast with the more familiar practice—first the selection of humours and then the devising of situations for their proper setting forth—he was denied the plagiary's opportunity, even if it had come to him and he had been willing. Further, it was almost an article of duty with him, as a critic of contemporary habit, not to seek out plots in Italian and French story-books and translate them into drama, or to tune them for English ears. He might on occasion borrow hints from *plays*, but he refused to be an 'adapter' or 'dramatizer' of material which had already served its purpose in novel or narrative poem. Only once, in his first extant play, *The Case is Altered*, did he borrow his plot; and even there, as if English Plautus must be more full-bodied than the Roman stage had required, he fused the *Aulularia* and *Captivi*. Part of the satire of *Cynthia's Revels* is directed against those that "feed their friends with nothing of their own." Though his text is strewn with a scholar's reminiscences, and though, even in episode and character, he draws from his predecessors—as in the kinship of Sordido with the "usuriers de Landerousse" in *Pantagruel*, or of the Silent Woman with the "femme mute" described by Rabelais in the same book [1]—he makes good his claim to originality. His use of the humours in his scheme of comedy precludes him from borrowing but in the narrowest way, and his independence of mind and his interest in the realities of English life as material for comedy saved him from the temptation. By declining to be a borrower he has invited the severest tests, which no one ever thinks of applying in cases of open theft from Cinthio or Holinshed. He hints suspicion of his own confidence by playing cicerone to himself so often—in inductions and prologues, in the body of his text, and, most painfully, in the 'intermeans' of *The Staple of News* and other pieces.

Finally, Jonson's method restricted him in his material for comedy. Though from Aristotle downwards the business of the comic Muse, as contrasted with that of her tragic sister, is character of a lower type ($\mu i\mu\eta\sigma\iota\varsigma$ $\phi\alpha\nu\lambda\sigma\tau\epsilon\rho\omega\nu$), it was felt by Dryden and others that Jonsonian comedy concerned itself exclusively with vulgar and domestic life in its lowest grades.

Jonson with skill dissected humankind,
And showed their faults, that they their faults might find;

---

[1] III. iii. and xxxiv.

But then, as all anatomists must do,
He to the meanest of mankind did go,
And took from gibbets such as he would show.[1]

Thus Jonson did mechanic humour show,
When men were dull, and conversation low.
Then comedy was faultless, but 'twas coarse ;
Cobb's tankard was a jest, and Otter's horse." [2]

Dryden is less concerned in condemning Jonson than
in showing the superiority, on the one hand, of Shakespeare's art, and, on the other, of contemporary taste—
"for humour itself, the poets of this age will be more
wary than to imitate the meanness of his persons " [3]—yet,
with allowance made for the poet's hyperbole and the
critic's condescension, the criticism is fair.   Jonson gives
us a full gallery of gamesters, roarers, cutpurses, gulls,
and bawds, all more convincing portraits than his
gentry or the high personages of his tragedies.   He
knew his Bartholomew Fair as well as any man, and
there most readily found the material for his realistic
and satirical purpose.   The Comedy of Humours allowed
but small choice, especially in its first stages, just as
did the 'Character' to the Earles and Overburys ; and
when in its later history, in changing circumstance, it
most openly affects the 'humorous' vein—as in Brome's
Sparagus Garden and more than one of Shadwell's plays—
its choice is still the same.   Higher and more artificial
society, the dukes and countesses of Mitis's protest
in *Every Man out of His Humour*, could not offer
then, or even in Congreve's day, so much variety,

---

[1] From a prologue to *Julius Cæsar*, ascribed to Dryden. See
Scott and Saintsbury's edition, iii. 103-104.

[2] Epilogue to the Second Part of *The Conquest of Granada*.

[3] *Defence of the Epilogue.*

though it might give better opportunities for plot. The dramatist who worked with humours relied, in theory, if not always in practice, on their natural contrasts rather than on the aid of an imposed action. Jonson's liking for "gibbet" folk made him less generous in plot; and, conversely perhaps, a dislike of the action favoured by the "farce - fools" of the popular stage encouraged him to seek a dramatic equivalent in the confessions and jostlings of the characters themselves. In one respect he paid dearly for his choice of lower types. He has given us no women comparable, even as studies, with the best of his men. Only once, as has been already said, he shows promise of some power. Realistic comedy had to go a long way before it thought of portraying women, not after the Shakespearian model, but with the care she bestowed on her men. It is not so much that Jonson's women are unpleasing as that they are indifferently drawn, or, if it be not unfair to saddle the dramatist with Fabian Fitzdottrel's views in *The Devil is an Ass*, indifferently understood. They are puppets rather than humours, even of the simplest kinds : wanton wives, good-natured shopkeepers, bawds, as a Fleet justice or a Smithfield apprentice might know them in passing acquaintance. If we except one or two, such as Mrs. Fitzdottrel or Widow Purecraft, it is only because they are a little more convincing than others. But they are ordinary folk, not of the dramatic stuff of his Rachel de Prie.

This sketch of Jonson's views on comedy is offered to the reader by way of prologue to an account of his plays, a procedure more excusable in his case than

H

in that of any other English dramatist. There is his sanction for this. If he felt that his work must be explained, at each venture, to his own age, what risks does he not run, three centuries later, when the stage has forgotten him and his art is rusty? It is his condemnation as an artist that he required, and requires, these aids; and it will be ours as critics if we judge without knowledge of what his problem was, and how he set himself to solve it. This knowledge may not help him much with some, perhaps many, modern readers who can find little enjoyment in him, and are content, with Meredith,[1] to leave him to scholars; but it cannot do him the injury which the mildew of commentary has done to others, even the greatest.

II

Jonson's fourteen extant comedies may be placed in three groups, corresponding with the reigns under which he lived. In the first group he gives us five— the transitional play (1) *The Case is Altered* (? 1598), followed in rapid succession by (2) *Every Man in his Humour* (1598), (3) *Every Man out of his Humour* (1599), (4) *Cynthia's Revels, or the Fountain of Self-Love* (1600), and (5) *The Poetaster, or His Arraignment* (1601); in the second other five, namely—(6) *Volpone, or the Fox* (1605), (7) *Epicœne, or the Silent Woman* (1609), (8) *The Alchemist* (1610), (9) *Bartholomew Fair* (1614), and (10) *The Devil is an Ass* (1616); and in the third, after an interval, these four—(11) *The Staple of News*

---

[1] "The comic of Jonson is a scholar's excogitation of the comic" (*On the Idea of Comedy*, p. 15).

(1625), (12) *The New Inn, or the Light Heart* (1629),
(13) *The Magnetic Lady, or Humours Reconciled* (1632),
and (14) *A Tale of a Tub* (1633). In the first he defines
his scheme of 'humorous' comedy and experiments
in literary satire; in the second, after a diversion to
tragedy, he produces his greater 'comical satires' and
masterpieces in realism; and in the third he returns to
his pet humours, recovering some of his old power in
his first effort before falling away in the 'dotages' of a
broken old age. Of these fourteen comedies, seven (Nos.
2-8 inclusive) appear with the author's revision in the
folio *Works* issued in 1616; five more (Nos. 9, 10, 11, 13,
and 14) in the second volume of the posthumous Folio
of 1640; and another (No. 12) in the one-volume Folio
of 1692. Nine, including *The Case is Altered*, had been
printed in quarto during Jonson's life, and all of these,
except *The New Inn*, between 1600 and 1612. There
are no problems of ascription or collaboration. Were
the marks of Jonson's style less clear and uniform than
they are, the literary personalities, in explanation, protest,
and quarrel, would remove all doubts as to the canon.

Jonson's neglect of *The Case is Altered*, if not as a
fault of his dramatic youth, at least as the expression
of his younger manner, shows the confidence he had
come to place in his theory and in his achievement. It
was, as we have seen, transitional in character, perhaps
unconsciously experimental. When Jonson found his
true purpose in his first *Every Man* play, he threw it
aside, as a painter would a first sketch that poorly
suggests the completed picture.[1] His pleasure in this
self-discovery and in finding his mission are remarkable.

[1] The 'copyright' view (p. 68 n.) is still only a guess.

For *Every Man in his Humour* so exceeds the expectation of a first effort, especially of a man of Jonson's temper and in conditions such as his, that it holds, by general consent, a high place in that kind of comedy of which he is the acknowledged master.   It is a striking advocacy of the reformed comedy, a vindication, to the utmost limits of defence, of an experiment in play-making to which he had been attracted by purely critical processes.   We think of Jonson offering it as proof that his theory could be translated to practice, even on the popular stage, and it may be that some of the disfavour shown to it by later readers who know little or nothing of his theory is due to the feeling that it fails in art and in entertainment because it is too conscious and deliberate.   It is a diploma piece ; more original perhaps than most, but with the fault of emphasis, almost mechanical, from which few escape.   It cannot be called 'spontaneous' (the word is Swinburne's), but its plot is 'simple,' even to tenuity ; it is not touched, except in an incidental way, by the passion for satire, which he had shown in *The Case is Altered*, and was to show more fully in all his later plays.   Its main purpose is the realistic presentation of a series of sharply contrasted characters.   As types these are all familiar : an old man concerned about a foolish son, a jealous cit and his wife, gulls of the town and country, a clown and his wife, a merry magistrate, with a company of minors (clerks, servants, and the like) to throw up their betters in relief—Londoners all, even under the Italian disguise of the first version.   It is not the least merit of Jonson's drawing of these humours that it is without the stiff lines and false

exaggeration to which a young writer, also a propagandist, might have been easily tempted, and without
the mannerism which weakens so much of his later
work. Knowell senior and Kitely best illustrate his
'humorous' method; the one blinded by anxiety for
his son's welfare to his own inconsistencies, the other
a victim to foolish jealousy; both made more ludicrous
by the complementary 'complexions' of others, as, for
example, Knowell is by the better-balanced but worse-
mannered Downright. And, as it were to remind us
that they are fools and that the showing up of their
folly is the purpose of comedy, they are given a
setting of plain fools, of gulls such as Master Stephen
and Master Matthew, with a worthy clown, Oliver
Cob. In that setting we have the first sketches in a
genre which Jonson made his own and used persistently
to the glory of the great family of La-Foole. Outside
this more 'mechanical' round of the humours stands
the famous Paul's man, Captain Bobadil.[1] He is mis-
judged by those who would take him for a mere
soldier-braggart of Plautine tradition, or do not see
that there is a difference between him and even the
best of Jonson's 'humorous' characters. For he is
more self-expressive, more independent of the devices
of setting on which the other personages rely as of
necessity, more truly than anywhere else in all
Jonson's work an original and living creation, of the
order in which Falstaff and the Knight of the Rueful

[1] This, now the accepted, spelling, is followed throughout
this volume, though Jonson prints Bobadill in the Folio as the
anglicized form of Bobadilla of the Quarto. It is, too, the more
natural English form, as Machiavel is of Machiavelli.

GEN. THEO. SEMINARY
LIBRARY

Countenance are the great patterns in different literary
kinds.   He has suffered by foolish comparison with
Shakespeare's masterpiece, and, as in the real world,
is known by the company he keeps, and offered the
cold compliment that he is their superior.   It is not
that the dramatist has drawn him better, and with
more affectionate care, than his neighbour humours, but
that he has made him differently; that the advance in
characterization is a direct effect of the freer allowance to Bobadil in the control of action and situation.
Yet he is a creature of the stage, not of life, in
the sense of which we think of Falstaff: an excellent
theatrical jest, never completely human, as we see
"the best of comical characters" under the cloak of
his stage rascalities.[1]   He interests us most, not because
he is so much more convincing than any other character of Jonson's, but because in him the dramatist
seems to succeed in defiance of his method.   Unfortunately, Jonson was never again so near escape
from the fetters of his own making.   Dickens liked
the character, and won applause from his public and
especially from Leigh Hunt by his acting of it on more
than one occasion.   We can picture to ourselves, without
the aid of Leslie's canvas, what this expert in broad
'humorous' contrasts made of the part, and be allowed
the modest suspicion that he missed some of the finesse
and gentler virtue of the "obscure gentleman."

In *Every Man out of his Humour*, the first of the
"comical satires," Jonson gives more formal expression
to his theory.   Its interest as a critical exercise is poor
compensation for its weakness as a play.   There is little

----

[1] See *supra*, p. 90.

or no plot; the characters are extravagant studies in realism verging on caricature, and suggest, when taken together, the action of cleverly handled marionettes. The elaborate description of each of the *dramatis personae*, the harping on the significance of the title, the long Induction on the doctrine of the humours and the history of comedy, and the running commentary of the *raisonneurs* Mitis and Cordatus are confession that the play is not self-sufficing—a confession less of feeble art in the author than of the tyranny of the new method. In the earlier play Jonson allowed his characters greater freedom : provided they remained true to themselves and served the general spectacular plan, they might move at will. A little chance jostling might help the plot in more than one way. In *Every Man out of his Humour*, however, Jonson has turned precisian in his own rules ; or, at least, his success in the first has given him courage to put his scheme of comedy to stricter trial. His thesis, made clear in the chatter of Mitis and Cordatus, is that humours find their remedy in their own excess. To make this 'catastrophe' more effective, he crowds the stage with a great variety of strongly defined characters and keeps them "in their humours" till the close of the fourth act. The un-ravelling in the fifth act is perfunctory. Jonson appears to feel this, in the defence put into the mouth of Cordatus when counselling Mitis to "prepare his expectation." Mitis had asked why the play bore its title, "when I saw all his actors so strongly pursue, and continue their humours." "Why," says Cordatus, with the voice of Jonson, "therein his art appears most full of lustre, and approacheth nearest the life ; especially when, in the flame and height of their humours, they are laid flat, it fills the eye better, and with more contentment."[1] The truth is that Jonson gets into difficulties by over-committing himself at the outset to the mood of Asper. He is too "peremptory," too keen to "anatomize," and to give "pills to purge," too bent on quizzing or shaming Marston (Carlo Buffone) or Brisk (Daniel) or Lodge (Fungoso) or Munday (Puntarvolo). In his zeal for emphasis he so crowds his stage that he has to ask himself "Is it possible there should be any such humourist?"[2] and he drags out his scenes to make the humours "perspicuous enough."[2] When the promised "general drought of humours among all our actors"[3] comes at the end, we wonder whether we should have observed it had Jonson let the play be its own interpreter. By this test the piece stands condemned as drama. Jonson's satirical humour was growing to a height; only when it was spent, or reduced to proper proportion, could he hope to re-awaken in English comedy the promise of his first effort. The characters do not call for individual mention. In them Jonson's realistic power is marred by excess; they do not prove to us that they are, or need be, such fools as we are asked to believe they are. This is, of course, the habit and fault of this type of comedy, but here what might be allowed to them by way of self-expression is choked off in tedious commentary. In this company of gulls, Fastidious Brisk, the "fresh Frenchified courtier," who is "humorous as quicksilver," seems to have been Jonson's chief literary care; but he is by no means, as Gifford held, a Bobadil

---

[1] At the close of Act IV.   [2] II. i.   [3] III. iii.

translated to Whitehall. The description of the "strange encounter," in IV. iv., may have suggested the kinship, but the Courtier is too much of a puppet to be mistaken for a further study in the superior comedy of the Captain. The personal satire in this rôle and the others is of some historical interest, but it does not help the dramatic, and neither Asper nor Macilente, whatever each may tell us of Jonson himself, is convincing as a stage character.[1]

Jonson gives still freer rein to satire in *Cynthia's Revels.* We have called it a critical argument rather than a play.[2] It cannot be classed with the comedies of humours, unless we force the application and call the popular literary taste of the age the humour which Jonson had chosen for ridicule. It is lifeless, inordinately long, and in certain scenes (witness V. ii.) weak in characterization ; and it may be fairly described in the words of its own Hedon and Anaides :

Hed.   See, see ! this is a strange play !
Ana.   'Tis too full of uncertain motion. He hobbles too much.[3]

Jonson's defiant defence in the Epilogue—

By God, 'tis good, and if you like't, you may,

has been generally mistaken as painful testimony to the effects of the water of the "Fountain of Self-Love" on the poet himself ; even his apologist Gifford admits its arrogance. But bully Ben, had he written a score of

---

[1] The 'In' and 'Out' of the titles of the two 'Humour' comedies promise a more violent contrast than the reader may find in Jonson's treatment ; for in both the leading characters start 'in' and end 'out.' But it is a question of degree, and in the second of excess in abnormality.

[2] *Supra*, page 16.   [3] V. ii.

Odes on Himself, must have his due.[1] When Mercury
in this play describes him, in the character of Crites, as
"a creature of a most perfect and divine temper, one in
whom the humours and elements are peaceably met,
without emulation of precedency," and rolls on in
panegyric, do we not there, and in other places too,
'smoke' the jest?[2] Let us not forget that the scene
of the play is Gargaphie—"which I do vehemently
suspect," says one of the eyases, "for some fustian
country"—and that the confusion in the action and in
the relationship of the characters (some of them both
allegorical and real), the hyperbole in description, and
the provoking digressions are intended to serve the
general plan of the literary satire. If Jonson is working
by any 'humorous' formula, he is trying to reduce the
follies of the day by ridicule of their own excess. He
is not the angry and soured man of later days; he
quizzes and tries to perplex; and in his Epilogue he
offers his roguery to be taken or declined as the Court
wills. The play is therefore beyond the range of
ordinary criticism as drama, as is so much of Lyly's
work, to which Jonson owes not a little, and here as
fully as anywhere. It is meaningless to the modern
reader without the contemporary context; as it may
have been meaningless to many in Jonson's day who
were indifferent to literary controversy or ignorant of
the offence of the Marstons and Mundays. It contains
a number of lyrical snatches and two masques, early

[1] He returns to this point in the speech of the "Armed Prologue" in *The Poetaster*.

[2] When the Perfumer says (V. ii.) "Taste, smell. I assure
you, sir, pure benjamin, the only spirited scent that ever awaked
a Neapolitan nostril," did Ben's audience see any point?

evidence of Jonson's poetic work. In this connexion
its chief importance lies, and we shall return to it again
when we come to speak of the masques. Its passages
of higher literary quality, such as the hymn to
Cynthia,[1] acquire their true interest in relation to
that courtly genre in which Jonson found his opportunity, as Lyly had found his. The lines on Echo, in
the first scene, and the speech by Lovel on the mind, in
The New Inn,[2] are in Hazlitt's opinion two of Jonson's
most poetical passages.[3]

In *The Poetaster* Jonson leaves mazy Gargaphie for
Rome. He does so, not because Rome is far away
and ancient and an escape from quarrelsome London,
but because by the fiction he could better indulge his
satirical mood, now embittered and personal. He
obtains the verisimilitude which he neither sought nor
obtained in *Cynthia's Revels*: he can strike harder at
real Englishmen dressed as Romans, and secure a more
effective outlet to his passion than a straightforward
libel can give. Though the play has, for the reasons
urged against its predecessor, small claim to the title of
comedy, that claim is certainly stronger. It was written
quickly, in fifteen weeks, a short time for Ben's
"laboured pen," and so escaped from the overdraw-
ing and digression incident to literary fun, as Jonson
understood the game; and it was sustained by the
pressure of personal conflict. The play and the apology
testify to the strength of that pressure, not only in the
attack on "illiterate apes" who had vexed him for
"three years," and in the recitation of the faults and

---

[1] V. iii.   [2] III. ii.
[3] *Dramatic Literature*, 1820, p. 171.

offences they found in him, his railing, his striking at
persons, his literary thefts, his slow art, his overstrained
satire, his lack of "pith and matter," but in his protesta-
tion that "his mind is above their injuries," that, though
he could "squirt their eyes with ink or urine," he is
indifferent, and, most of all, in his closing intimation,
that he forsakes the comic Muse who has proved so
"ominous" to him.   An "Arraignment," announced by
speeches by Envy and a Prologue in armour and ending with a farewell to comedy, is a serious confession
by a satirist, and might well be the undoing of any
dramatist.   It is surprising that the play is as good as
it is, notwithstanding its sputterings of wrath, and its
stretches of dull writing, as in the love-scene between
Ovid and Julia, in the apostrophe to Poesy (in the vein
of the suppressed passage in *Every Man in his Humour*),
and in Caesar's and Virgil's mouthings.   This seems to
be due to its better sense of climax, a commendation by
no means inconsistent with what has been said about its
dramatic weakness.   The movement of the first four
acts suggests a plot where there is hardly any, and
the fifth act, notwithstanding obvious objections to the
trial-scene, gives a satisfactory conclusion.   This appeal
of the play is remarkable, inasmuch as the characters
are undistinguished and the 'points' obscure to all but
literary antiquaries.   Tucca, the "notable shark" and
coward, the most strongly drawn of all the people in
the satire, may please the gallery, but he is a sorry
kinsman of the humane Bobadil.

When, after four years, Jonson returns to the comic
stage with *Volpone*, he betrays the effects of his sullen
retreat to tragedy.   Personal animosities have lost

their bitterness, though, in the Prologue and once in the play,[1] the insults on his slow art, his collaboration, and his plagiarism still rankle. Yet he would claim that

> All gall and copperas from his ink he draineth,
> Only a little salt remaineth.[2]

In the Dedication to the Universities, he declares that those who cater for "the multitude" may "do it without a rival, for me," and promises, "if my Muses be true to me," to "raise the despised head of Poetry again, and stripping her out of those rotten and base rags wherewith the times have adulterated her form, restore her to her primitive habit, feature, and majesty, and render her worthy to be embraced and kist of all the great and master-spirits of our world." There is temper in this mood, but more dignity, or at least a staying of personal clamour against poetasters. Jonson's resolve carried with it one serious risk, that he might overstrain the functions of comedy, as reserved for the lighter faults of men ; and another, more personal to himself, that he might throw the weaknesses of his 'humorous' method into stronger relief. The theme of *Volpone* is the familiar story of the machinations of a cunning, greedy man and his clever parasite, the follies of their dupes, and the final undoing of all parties; but Jonson, notwithstanding his liberal allowance of good fun, tunes it to a pitch unexpected in comedy, and in one place at least, where Corvino (not the wittol of Restoration comedy) would force his wife to shame, strikes the note of tragedy. All the chief characters, indeed all except the English knight and his lady and the unhappy Celia, are so ill-conditioned,

[1] II. i.   [2] Prologue.

that they forbid the 'sporting' sympathy on which comedy, by Jonson's own rule, must rely. Their deeds are "crimes" rather than "follies." The Fox and his friends are never mere mischief-makers; they are villains of the stuff of which tragedy makes use, but without the dignity conveyed in her treatment, playing with a natural frankness, with no suggestion of the discrepancy between real and assumed character which gives comedy its great opportunity. It matters not that there is a happy ending to the sorrows of minor characters. The excess in depravity is here never a reasonable cause of entertainment, as it might be, and can be shown to be, in certain plays, when a character admitting poor defence on general grounds may be useful in serving the purpose of innocent pleasure. The satirical intensity rarely, if ever, permits that laughter at vice, which is "the greatest of all possible incongruity." [1] The piece is a dramatic satire, or, better, a satirist's comedy. Not a single character in it is real, even in the sense proclaimed by Jonson himself. Everything is drawn to exaggeration : the scene is laid in Venice, the mother-city of splendid vice; there is one continuous suggestion of luxury, in Volpone's surroundings, in his wooing of Celia in terms out-Marlowing Marlowe. The intrigue is slight and the *dénouement* is reached by the weak dramatic device of making triumphant villainy over-reach itself or be suddenly pricked in conscience ; but the play, thanks to its observance of the unity of time, moves easily, notwithstanding such minor faults as the unnecessary tedium of the Fox's rôle as a mountebank,

[1] Morgann, *u.s.*

or the inexplicable entry of Bonario into the Magnifico's house, and it gathers some dramatic strength, if only in a reflex way, from the cumulative extravagance of the satire. Jonson's introduction of Sir Politic Would-be, his wife, and Peregrine in a comic underplot with little or no connexion with the main story is a confession and amends to Comedy for giving in her name this un-relieved sketch of human depravity. The soul of the piece is the parasite Mosca, Volpone's "witty mischief." But we suspect his humanity, as we suspect Volpone's, and, it may be, Voltore's, and Corbaccio's, and Corvino's, and only listen to him with the respect we give to a well-contrived hyperbole.

Jonson escapes from this sombre mood in *The Silent Woman*, where he is gentle and merely incidental in his satire. The characters, unlike those in *Volpone*, are, in Dryden's words, "all delightful"; the theme is again one of heirship, but of a spark to an eccentric uncle, not of vultures and ravens out to spoil the fox; and the play, by its dealing only with follies, is, notwith-standing an occasional descent to farce, more strictly than any other play a comedy. It is said to have been the most popular of Jonson's on the stage, and for a long time after its revival at the Restoration. Dryden's blessing in his famous 'Examen' must have helped it, for it was praise indeed that were it translated into French the question of the pre-eminence of the English stage would be finally resolved. It appealed to Dryden's critical taste as a successful application of the rule of the Unities to English drama; and to his classical sense of orderliness and coherence, by the 'rising' interest of the action, by the preparatory hints of characters before their appearance, and by the proper perspective of such subplot as is allowed. It gives him his opportunity of discoursing on dramatic humours, as Jonson's "peculiar genius and talent." But the secret of its power from the Restoration onwards, at which Dryden also hints, though in a sort of by-commendation, lies in the fact that Jonson "has here described the conversation of gentlemen with more gaiety, air, and freedom, than in the rest of his comedies."[1] For this reason the play, unique in the Jonsonian canon as a sustained effort, suggests a more intimate relationship with the Comedy of Manners of the close of the century than is openly claimed by copyists like Shadwell. It gives a very clear hint of what Jonson might have achieved had he not been so possessed by theory and the angrier mood of satire. It is condemnation of his accustomed method, on personal grounds at least, if not on technical. This is confirmed by the fact that the weakest parts of the play are those in which he relies on emphasis in characterization and contrast as in his earlier work, and so brings good comedy sometimes perilously near farce. For it appears inconsistent with his own view of 'humorous' comedy to find a subject in Morose's dislike of noise and his eccentric efforts to escape from it, and to make a cold in the head the sole provoker of fun, even in a minor rôle; and we feel now and again that what Dryden calls the "several concernments" of the characters, and defends, together with the "singularity" of Morose himself ("that stiff piece of formality," in Truewit's phrase), from the charge of exaggeration, are drawn too mechanically. Yet we cannot say, if we

[1] *Essay of Dramatic Poesy.*

consider the general effect of the piece, that they interrupt the easy crescendo of good fun, or that La-Foole, Daw, the Otters, and their friends are only tiresome recastings of Jonson's familiar stage-gull. The play saves itself by its good humour (taking the word as we now use it), a quality which subdues pleasantly the satire on women, especially on the "ladies collegiate," as well as the Jonsonian pedantries in the argument for Morose's divorce in the fifth act. Its quizzing of feminine affectations, with a gusto and grace rare in our author, and perhaps in his time, supplemented its commendation to the 'next age' for its conversational ease; and the fact that it is written entirely in prose, lighter in movement than the samples introduced in the two *Every Man* plays, is of some significance when we follow the later development of English comedy and the history of its stage reputation.

The Alchemist shows Jonson once again in his characteristic manner, but in some ways a gainer by his experience in *The Silent Woman.* It is a satire, but in lighter vein than *Volpone,* not a general attack on ugly humanity. It is a 'humorous' shaming of a fine variety of gulls victimized by the charlatan 'philosophy' of the day; and Subtle and his *famulus* Face are parallels with the Fox and his 'fly' only in their parts as provokers of the fools to folly, not in the vindictiveness of their scheming. If it has some of the seriousness incident to a comic 'tract for the times' or comedy of the Dickens kind, if it returns to blank verse as an escape, as it were, from familiarity and awes the reader with its technicalities and learning, it avoids the exaggeration and digression which Jonson could never resist when in

I

his angrier mood. Its plot is of the simplest, observing
all the unities, and especially 'place,' with even greater
strictness than in *The Silent Woman*; the action proceeds
easily in the rooms of Lovewit's house and outside his
front door, from the lively squabbling of the impostors
in the opening scene to the crisis of Lovewit's unexpected return in the fifth act. What there is of farce
is not allowed to get out of hand. The wealth of
detail, all the "crosslets, crucibles, and cucurbites" of
alchemical quackery, is handled with ease. If this is
disturbing to the modern, and, to his mind, perhaps the
damning of the play, it supplies the realistic touch which
Jonson's art demanded and James's London could enjoy.
In the characterization even the modern will admit
that Jonson recovers something of that 'universal'
quality which he so often loses in close contemporary
settings. The play gives small opportunity for the
cheaper contrasts of humours to be found in some of
the earlier comedies. There are, as in *Volpone*, two
groups, the gulls and their undoers, the latter fools too
in thinking that their knavery will not be laid bare.
Jonson shows finesse in particularizing the characters.
The three conspirators, Subtle, Face, and Dol Common,
are cheats of different patterns, and the gulls each after
his own kind, from the sensualist Sir Epicure Mammon,
always expectant, Kastrill, the heir and noodle, and the
moral humbugs Pastor Tribulation Wholesome and
Deacon Ananias, to Dapper, the silly law-clerk, Abel
Drugger, the impressionable tobacco-man, and the brain-
less Dame Pliant. The studies of the Amsterdam
Puritans and Sir Epicure Mammon show Jonson at his
best : the first for the mordant satire and snuffling

realism, the second as a literary *tour de force*, bodying
forth a character which is not farcical, as some would
hold, or burlesque, as with others, but dramatically true.
Each dupe is agog for the philosopher's stone and the
elixir, to serve his particular desires. Sir Epicure has
the Tamburlaine relish in his pleasures, and yields
himself to the quacks only because of the magnificence
which the stone puts within his reach ; as Tamburlaine
himself would have done, and in the same terms, had
he met his Subtle and Face. It is the comedy of
drunken ambition, made foolish by its excess, and yet
more foolish by its indifference to the problem why the
Subtles, with omnipotence in their hands, should drudge
for gross knights and deny themselves even a share of
the Ophirs of their own making. In no other character
has Jonson turned what may be called the inconveniences
of his dramatic style, his aggressive learning, his bookishness, his literary elaboration, to the simple universal
purposes of comedy. 'Alchemy' is no more than the
name of this good Ship of Fools : in any bottom this
company would make voyage for laughter. Jonson's
triumph is the greater because in this company there is
no dully wise man or woman to point the comic lesson
of this complex foolery ; for Surly, the traditional 'knowing one' of comedy, set to catch the other knowing
ones, proves himself an ass, and the colourless Lovewit,
a walking-gentleman who turns up at an awkward
moment in his disordered house, is content to think
himself happy with the unknown widow for wife and
the tricky Face restored to confidence.

Jonson could not congratulate himself that his
Alchemist, notwithstanding its popularity, had succeeded

in stemming the "concupiscence of dances and of antics" by giving a practical example in comedy of what art claims by "election and a mean." So he turned again to tragedy in angry protest against the "jig-given times."[1] Not till three years after the production of *Catiline* did he try to shame once more in lighter vein the degeneracy of the comic stage.

Bartholomew Fair is in intention a satire, alike on the Puritans and on the stage trashery they condemned in their own narrow unliterary way, conveyed in a series of rough adventures at the annual revel at Smithfield. But the satire does not brag itself as in the earlier comedies, and the dramatist is more reticent and of better temper in the standing matters of quarrel with his public, as set forth in the ludicrous indenture between him and them, and in Justice Overdo's general invitation to supper at the close.[2] Indeed there is some reason for thinking that Jonson was attracted to the subject as a study in vulgar realism.[3] This is suggested to us by the Stage-keeper of the Induction, ingeniously introduced by Jonson as a sort of bitter *apéritif* before the long feast. "When't comes to the Fair once, you were e'en as good go to Virginia, for anything there is of Smithfield. He has not hit the humours, he does

---

[1] Cf. his friend Selden : "In our Court in Queen Elizabeth's time gravity and state was kept up ; in King James's time things were pretty well ; but in King Charles's time there has been nothing but Trench - more and the cushion dance, *omnium gatherum, tolly polly, hoyte cum toyte* " (*Table Talk*, LXXXI.). On the tyranny of the Jig see Mr. W. J. Lawrence, *Times Lit. Suppl.*, 1919, p. 363.

[2] "My intents are *ad correctionem, non ad destructionem ; ad aedificandum, non ad diruendum.*" [3] *Supra*, pp. 33, 94.

not know them; he has not conversed with the
Bartholomew birds." The lament that there are no
'sword and buckler' men, jugglers, 'educated apes,' and
other wonders is but the playwright's promise of as
good a show of gingerbread and roast-pig and puppets, of
ballad-men and cutpurses and green ladies as the theatre
had seen or was likely to see again. The defence of the
play against the obvious charges that it is too weak in
plot, too rich in detail, too crowded, that it is not true
comedy because of its deshabille or reasonable farce
because of its length, must be that it is intended first
and foremost as a transcript of real life. Of no
other play of Jonson's may it be said he relies less on
artifice, especially in the exaggeration of qualities or
'humours.' Zeal-of-the-land Busy is a living character,
in a sense inapplicable to Butler's immortal figment, and
not because of any advantage derived from its being
dramatic; a sketch of sonorous hypocrisy both histori-
cally and universally just.[1] Nor is there much, if any,
artificial heightening in Cokes's difficult rôle of sublime
idiocy. If the play be sometimes too coarse—never a
cardinal blemish in Jonson, as in so many of his age—
here again let realism be his defence. We could not
accept the reformation of Ursula and Joan Trash to
impossible decencies. Nowadays we incline to commend
the play only as an antiquarian document of unusual
interest; it is too 'local' and allusive, as well as too
coarse, for the modern reader and playgoer; but it held

---

[1] Jonson's friend Selden refers in his *Table Talk* to Rabbi Busy's
disputation with the puppet in *Bartholomew Fair*, and adds
commentary which probably reflects his conversation with the
dramatist.

the stage in Jonson's generation, and long after the short revenge of the Puritans on the theatre for its "confuting" of the Rabbi Busys and its mockery of their "famelic sense" for the pigs-fry of Smithfield. Yet its success in the past, and its interest to us, cannot be explained by its dramatic qualities. We take it as we would take Vanity Fair itself, as a miscellany of entertaining rogues and strange toys for afternoon pastime.

We miss this freshness in *The Devil is an Ass*. The theme is still gulls and gullery, but narrowed down to a contemporary interest in 'projectors,' the ancestors of South Sea and other Bubble-makers, and demonology; and the characterization is in the early 'humorous' manner. It is a tired rather than a tiresome play, but with passages of the old liveliness; and it is excellently written, as Jonson himself hints through Gossip Tattle in his next play.[1] Meercraft, who talks in 'millions,' is, in his trickiness, something more than a puppet-copy of Face. His victim, Fitzdottrel, so happily named, and as happily by the sobriquet "his Grace of Drownd-land," is an amusing creature of silly greed and ambition, who "will still be an ass in spite of providence"; but he is never more than a mouthpiece of satire, garrulous enough to make King James nervous lest the public hear too much about certain Court doings.[2] And the 'Devil,' that is, Pug, the foolish imp who devised for himself an escapade on earth, proves himself also an ass, and the greater ass in thinking, contrary to good advice from headquarters, that in 1616 the capers of the Morality-Play Devil and Vice of 1560 were still in

[1] *The Staple of News*, I. ii.   [2] II. i., and *Convers.* xvi.

fashion and effective. The centre of this satirical
play is Satan, who, in the first act, gives Pug good
advice and blessing, and in the last his curse for dis-
gracing Hell's good name for intelligence. In these
brief 'entrances' Jonson shows a tantalizing restraint.
Nowhere has the spirit of comedy so subtly, and yet so
harmlessly, touched Jonson's art; but it is only a touch,
and we wish for more. The play has a prospective
literary interest in the domestic cynicism of Lady
Eitherside and her friend Lady Tailbush (IV. i.)—a characteristic noted by Gossip Mirth in *The Staple of News*
(I. ii.)—and in Master Ambler's adventure (V. ii.). By
way of contrast it gives us, in Mrs. Fitzdottrel, a pattern
of fidelity more amiable and more fully described than
is usual in Jonson's comedies.

When Jonson returns to comedy, nine years later,
he is still interested in the conventions of the old
Morality and in their entanglement with the realities of
modern life as an aid to his satirical purpose, but he
has learned to use them with subtler art. This is at
least true of *The Staple of News*, for whereas in *The Devil
is an Ass* the devil-scenes are but a frame to the action
—Pug, throughout that action, being disguised, and
rather more of a fool than an expert in wickedness—
in *The Staple of News* abstractions such as Pecunia and
her household, Mortgage, Statute, Band, and 'blushet'
Wax, the five and only women of the play, mix with
frankly human folk like the Pennyboy family and the
unscrupulous Fitton. It is still a habit with Jonson to
give descriptive names to his characters or humours, as
Picklock for the Man-of-law, Lickfinger for the master
cook and parcel-poet, and the like, though he rarely

declares an allegorical intention, either wholly or in
part. Here, however, and most clearly in the case of
the "infanta of the mines," he attempts the double task
of maintaining their symbolic character and preventing
an undue suspicion of their unreality among their real
neighbours. For this reason the play has been condemned by many, and for it praised in the highest
terms by Swinburne.[1] There is safety in the middle
view that, while it is more remarkable than its predecessor, both for its daring and achievement in this
respect, and too sustained in the vigour of its satire to be
classed with Jonson's 'dotages,' it is no more than an interesting experiment by a writer ill-suited for the work by
his practice in poetic masque and in realistic comedy. If,
as Swinburne has justly pointed out, the Gossips of the
'intermeans'—Mirth, Tattle, Expectation, and Censure
—out-distance the *raisonneurs* in *Every Man out of his
Humour* as "genuine and living sketches," it is simply
because they have little or no claim upon us as abstractions,
whatever the dramatist may call them. In the 'Prologue
for the Stage,' Jonson attempts a plea for his experiment
by asking his audience to use their ears rather than their
eyes; and would seek to rescue the theatre from its
Hyde Park and Phœnix realities by taking advantage
of the poetic opportunities to be found in allegory, or
in ecstatic language like that of Lickfinger and his
friends in the fourth act, too serious to be burlesque,
even in their mouths. Posterity sees how foolish the
claim was, and that what dramatic credit remains to
him from his later work rests solely on his loyalty to
earlier purpose. The play has a double satirical motive,

[1] Following Gifford, but going further.

the folly of the search for wealth and the mob's mad-
ness for silly gossip. The latter is described in an
amusing way in the transactions of the staff of a "brave
young office" called the Staple of News, who purvey
fictions of the most extravagant kind to gaping sub-
scribers.[1] The satire is literary rather than dramatic,
as it is also in the scheme for the foundation of Canters
College,[2] a *jeu d'esprit* in parallel with the Ladies' College
in *The Silent Woman*; and it is made the occasion
for return to familiar topics such as alchemy and the
brethren of Amsterdam.

Two matters of interest, not peculiar to *The Staple of
News* but indicated with some prominence in it, may
be mentioned : the first, the employment of personages
outside the action, to explain and comment upon the
piece; the second, the author's pointed references to
previous work. Jonson offers, in what he here calls
the 'intermean,' a generous supplement to the more
formal declarations of the prologue and induction. He
had already supplied a model in *Every Man out of his
Humour*, in the critical bouts of Asper, Cordatus, and
Mitis. Though the device is convenient to some kinds
of lighter comedy, and especially to burlesque, as shown
in Sheridan or in the more frivolous practice of our
own day, it is a confession of weakness in comedy so
carefully planned by such a 'serious' comic writer

---

[1] The Ingenious, who honour Shakespeare's Puck as the first
telegraphist, will find clear anticipation of certain modern engines
of war in Vitellesco's egg and the 'invisible eel' (III. i.), as they
will discover in Shirley's masque of *The Triumph of Peace* the
modern threshing-machine, the multiple cooking-stove, and the
diver's dress !

[2] IV. i.

and realist as Jonson. Even when its personalities and
schoolmasterly wisdom are not oppressive, it spoils the
dramatic illusion and insults the reader's intelligence.
Jonson can never forget to be critical and let his work
justify itself. All his plays are streaked with commentary on himself and his fellows; but it is significant
of declining dramatic power that what in the earlier
play has the excuse of a formative and militant effort,
is in the later work of *The Staple* and *The Magnetic Lady*
so calmly elaborated, that, cuckoo-like, it starves the
fable of its dramatic interest. The second characteristic
can be found in nearly every play. The reader of *The
Staple* will recall the account (may we say advertise-
ment?) of *The Devil is an Ass* at the end of the first act,
will note the repetition of names, as Ambler from the
same play and Zeal-of-the-land Busy from *Bartholomew
Fair*, and, turning to other comedies, will discover
many associations, varying from mere echoes of name
and episode to declared literary kinship as in *Every
Man out of his Humour* and *The Magnetic Lady*. In the
last of these, for example, we have not only a restating
almost in identical words (I. i. Intermean) of the early
protest in the Prologue to *Every Man in his Humour*,
but, in another place, a direct reminder (II. i. Intermean)
of an earlier utterance, in the words "Oh, he told you
that in a prologue long since."[1] This linking up of
different works in a long career, together with a
persistent habit of explaining the titles chosen for each
and the author's references to himself by name, is
perhaps unique in dramatic literature. But Jonson's
artistic consciousness and egotism are perhaps also

[1] In *Bartholomew Fair* and also in *The Silent Woman*.

unique; and they explain his continuous interest in his own development.

In *The New Inn, or Light Heart*, Jonson casts allegory aside, not, as might be expected, to recover the directness which the Comedy of Humours had lost by this connexion, but to indulge an old man's whim for romance, of a kind; but romance only in its disorderly weaving of an impossible plot, and hardly to be so called, if we think of *The Sad Shepherd.* This hint of reaction is its chief interest. As a play it is as poor stuff to us as it was to the Londoners who hissed it off the stage before the actors had done. To find, with Lamb, some "beautiful passages" (surely an easy task anywhere in Jonson), or with Hazlitt to commend the sketch of the host Goodstock, cannot make us forget the improbabilities of the plot, the faults of structure, the forced device of disguise, the tedious wit of the dialogue (as in the tailor-metaphors of Lady Frampul and her maid in II. i., or the inkhorn fun of Tipto and Fly in II. ii.), the scuffling scenes—so much "balderdash and bonnyclatter," for the "good wine" promised. The laboured lines on Platonic Love in the third act derive their interest merely as an index to a contemporary literary fashion, and, taken with the repetition in the masque of *Love's Triumph through Callipolis*, are evidence of a failing in originality. This sad *Light Heart* is a 'dotage'; and all our resentment against Owen Felltham for lack of good taste in attacking the stricken poet cannot tempt us to call his censure unjust. Even the friendly Tom Carew saw that Jonson's comic Muse had "declined" far from the "zenith" of *The Alchemist*, and could only

> foretell a red
> And blushing evening, when she goes to bed.

The reception of the play was the occasion of a fierce
outburst in a Preface 'To the Reader,' in a "char-
acterism of the chief actors," an early, if not our
earliest, snatch of stage - criticism, and in the unparalleled *Ode to Himself*, showing "the just indignation
the author took at the vulgar censure of his play by
some malicious spectators." This is the old Jonson
calling upon himself once again to leave the "loathed
stage"; but his vision is blinded by disease, and we
turn from confessions of "shrunk" nerves and disordered
vanity to the hope of his "blushing evening." The
critical reader will stop for a while at the passage
in the first scene describing the Lord Beaufort and
give it an autobiographic value as a tirade against the
'bold bawdry' of medievalism and as an apology for
Ben's ancients.

In *The Magnetic Lady* Jonson is frankly retrospective,
in his return to the Humours, in his purpose to make it
a sequel or finale to his varied efforts in comedy of that
kind,[1] and in his summing up, with the aid of his old
device of the intermean, of his critical quarrel with the
public. There is little in his ingenious plea to 'reconcile'
the Humours, for the function of comedy is, on his own
showing, the reconciliation of the individual humour to
its original tenor and of the group to a reasonable and
comfortable relationship. The play has the deeper significance that, notwithstanding all the ups and downs of
his career, Jonson remained in advanced years true to
the faith of his youth, and zealous in its defence. That

---

[1] See the passage quoted *supra*, p. 51.

faith had, as we have seen, lost some of its first purity under the temptation to sacrifice realism to allegorical ornament. In *The Magnetic Lady* he tries to return to the old way. But there is little or no 'life' in the Compasses and Loadstones; they are narrative rather than dramatic humours, neither self-expressive by their own action nor explained by the action of others. Captain Ironside — Rudhudibrass de Ironside — is a bookish travesty of earlier successes in the portraiture of the soldier; and at once invites comparisons. We seem to read a consciousness of effort in and between the lines, and most clearly in the all-too-necessary commentary of Messrs. Damplay and Probee and the boy of the house, John Try-gust. Even the affectionate James Howell made bold to tell his 'father' Ben that whereas he was "mad," that is possessed of "divine Fury," in the *Fox* and "madder" in the *Alchemist*, he was "not so mad"[1] in this piece. The dialogue drags, and the verbal wit rarely rises above the level of Gossip Polish's malapropism of 'Armenians' and 'Persians' for Arminians and Precisians. The play could not, if indeed anything could, save Jonson from the enmity of the Gills and Joneses or let him make his peace with playgoers who grumbled at the name given to a chambermaid or pretended to be squeamish over the actors' gag. When he told his audience that "a good play is like a skein of silk, which, if you take by the right end, you may wind off at pleasure . . . but if you light on the wrong end you will pull all into a knot," and that the duty of spectators is "to await the process and events of things, as the poet presents them,

---

[1] *Familiar Letters*, ed. Jacobs, p. 267.

and when he shut the mouths of the more critical with "Let us mind what you come for, the play," it was not unreasonable for them to ask whether the poet had given them good silk and an orderly skein to unwind, or whether so much pother of defence was not like the crying up of indifferent wares. They asked these questions rudely ; yet we cannot say that *The Magnetic Lady*, as we read it now, proves them to have been too fastidious.

It may be that *A Tale of a Tub* was "not liked" by the Court for other reasons than its rustic setting and its open mockery of Inigo Jones. Few nowadays will be generous enough to commend it as a play. If it has the interest of a 'sport' in Jonsonian comedy, it is so only in a superficial way, though, with *The Sad Shepherd*, it seems to show some change in outlook. It is noteworthy that in both these plays Jonson turns to the country and simple life, but in the *Tale* there is no babbling o' green fields, no restirring of the old fervours of romance. It is, as the Prologue calls it, a "ridiculous play," seeking relief in the contrasts of an antique English revel ("from old records") and the fun of village folk,

> to show what different things
> The cotes of clowns are from the courts of kings.

Its setting is little more than a *literary* device, the re-dressing of the bourgeois humours of *Bartholomew Fair* in country habit. It aims as deliberately at realistic effect in its use of dialect and proverbs, and it is essentially satirical in purpose. If Jonson's choice of subject reflects the awakening interest in ballads and popular literature, it was made by him merely to trick out an old theme afresh, not, as in *The Sad Shepherd*, to escape to fresh artistic conditions. We have assumed that it was written in Jonson's closing years, in difference with some who, perhaps unduly impressed by its literary weakness, consider it to be one of his earliest dramatic efforts, afterwards republished in his decline for its attack on his colleague the architect. The setting of the action early in Elizabeth's reign makes the play an antiquarian study at any stage of Jonson's career, and allusions to the "Queen," of which much has been made, are as inappropriate to Jonson's first decade of authorship as to 1633 when the play was acted. Until evidence is forthcoming of an earlier text, we shall consider it an old man's jest, made, as Gifford puts it, "to relieve the tedium and misery of long disease"; written rather in whim than to further his literary propaganda or revive his jaded reputation on the stage; a general satire on his neighbours in the guise of yokels, and incidentally more pointed against Inigo Jones,[1] because the quarrel was fresh and illness had made him fretful. It is "a Tale of a Tub, sir, a mere tale of a tub,"[2] a diversion partly for the great fishes which threatened his peace, partly for his own entertainment. But this laboured farce with its unlovely Awdrey and its buzzards of Totten could contribute nothing to his fame.

[1] There may be, too, some reminiscence of Jones's device in the first antimasque in *Pleasure reconciled to Virtue*, and of the reference to it in the supplementary antimasque *For the Honour of Wales*.

[2] Though there is a Squire Tub who claims to be *subjectum fabulae* (V. ii.), and mysterious association with some architectural device of Inigo's (IV. ii., V. iii.), the play would still deserve its name without these.

CHAPTER V

THE MASQUES

I

JONSON'S reputation as a comic dramatist was hardly greater than as a writer of masques, yet posterity has endorsed the one, if with a grudge, and has quite forgotten the other. There can be no complaint against this, for the masque is a halting instrument, and even in Jonson's or Milton's hands—if *Comus* be of this kind—could not achieve, when considered as a whole, what we would rank among the greater things of literature. Bacon calls it a "toy," and apologetically includes a short account of it among his "serious observations," and, though he loved show as dearly as any man, even as the princes who "will have such things," pleads that it should be "graced with elegancy" rather than "daubed with cost," with song and dialogue than with mere display.[1] Jonson was proud of his work in these "toys," and was convinced that "next himself only Fletcher and Chapman" could make them.[2] We must not forget that his long devotion to this form was more than the following of a fashion or for the gaining of

[1] *Essay* xxxvii. [2] *Convers.* iii.

Court rewards. Our knowledge of his character at once condemns the suggestion that he entered on this career with indifference to his art or to selfish ends. He brought to the task experience and learning, and, above all, a purpose as deliberate and defined as in his fight for a reformed comedy. Jonson had no chance successes. His position as the true creator of the masque and the unchallenged master in the genre was a personal triumph, won in loyalty to ideals and methods of his own making.

This triumph is the more unexpected by us, if it was not so by his age, because it was obtained in an art in many ways alien to his genius as we understand it, and especially unsuited for the discipline which he imposed on all his work. Court festivity was not the happiest occasion for literary 'messages' and protests, much less for any that Ben was likely to urge; and the jostling of scene-painters, musicians, and dancing-masters for their share of royal favour must have broken the heart of the bravest poet. In one respect he saw eye to eye with his fellow-craftsmen, that the masque was the expression of the sensuous side of art, that it should be a 'revel' in colour and movement and imagery, should express moods which were impossible on the popular stage, and incidentally, for the gratification of the Court and some badly used poets, should show open defiance to the tyranny of Zeal-of-the-land Busy and his friends. For the Prynnes were stirring; and

> at no time did the laws,
> However understood, more fright the cause
> Of unbefriended poesy.[1]

If Jonson took a more exalted view of the functions of

[1] Shirley's *Example*, 1634.

K

poetry and of its rights than many good men who had no
Puritan sourness in their taste, and, when maintaining its
place in the masque, appears severe in comparison with a
writer like Campion, there is no reason why we should
obscure what was really a fundamental difference between
him and the mere moralist.   But to Jonson the masque
counted for more than this.   It allowed him to indulge
that "poetical vein" which had had small place in his
realistic and satirical work.   In it he had freedom for
spectacular fancy and the poet's enthusiasms.   He could
sing, marshal his splendid goddesses, call up his grotesques,
mix, when he willed, the real with the whimsical, be
the poet *sans gêne*, as he could not dare to be even in
the luxurious moments in Volpone's chamber.   The
masque was thus to him the complement to the comedy
of humours.   He had a second reason, almost identical
with that which spurred him on his venture with comedy,
that there were interests of a literary kind to be served,
that by good writing and careful planning the mere
'jiggery' of the Banqueting Hall might be transformed.
It was a handsome and characteristic plea for the self-
sufficiency, if not the pre-eminence, of the literary part
of the masque, for the 'book' as against the 'setting.'
In the satirical dialogue of *Neptune's Triumph* the Cook
would argue with the humble Poet that, as it is his
"place to know how to please the palates of the guests,"
it is the latter's "to know the palate of the times."
"A good poet differs nothing at all from a master-cook."
The Cook's argument that both are bound to satisfy
the public taste is humorously developed, but it does
not touch the problem which lies in the background
of the satire — and is teasingly left there — whether

the Cook is not as much the arbiter of taste as its flunkey.

A play, lost to the modern stage, may live as literature, or, at the worst, as literature of a kind, but the masque stripped of its scenic splendour is only a sorry relic. Literary quality of a high order was not called for, and, we may say, was not of the essence of it. What might be infused by a writer of Jonson's talent cannot now be rated at its original power when read as a fragment of a complicated production, intended to be seen as well as heard, but now irrecoverable even with the aid of the antiquary. If the masque is open to the criticism that it is, like the later opera, a hybrid of the arts, and from the point of view of any of these necessarily inadequate, it has other drawbacks when considered exclusively as literature. It is of necessity artificial, more so than the pastoral, and is judged not less severely, perhaps with better reason, than that kind. It also relies so much on tradition in the selection and use of material, more especially with Jonson, whose purpose was to show how he could turn that material to fresh account, that we are at once put out of sympathy, except when, with Charles Lamb, we stumble on occasional passages showing "poetical fancy and elegance of mind." Further, the writer of a masque was compelled to work within narrow compass, a difficulty greater for him when relying on the co-operation of others for full expression than when making, let us say, a sonnet, where the complete effect is under control, single and literary. Yet Jonson faced all these problems with confidence.

This is not the place to discuss the history and

relationship of the masque and kindred forms, except
in so far as these help us to understand Jonson's work.[1]
The problems of development and the differentiation
of type present difficulties of the kind familiar to the
student of the early popular drama. It is hard to find
a perfect definition for each of the varieties, or two
examples which satisfy the same conditions; and it
is as vain to seek for a strict genealogical or chrono-
logical sequence as it is in the case of the Miracles
and Moralities. In fact, the deeper we go into the
evidence the clearer it becomes that there was no precision in the naming of the various forms of Mumming,
Disguising, Masque, Entertainment, Barriers, and Device.
We may fix on certain general differences. We may
say that the first was a performance by masked men,
who, in ceremonious manner, rarely by dancing, and
always without speaking (cf. 'Dumb Show'), carried
out a simple action : that the Disguising was a dance
executed by two sets of performers, men and women,
each making a separate entry and then dancing together,
and that it was in costume ('disguised') and sometimes with vizards : that the Masque, in its later phase,
as a 'novelty' to be distinguished from the 'disguising,'
was a dance performed by costumed persons, from eight

---

[1] Accounts of the English Masque have been given by A.
Soergel (1882), H. A. Evans (1897), R. Brotanek (1902), and
P. Reyher (1909). M. Reyher's volume, entitled *Les Masques
Anglais, étude sur les Ballets et la vie de Cour en Angleterre*
(1512–1640), is in every way a remarkable contribution and one
of the most striking examples of recent French erudition and
good sense in the treatment of English literary history. M.
Castelain's *Ben Jonson* (1907) contains an interesting chapter on
the subject.

to sixteen in number, not necessarily masked, with partners selected from the circle of spectators, both lords and ladies; that during the display each dancer spoke to his neighbour or neighbours, informally rather than in set speeches; and that the whole was structurally a composite of the old professional disguising with the domestic dance or formal 'ball,' and was intended as a ritual of courtly gallantry. The terms Entertainment, Barriers, and Device were broadly distinguished thus: the first as descriptive of a speech welcoming a great personage, generally offered in the open, and with such decoration of setting and action as place and occasion permitted; the Barriers as a make-believe tourney between bodies of knights, on a like occasion, and with like accompaniments; and the Device, used first as a general term, like 'disport' or 'shows,' for disguisings, pageants, and other festive spectacle, but later, as with Robin Goodfellow in *Love Restored*, when the Masque had been strictly defined and its relationship with the regular drama established, often merely as a name to differentiate the show (whether Masque or Entertainment or Barriers) from an ordinary stage play. Though these main differences hold throughout, they are confused by the changing nomenclature (witness the passage between Notch and the Groom in Jonson's masque of *Augurs*, 1622) [1] and the appearance of mixed forms, and by the frequent

---

[1] *Notch*—. . . Our desire is only to know whether the King's Majesty and the Court expect any disguise here to-night.

Groom—Disguise! what mean you by that? Do you think that his Majesty sits here to expect drunkards?

Notch—No. . . . Disguise was the old English word for a masque, sir, before you were an implement belonging to the Revels.

synchronism of some of an earlier type with those of
a later. We therefore confine ourselves to the consideration of those in which Jonson and his age were
interested, the Masque, the Entertainment, and the
Barriers. If these have any literary value, it must be
sought for then, say between 1603 and 1640, when the
Court encouraged the best talent.

From first to last, even in Jonson's hands, the foundation of the masque was the dance. "Surely," says
the Shepherd to the intruding Fencer in *Pan's Anniversary*, "the better part of the solemnity here will be
dancing." All the rivalries of poets, architects, and
musicians for the glorification of their arts were of no
account without the dancing-master. He could produce
a masque without them ; they never without him. It
is true that by allowance the aids of song and dialogue
and scene were elaborated often to extravagance, but
they never lost their ancillary place, and Jonson's
strong plea for the poetic part was not so much that
the poet should be supreme as that he should not be
made to yield place to the carpenter and scene-painter.
In his writing he never forgot that his verse or prose
must express rather than control the festive movement,
whereas Inigo Jones, in the enthusiasms of his great
talent as much as in his animosity to Jonson, seemed
to forget that he had only a share which some might

Groom—There is no such word in the Office now, I assure you,
　　sir. I have served here, man and boy, a prenticeship or
　　twain, and I should know. But by what name soever you
　　call it, here will be a masque, and shall be a masque, when
　　you and the rest of your comrogues shall sit *disguised* in
　　the stocks.

not call the chief. A second point to be remembered is that the masque was exclusively the business of the Court, though in its prime some relationship was established between it and the popular drama, either by the appearance of masques or masque-like interludes within plays or by the borrowing by masque of certain devices from the common theatre. In its earlier phases down to the close of Elizabeth's reign it is strictly a Court amusement, varying in quality with the ebb and flow of royal favour. Its remarkable development in the seventeenth century was due directly to the strong encouragement given by James and Charles and their Queens—a fact, in the case of the first, which may astonish those who cling to the legends of Northern meanness and Puritanic restraint and are ignorant that James, fifteen years before his coming to England, had written a masque [1] or *Epithalamion*. Never in England was an art, essentially of the lighter vein and greedy of display to extravagance, so handsomely served as was the masque by the first Stuarts. Although writers were attracted whose experience had been wholly won in the public theatre, it retained its courtly character to the last. Its splendour owed everything to its princely associations, as Jonson tells us in *Hymenæi*, when acknowledging how these had encouraged poets. In it, says Daniel in his *Tethys Festival*, in praise of Inigo at the expense of Ben, "the only life consists in show"; and Jonson himself, sometimes, as in *Love's Triumph through Callipolis*, seems to have held his hand lest any poetic tedium might interrupt the orgy of spectacle. If we cannot recover that splendour, there is at least

---

[1] Apparently the only Scottish example extant.

no excuse for forgetting this distinction and hastily applying our knowledge of the playhouse drama as a test of these fantastic pieces. In the third place, we should keep in mind that the masque was an occasional work, "a transitory device," as Jonson styles it in *Hymenœi*, written to celebrate some domestic matter of Court or to enhance some annual festivity. With rare exceptions, the performance—or the first perform-ance, if the piece survived for a second presentation—took place at Christmastide, early in January, and most often on Twelfth Night.[1] This fact not only illustrates its close connexion with the Court, but shows how different the conditions in which it was produced were from those affecting the free lances of the theatres, who had their choice of times and subjects and could defy their Henslowes with greater ease than the masque-writers could the powers of the Banqueting Hall.

That rugged Ben, the unlikeliest of courtiers, took so kindly for a time to this discipline is not less surpris-ing when we consider how straitly his dramatic fancy was leashed by the literary form of the masque. But he undertook the task with open eyes and with a clear missionary intention. The interest of his venture to us resolves itself into admiration of his ingenuity in recon-ciling the claims of traditional form with his insistent

---

[1] The Poet in *Neptune's Triumph* describes himself as "a kind of Christmas engine ; one that is used at least once a year, for a trifling instrument of wit or so." This time of the year was more suitable for display, as Daniel shows in his *Tethys Festival*, per-formed in June 1610, where he tells us they had to dispense with the torchbearers, "who might have added more splendour" (and who indeed supplied most of the light), because " they would have pestered the room, which the season would not well permit."

originality. It was doubly characteristic of him to maintain that a norm was desirable and that he should define it. He could justify his confidence, for he both made the masque and controlled its short career. The first of these commendations is not discredited by the fact that the main lines in the form of the later masque which we are about to describe can be traced a century earlier, if *The Booke . . . of an Earles House,* quoted by Collier, be above suspicion.[1] The comparison of any of his masques, even his first, with any that went before will supply the measure of praise to be given to him as a creator.

The basis of the masque in its final form was, as from the first, the dance, performed by a body of 'masquers' in various movements among themselves and with the spectators. These movements were three in number: the *First Dance* or *Entry,* immediately after the company had made its *Grand Entry,* or *Triumph,* or *Procession* ; the *Second Dance* or *Main Dance*; and the *Third Dance* or *Last Dance,* or *Going out,* or *Going off,* before they retired from the lower stage or floor to their seats at the upper end of the hall. These dances were confined to the masquers, whether professional performers or (as a rule) members of the Court, and were rehearsed under the care of instructors like Thomas Giles and musicians like Alfonso Ferrabosco. Between the second and third, two supplementary dances were given, the first called the *Measures,* a stately movement or base-dance, 'with the men' if the masquers were women, or by 'taking forth the Ladies' if they were men, and the second, *The Revels,* a lively movement or round-dance,

[1] *Annals of the Stage* (1878), i. 24.

also with partners, sometimes described as *The Galliards and Corantos*, probably unrehearsed, and continued at will. These five dances (three formal and two 'intermixed')[1] constituted the masque in its simplest form, as they did the *Main* or *Grand Masque*, when a prelude to the *Grand Entry* was added and elaborated with its own dances. The musicians accompanied the dances and rendered songs throughout, generally one by way of 'overture' as the masquers descended, one between each of the three chief dances (frankly described in some cases as a device to give the dancers breathing-time), and sometimes one as a departing chorus. Occasionally a patch of dialogue took the place of a song, but only when by the development of the preliminary portion speaking personages were available. It will be seen therefore that as far as the principal masque is concerned, and for that matter the grand masque, even in its latest form, there was small opportunity for literary embellishment. Three short songs, or four if there was one at the end, or a few lines of explanatory dialogue, were the sum of the poet's allowance. He could not stay the frolic of the dances by tedious monologue or too much dramatic interlude. Even Jonson, when he varies the rule, and that rarely, as in *Pan's Anniversary*, only transforms the 'last dance' to a fantastic revel or 'antimasque' and inserts no more dialogue than is necessary.

Jonson had therefore to find an outlet elsewhere. The only place was at the beginning, where already by the example of Gascoigne and others the prologue of the Morality had become more elaborate as a description

_____
[1] So referred to in *Hymenæi*.

of the ensuing spectacle and as a literary effort. In a
slight sketch, more dramatically drawn, he could not only
give, in the formal verse of a Presenter, a special meaning to the festivity, and determine the character of the
dressing and action of the dancers. He could thus
improve the masque and win some credit for poetry.
Unfortunately for him, his opportunity was in due
course also his fellow-inventor's. Jonson began by
making the whole stage-management his business. He
could not well do otherwise, for he was devising a new
thing of a literary-spectacular kind, and he was the only
man to say what properties and 'motions' were required.
In his earliest masques he gives elaborate particulars of
the *mise-en-scène* and makes generous acknowledgement to the artificers of their attention to his wishes.
But it was a risky partnership, even in happier circumstances than Ben and Inigo found themselves, and it
was perhaps not altogether said in malice by Daniel, for
Ben's ears, that "in these things wherein the only life
consists in show, the art and invention of the Architect
gives the greatest grace, and is of most importance :
ours, the least part and of least note in the time of the
performance thereof; and therefore have I interserted
the description of the artificial part, which only speaks
M. Inigo Jones." [1]

In this prelude, which, were it not for confusion
with 'antimasque,' we might call, with Daniel, the
'antemasque,' [2] Jonson gave free play to his fancy
and controlled the presentation. He selected his motive
(or took the hint from high quarters), planned the

---

[1] Preface to *Tethys Festival*.
[2] "The ante-maske or first show" (*ib.*, ed. Grosart, p. 311).

scene, and arranged the characters, the dialogue, and songs as he might have done for one of his comedies; but he kept in mind, as distinctive features of his task, the peculiar conditions in the Banqueting or other hall at Court as compared with the stage of a theatre, and the terpsichorean character of the main performance. As the dancers invariably made their 'Grand Entry' in disguise and the disguise generally varied with each performance, it was easy for the poet to devise a scene which should determine and explain the masquerade. It was possible either to 'write up' to the properties, if the Master of Revels had some special costumes to display, or, when the royal purse was empty, had to use what he found in the wardrobe; or, on the other hand, as was happily allowed to Jonson throughout most of his career, to decide on the plot and on the various decorations to be carried out by others. It will be found on examining the theatrical details of Jonson's masques that in nearly every case the poet had the fullest freedom in the choice of subject, and the architect in the means for carrying out the invention.

If we turn for a moment to the mechanical arrangements for the presentation of a masque we shall better understand its literary form. In no two cases was the stage plan the same, for the Master Surveyor had to build as well as paint, but a general reconstruction can be offered from the evidence of the masques themselves and from extant sketches by Inigo Jones. Let us imagine an oblong hall, lying north and south; and let us divide it roughly into two parts, the southern half for the spectators and the 'dancing place,' the northern for the acting and scenic display. In the former, near its lower end, stood the 'State,' where the Court sat, and, along either side, the 'scaffolds' (what we should now call boxes) for the ambassadors, nobility, and other favoured persons. In the centre, sometimes on the floor-level, sometimes on a low platform, was the dancing-place, on which the movements of the Main Masque— the Entry, the Main, and the Going out—were performed. Round this space or platform, at different places, the musicians placed themselves. From the centre of the side of this space, farthest from the 'State,' a flight of steps or 'degrees' led into the northern half of the hall, up to the stage which extended from wall to wall, and which was in Jonson's time framed by a proscenium, specially designed for each piece. A removable screen or curtain appears to have been sometimes drawn between the two halves of the room at the point where the steps met the dancing-place, but when the device of the proscenium was adopted, the curtain took the place it still retains in the public theatre. The stage was not deep, and behind it rose one or more platforms, the first reached by two short flights. On this higher level, in the centre, were the seats of the masquers, who remained undiscovered in a cliff or 'concave shell,' or behind a suspended cloud, or in some other scenic contrivance till the crisis of the performance arrived and they made their Grand Entry downwards to engage in the First Dance in the area in the midst of the 'State' and scaffolds. Behind the masquers' seats, and still higher, was generally another platform for some of the musicians who discoursed the 'loud music,' and for the working of mechanical devices in connexion with the spectacular disclosure of the masquers after the preliminaries on the lower stage were concluded. This building up of the stage in various tiers was an arrangement derived from the earlier practice of presenting the 'show' on a 'scaffold' or 'pageant,' of the kind used in the itinerant Moralities, rolled into the hall and hidden by a 'screen.' The device lent itself readily to the elaboration of spectacular effects, especially when the tiers were fixtures, and could be erected to any plan. It may have lingered till the masque itself died, but there is some presumption that with the advance in the use of movable scenery, and in the suggestion of perspective by side-scenes, it was supplanted by a single floor or stage, as shown in Jones's drawing for the 'Pastoral of Florimene,' presented in December 1635.

There was small opportunity for dramatic action and dialogue between the opening 'set' and the discovery of the masquers. For neither could these worthies sit hidden too long in their 'work,' nor would the spectators wait too long for the true masque to begin with its stir of the hautboys and the moving feet, the choruses and flare of torches. If they waited, they must have something more than set speeches between ancient kings or abstractions as in the old Morality, or part songs by Triton, and the nymphs, and the like; something to suggest what was coming. The motive might be one of contrast, presenting shades on the banks of Styx before Youth joined in the revels, or hags at their incantations as a prelude to the entry of Queens in their chariots; it might, in realistic mood, deal with the gossip of the buttery-hatch before Apollo introduced his band of Augurs; it might interest the audience in the comic chatter of hangers-on and menials known to all present, before calling forth the stately abstractions or troops of elves ; it might be plainly satirical or quizzical of heralds and printers, before the audience found themselves transported to the New World in the Moon. The author's one problem was the quick and effective arrest of the attention of a frivolous audience, not the easiest of tasks with the rivalry of arts that could make a more direct appeal to sense. To meet this necessity and to give poetry her pride of place constituted Jonson's dilemma. He solved it as well as any man could hope to do by his use of the antimasque.

This term has been frequently misunderstood, through confusion with 'antic-masque' and 'antemasque,' both of which are found contemporaneously ; and it has been urged in support of each that the manner was 'antic' or grotesque, and that the antimasque generally and properly preceded the main masque. Jonson himself has put the matter beyond doubt, in two passages, in the 'directions' in the masque called by Gifford *The Hue and Cry after Cupid* and in the masque of *Queens* following immediately thereafter. "At this," he writes in the first, "from behind the trophies Cupid discovered himself, and came forth armed, attended with twelve boys most anticly attired, that represented the Sports and petty Lightnesses that accompany Love"; and later, "wherewith they fell into a subtle capricious dance, to as odd a music, each of them bearing two torches, and nodding with their antic faces, with other variety of ridiculous gesture, which gave much occasion of mirth and delight to the spectators." So far, only the antic character is described, and with special reference to the dance which was directly suggested by the morris and which continued many of its features; but at the opening of the next piece Jonson turns to the subject again in more explicit terms. "And because her Majesty (best knowing that a principal part of life in these spectacles lay in their variety) had commanded me to think on some dance, or show, that might precede hers, and have the place of a foil, or false masque, I was careful to decline, not only from others, but mine own steps in that kind, since the last year I had an antimasque of boys; and therefore now devised that twelve women in the habit of hags or witches, sustaining the persons of Ignorance, Suspicion, Credulity, &c., the opposites to good Fame, should fill that part, not as a masque, but a spectacle of strangeness, producing multiplicity of gesture and not unaptly sorting with the current and whole fall of the device." Bacon calls these pieces Antimasques, and adds "they have been commonly of Fooles, Satyres, Baboones, Wilde-men, Antiques, Beasts."[1] Twice in the masque of *Augurs* Jonson uses the form 'antic-masque' ("Our request is . . we may be admitted, if not for a masque, for an antic-masque"), and again in one of Vangoose's speeches, but with a flavour of pun, and adapted to the taste of Notch and his friends of the buttery-hatch or to the satirical purpose of the mountebank.[2]

The essentials, therefore, of the antimasque are, on Jonson's showing, that it shall be a 'foil' to the masque,

[1] *Essay* xxxvii.

[2] Other examples are rare. One will be found in the anonymous *Masque of Flowers* (1614) printed by Evans, pp. 105 *et seq.* Cf. also the two forms in the two editions of Chapman's *Masque of the Middle Temple and Lincoln's Inn* (1613).

and that it shall "sort with the current and whole fall of the device." The idea of contrast is developed with great variety. There may be a simple antithesis of situation and character—a visitor from Saturn (*Time Vindicated*), or Jupiter (*The Fortunate Isles*), or Heaven (*Love's Triumph*) to wonder at the ways of James's London and criticize, as the *compères* and *commères* used to do in the modern *revues* before these fell on evil days. There may be, as *dramatis personae*, such commonplace beings as projectors, or amorists, or braggart soldiers, or newsmongers, or travellers, or scapegrace courtiers, or roarers, or bawds, to give point to the splendour of the allegorical or mythological spectacle which followed. If the same performers are to appear in both, they may be introduced as tattered gipsies or moping shades before they flaunt their finery and health in the frolic of the Grand Masque. If the Grand Entry is the apotheosis of Beauty, let the prelude be a revel in the ugly and horrible; let witches and their ill-smelling cauldron precede the advance of great Queens in a cloud of perfume. Because the dances of the masque are cunningly devised movements, stately and decorously gallant, let the grotesques of the antimasque amaze the spectators by their licence or make them laugh at their foolery. If the masque is a pretty allegory of "the rites done to the goddess Chloris," let the company be told in the prelude that hell is topsy-turvy, that Ixion is loosed and leading lavoltas with the Lamiae, and that the Furies are at nine-pins. This balancing of effects gave Jonson's special talent its opportunity. For the masque being essentially an expression of Beauty, generally in its more gorgeous heroic aspects, the

L

contrast had to be found in plainer and less lovely
realities, to which Jonson, as a satirist of the sterner
sort, as a student of real life, and as a writer trained
in the tradition of the theatre, could readily turn.
Through his theory of excess in the humours and of
their contraries he found an easy way to the antimasque;
and the use of the masque in drama and familiarity
with the princely and 'rude mechanical' contrasts in
plays like *A Midsummer-Night's Dream* prepared his
courtly audience for the venture. It must be observed,
however, that a strict antithesis of characters was by
no means necessary or always attempted. Jonson, it
is true, often worked by direct contraries, most plainly
and confessedly in his masque of *Queens*, where twelve
hags serve as introduction to twelve queens, and in a
hardly less marked way in *Oberon*, *Lethe*, *Love's Triumph
through Callipolis*, and others; but this spectacular
contrast might be little more than an 'accident' of the
essential purpose of the antimasque to stimulate interest
in the Grand Entry and ensuing display, and to relieve
their traditional formalism.

There were risks, as Jonson knew, in this association
of the masque and the antimasque. He shows this in
the satirical dialogue between the Poet and Cook in
Neptune's Triumph, where the former, having confessed
that he has no antimasque, and indeed does not

> think them
> A worthy part of presentation,
> Being things so heterogene to all device,
> Mere by-works, and at best outlandish nothings,

is offered the strangest olio of flesh, fowl, and vegetables
for his prologue; and again in his satire of Vangoose in

the masque of *Augurs*, " O sir, all de better vor an antick-
mask, de more absurd it be, and vrom de purpose, it be
ever all de better.   If it go from de nature of de ting,
it is de more art : for dere is art, and dere is nature."
Yet in no case, in his long series of masques, is there
any doubt of the dramatic propriety of the antimasque,
even in its most extravagant mood.   His mastery in
this respect is well shown in *Neptune's Triumph* and *The
Fortunate Isles*, in which the subject and characters of
the main masque have a strong family likeness, but in
which the antimasques have little or nothing in common.
The plea for a strict relationship between the two parts
was not therefore, as over-refined classicism might insist,
that there could be only one proper contrast to a given
subject.   A master-hand at least could show that there
was no limitation to ingenuity in the antimasque without
hurt to the true sequence.   It was also possible, as is
shown in *Love Restored*, to use to good effect what
appears to be inappropriate, or might be as appropriate
in any other setting.   Even to make fun of the public's
curiosity to see masques and of the Court's exhausted
treasury may be the best introduction to Cupid and his
gay masquers.   "Alas," says Plutus, "how bitterly the
spirit of poverty spouts itself against my weal and
felicity ! but I feel it not."   Then the Triumph enters.

The public liking of the dance fun of the antimasque
tempted some writers to over-elaboration (D'Avenant
topping the list in his *Salmacida Spolia* of 1639 with
twenty antimasques), to extension of the satirical
dialogue, and even to the intrusion of a second antimasque
within the body of the masque proper.   Jonson supplies
instances of all, but sparingly.   The eight entries in

Chloridia are exceptional. They appear with sinister significance in this his last masque, which marks the crisis of his quarrel with Jones and his partisans. His use of a second antimasque, that of the Thebans in *Pan's Anniversary*, makes for his own theory rather than against it, for there it takes the place of the "Going out," and knits the masque and antimasque more closely. Further, as the antimasque was not necessarily an *ante*masque, there was no reason why it should not appear within the masque, fully associated with it, and not in the way of a Morality Interlude. It is more surprising that Jonson's trial in *Pan's Anniversary* was not repeated more frequently, especially as the antimasque was acted by professionals, sometimes from the theatres, who would have relieved the Court revellers and given them breathing-time. But the main tendency was towards dislocation, and the antimasque took a position as art and entertainment analogous to that of the prologue and epilogue in relation to the late seventeenth century plays. This dislocation, as Jonson saw, served both parts ill, even to their undoing, for the masque tended to grow dull and formal in its extravagance without the provocative aid of the antimasque. The latter fell away to occasional satire, farce, or grotesque spectacle. Yet when Jonson gives us in his later masques scenes of pure comedy, which might be transcripts from his studies in the Humours, he seldom fails to make clear their appropriateness to the succeeding spectacle.

II

Jonson's career as a masque-writer begins in 1605, with the production of the Queen's first masque, *Blackness*, but he had already tried his hand in *Cynthia's Revels* (1600). In his day, and till the close of the seventeenth century, masques within, and as part of, plays were not uncommon. At least seven of these connected pieces had appeared before 1600 : one in Kyd's *Spanish Tragedy* (I. v.), one in Greene's *James IV.* (V. ii.), three by Shakespeare, in *Love's Labour's Lost* (V. ii.), *Romeo and Juliet* (I. iv. and v.), and *Much Ado* (II. i.), one in Munday and Chettle's *Death of Robert Earl of Huntingdon* (II. ii.), and one in Middleton's *Old Law* (IV. i.). Between the production of *Cynthia's Revels* and Jonson's death there are about forty-five extant plays containing masques by dramatists of repute, including Shakespeare, who adds to the three already named *Timon of Athens* (I. ii.), *The Tempest* (IV. i.), and *Henry VIII.* (I. iv.). Jonson, however, contributes only once again, and not till 1633, in the satirical and rather informal scene in the fifth act of *A Tale of a Tub.* There are many reasons why the masque thus intruded itself in the ordinary drama ; it had a decorative value in tableau or grand finale, as is shown by its coming in generally at the end of a scene or act, or of the play, and it supplied that atmosphere of faery and courtly gaiety which Lyly had been the first to throw round the drama ; as a 'play' within a play it helped the main action ; it had the interest of a fashionable practice, all the greater because that practice was at Court, about whose doings the twopenny gallery was

always curious and had heard a little from the favoured
burgesses who had been admitted by the Lord Chamberlain. It may have been of special concern to those
dramatists who, unhonoured by commands to write,
wished to show their quality in the art or to use it as
a vehicle of satire; but, above all, it supplied an easy
device for the development of the plot, when the
disguise of the dancers aided or confused the purposes
of gallantry, or gave an introduction, as in Romeo's case,
or helped conspirators to achieve their tragic surprise.
That this last reason, its dramatic usefulness, is the
most cogent, seems to be supported by the fact that the
majority of these imbedded masques are of the simpler
type, concerned exclusively with the stir of the entry of
the masquers, the disguise, the opportunities given to
the couples of talking apart, the music and banqueting.
Some are no more than a dance of persons whose
vizards and disguises are assumed solely for the ravelling
or loosing of the situation. There were seldom any
scenic effects, even on a rolled-in scaffold. Nearly all,
and certainly all Shakespeare's, including the mythological 'show' in *The Tempest*, were performed in
procession and dance, with song and dialogue, on the
floor of the 'scene' or the ordinary stage. They were
merged in the play and were a real part of the action
rather than an intruded spectacle. Jonson, on the
other hand, anticipates in *Cynthia's Revels* the more
elaborate manner of the Court masque. It may appear
remarkable that he whose later worries were with
people who were all for spectacle, should have from the
first made no use of the simpler form; but his quarrel
was only with their methods and what he chose to

consider their aggressiveness. He never entered a general plea for restraint in the preparation of the masque, and, when left to himself, was no niggard in device.

It was therefore certain that when Jonson turned to the individual masque he would champion its rights to the full. Possibly, the self-confidence gained in his *Cynthia's Revels* would have given us the masque of *Blackness* and its successors, had Davison and Campion never written their masque of *Proteus* for the Gray's Inn Revels of 1595, or Daniel his *Vision of the Twelve Goddesses*, nine years later. These two pieces, which with other three, anonymous, constitute the known earlier work in this kind,[1] show that the main characteristics of the 'staged' masque of the early seventeenth century are already present, in the framework of song and dance, in the importance of the Grand Entry with its surprise and spectacular effect, and in the free decorative use of allegory and scholarship; but they lack the dramatic quality which Jonson was to give, and when compared, especially in the opening dialogue, with his masque of *Blackness* confess their closer kinship with the old rather than with the new. The vogue of the masque at Court and in great houses is shown by the fact that between the date of the production of Jonson's first masque and his death more than seventy pieces were written; and it is reasonable to assume that there were others which

[1] "The Queen's Masque in honour of the arrival of Prince Henry" (1603), the Indian and Chinese Masque, and the "Masque in honour of the marriage of Sir Philip Herbert and Lady Vane" (both in 1604). The *Gesta Grayorum* contains, with *The Masque of Proteus*, the so-called masques of Amity and of the Helmet. These are however only 'shows.'

have not survived or are at present unknown. Of this
number of extant masques twenty-five are by Jonson;
and as many are anonymous. Five are the work of
Campion. Of the other known writers, including
Daniel, Chapman, Marston, Beaumont, Middleton, no
one has more than two. The twenty-five by Jonson
represent nearly fifty per cent of the whole produced
during his career as a masque-writer, that is, between
the appearance of the masque of *Blackness* and *Chloridia*.
This outrivalling of his neighbours in fertility as well as
in quality is the warrant for considering the masque as
a Jonsonian creation.

Before the appearance of the masque of *Blackness*
Jonson had written, besides the masque in *Cynthia's
Revels*, three of his eight *Entertainments*. These may
be referred to at this place as they have a close artistic
association with his masques,[1] the earlier showing in
several respects a sort of studio-practice in the effects
worked up in the true masque, the later reflecting his
experience in the fuller genre. The first three help us
to understand why Jonson, notwithstanding certain
obstacles of a personal kind, quickly won the favour
of the Court. His first and best Entertainment, *Of
the Queen and Prince at Althorp* (25th June 1603),
generally known as *The Satyr*,[2] is strongly suggestive
of the masque in the variations from the old-fashioned
Speech, in the substitution of two lively movements

---

[1] Jonson's three *Barriers* are referred to *infra*, in connexion
with the masques with which they were directly associated in
performance. He may have written others. Cf. the short *Speech
at a Tilting* (*Underwoods*, XXIX.).

[2] Gifford's variant of the second title 'A Satyre,' in the Folio
of 1616.

for the formal address, in the introduction of dances, fantastic for the fairies and lively for the morris-men, in the 'flyting' of Mab and her elves with the Satyr, in the vein of the later antimasque, and generally in the fulness of the poetic invention. In his next, *King James's Entertainment in passing to his Coronation* (March 1604), which he shared with Dekker, he relapses to the pedantries of the old allegory and, doubtless in compliment to the King, makes his lines hobble with learned allusions. The third, for the King and Queen at Sir William Cornwallis's House (May 1604), called by Gifford *The Penates*, is a slight piece, but it has the interest of anticipating in the speeches of Mercury Jonson's use of prose, and in the part-song of Aurora, Zephyrus, and Flora his quality as a lyrist. Maia's verses make us think of *L'Allegro* and speculate on Milton's knowledge of them. The *Entertainment of the Two Kings of Great Britain and Denmark*, given at Theobalds in July 1606, a short piece in Latin, with eight lines in English, is unimportant ; and the next, for King James and Queen Anne, also given at Theobalds, in May of the following year, is a short and rather stilted dialogue between Genius, Mercury, and the Fates, concluding with a song. We have no more Entertainments from Jonson's pen until 1633 and 1634, unless we consider a nondescript piece of 1626, loosely called *The Masque of Owls*, one of the kind. It is a monologue by Captain Cox "in his hobby-horse," who introduces in order six figures of owls and describes each in a satirical character-sketch. Jonson's last efforts were *Love's Welcome*, produced at Welbeck before Charles, when on his way to Scotland in 1633, and

another with the same title, in 1634, at Lord Newcastle's place at Bolsover. They are of small account,
but they show the effect of his long practice in the
masque, and especially in the antimasque; in the
first, in the dialogue between Accidence and Fitzale,
the quintain revelry of Green-hood, Blue-hood, and
other 'disguised' persons, and the bagpipe dance, and
in the second, in the burlesque entries and dances of
Dresser, the plumber, Quarrel, the glazier, and others,
preceding a dialogue between Eros and Anteros, and
in the satire of Inigo Jones in the character of Coronel
Iniquo Vitruvius. An undated *Interlude* (ascribed to
Jonson) on the occasion of a christening at the Earl of
Newcastle's is in the style of antimasque, in its chatter
between a wet nurse, a dry nurse, and a midwife, with
no reserve in realism and little merit in the dialogue
or in the watermen's song.

Jonson's reputation as the author of the two *Every
Man* comedies, with *Cynthia's Revels* and *The Poetaster*,
probably commended him to Lord Spencer of Worm-
leighton for his entertainment of the Queen and Prince
Henry, but it was his success at Althorp and his
compliment to the King at the coronation show in
the City of London and again at Highgate that won
for him the coveted honour of presenting the Queen's
first masque. If the trouble over *Eastward Ho* had
been earlier, and there had been time to command
another poet, Ben's prospects at Court might have
vanished. It may be that James's forgiveness for an
offence in which Jonson had but a small share was a
confession that he could not afford to lose a man so
much after his own heart. Jonson would have con-

soled himself without difficulty. He had his mission to the theatre, and *Volpone* was ready for his patrons at the Globe.

The masque of *Blackness*, the first of Queen Anne's festivities after her going south to England, was produced with great splendour. The "bodily part," including a first attempt at scenic perspective, was designed by Inigo Jones, but Jonson imposed his plan, even to details, and he has left us a full account. The first paragraph of the preliminary note in the printed edition is really applicable to all the masques, and is characteristic. "The honour and splendour of these spectacles was such in the performance as, could those hours have lasted, this of mine now had been a most unprofitable work. But when it is the fate even of the greatest and most absolute births to need and borrow a life of posterity, little had been done to the study of magnificence in these, if presently with the rage of the people, who (as a part of greatness) are privileged by custom to deface their carcases, the spirits had also perished. In duty therefore to that Majesty who gave them their authority and grace, and, no less than the most royal of predecessors, deserves eminent celebration for these solemnities, I add this later hand to redeem them as well from ignorance as envy, two common evils, the one of censure, the other of oblivion." To explain his Ethiopian setting to meet the Queen's wish "to have them blackmoors," the authority of "Pliny, Solinus, Ptolemy, and of late Leo the African" is advanced, and notes in Greek and Latin are appended; and when he comes to the properties, he is careful to tell us that they are as "described by the ancients."

Clearly he had an eye for posterity as well as for the revellers and Master Jones. And if posterity, not being Jacobean in temperament, is not less bored by Leo the African than some of James's Court must have been, it can still find pleasure in the simple motive and in the verse. Jonson was commanded to prepare a sequel, the masque of *Beauty* (10 Jan. 1608), known also as the *Queen's Second Masque*. He tells us that he was asked "to think on some fit presentment which should answer the former." The connected story of both pieces can be epitomized in a few words. The ladies of Niger, hitherto proud of their black beauty, had fallen into "black despair" on hearing, through "poor brain-sick men, styled poets," that before the age of Phaëton they were "as fair as other dames"; but by an oracle they had been told to seek consolation in a land "whose termination (of the Greek) sounds Tania." So, after passing Mauritania, Lusitania, and Aquitania, they reach Britan[n]ia, or Albion the fair, "ruled by a sun,"

> Whose beams shine day and night, and are of force
> To blanch an Æthiop and revive a corse.

They dance with the Tritons on the shore, till, "accited to sea," they return, with the promise given by their moon-goddess, that in their native African lake they will be allowed to lave themselves to 'perfection,' and that they will return next year. In the second masque, Januarius, who laments their overlong absence, is informed by Boreas that the fault is not theirs, that they are transformed, and that Night,

> mad to see an Æthiop washéd white,
> Thought to prevent in these ; lest men should deem
> Her colour, if thus changed, of small esteem.

On this pretty plea she had sent the dames tossing on
a floating island. Boreas is dismissed, and the gentler
Vulturnus finds the isle and wafts it with its Throne of
Beauty and the ladies to the English shore, where he
commits all to the care of aged Thames. The close
association of the two pieces is important, in their plot,
in their performance by more or less the same company
of Court ladies, headed by the Queen, and in their
later publication by Jonson together in one quarto;
but chiefly in their use of the device of contrast, as
suggested by the Queen. This last is of some significance as revealing at the very outset the principle which
Jonson used to good purpose in the antimasque. The
interruption of Jonson's plan for the presentation of
the second masque and the interpolation of another by
him in 1606 and of one by Campion in 1607 do not
appear to have attracted attention. The date is fixed
in the first and is again referred to in the second
("thence assigned a day for their return"); and the
opening words of the Preface read—we might think
rather petulantly—"Two years being now passed that
her Majesty had intermitted these delights, and the
third almost come, it was her Highness's pleasure again
to glorify the Court. . . ." Jonson may have fretted,
but the delay was a covert compliment, for in the
interval the Queen, who claimed the masques as her own
and had arranged that the "same persons" were to
dance in both, had given birth to two daughters, Mary,
on 8th April 1605, and Sophia, on 22nd June 1606.[1]

[1] The first died on 16th December 1607 and the second on
23rd June 1606. We hear later of the Queen's gout preventing
her dancing.

It is therefore not unlikely that Jonson wrote or planned his masque of *Beauty* at an earlier date than has been assumed.

Hymenæi, presented on 5th January 1606 in honour of the marriage of the boy Lord Essex, is not therefore an interloper in any literary sense, and we are excused the task of explaining the break in continuity. It strengthens the evidence of Jonson's liking of balance, for he introduces two groups of masquers, one of eight men, representing the four Humours and the four Affections, followed by another of eight ladies, representing the powers of Juno, "the governess of marriage"; and in the Barriers, played next day, he found further opportunity, on traditional lines, in the word contest between Truth and Opinion, and in the tourney of the champions. As a piece it is of indifferent quality. The verse, especially in the adaptations of Catullus, has a forced air. Jonson may have felt relieved rather than piqued, when, the Queen still delaying her return from Niger with unblackened face and arms, Campion and his musicians were entrusted on 6th January 1607 with the festivity in honour of Lord Hay's marriage; all the more, as it turned out he had to do honour to Lord Haddington, on 9th February 1608, immediately after he had presented his masque of *Beauty*.

The Haddington piece, happily named by Gifford *The Hue and Cry after Cupid*, makes some amends for the stiffness of Ben's first nuptial masque by its lyrical quality. One passage—the second stanza of the first Grace—has been described as "simply magnificent," a Swinburnian ecstasy which most readers will be content to let pass without adjustment. Moschus had proved

a better model than Catullus. The historical interest
of the piece is that it is Jonson's first experiment in
antimasque, in the entry of Cupid with twelve boys
"most anticly attired" and in their "subtle capricious
dance." The device so commended itself to him that
in the next year's production, the masque of *Queens*, he
reminds his readers of this "antimasque of boys," and
proceeds to elaborate the idea in his twelve witches,
"not as a masque, but a spectacle of strangeness."

In the masque of *Queens*, Jonson recovers the freedom
of invention which he had lost in preparing 'occasional'
pieces like *Hymenœi* and *The Hue and Cry after Cupid*.
Her Majesty is again patron and his chief 'celebrator'—
"it increasing now to the third time of my being used
in these services to her Majesty's personal presentations."
This masque was performed on 2nd February 1609
with great magnificence, and it still ranks as one of
Jonson's best. When he wrote it, he was indulging his
"high serious" mood. Just a year before, he had made
his pronouncement to the Universities, in the dedication
of the quarto print of *Volpone*, on the rights of poetry
and the offices of the poet ; now he chooses for his argument "a celebration of honourable and true fame, bred
out of Virtue," and promises to observe "that rule of
the best artist, to suffer no object of delight to pass
without his mixture of profit and example." The
motive is simple, that Virtue is the one excelling and
undying joy of men ; reminiscent in many ways to us,
both in the poet's utterance and in the contrasts of
setting, of the Miltonic exhortation, "Love Virtue ; she
alone is free." The plot is of the slightest. The revels
of the witches are suddenly dispersed before a Vision of

the House of Fame with twelve great Queens, including
her Majesty as Bel-Anna, Queen of the Ocean. "A
person, in the furniture of Perseus, and expressing heroic
and masculine Virtue," does honour to the "bright bevy"
of Queens; Fame appears and speaks; the Queens
descend, ride round in triumphal chariots, and thereafter,
with dance and song, bring all to a conclusion. Jonson
applied himself to the first part, at the expense of the
second, which, though by no means indifferent writing,
leaves most to spectacular aids. The first part or
antimasque, on the other hand, had, as he understood
it, to be self-expressive. It was his first experiment
in the fuller form, with dialogue, and it called for
special care. He brought to the task his experience as
a student of the harsher and uglier realities which he
was using to satirical ends in comedy. Its length is a
confession of his zest; but it is not so excessive as
to weaken the general effect. Some contemporaries,
always grumbling at his work, complained of its congested learning and the meticulous bookishness of the
witchcraft, or laughed at the annotation. Later critics
have made comparisons with Shakespeare's masterpiece
(written in 1606 but not printed till 1623) to the dis-
advantage of the Dame and her eleven hags as rivals
to Hecate and her three, and of Jonson himself on
the score of plagiarism. It is wiser to decline such
criticism, and to remember that the poets worked in
different kinds, that Jonson had not the full dramatic
opportunity of the other, and that—to name the chief
blot in modern eyes—the identification of each witch
with an abstraction had a traditional excuse and is
tolerable in work which is mainly spectacular; and, in

the matter of indebtedness, to keep in mind that there
were more than enough of witches and cauldrons at the
service of any Jacobean poet without his having to
borrow from his neighbour.[1]   Verses like these—

> A murderer yonder was hung in chains ;
> The sun and the wind had shrunk his veins ;
> I bit off a sinew : I clipped his hair ;
> I brought off his rags that danced i' the air—

are the masque's security against censure.

Oberon, accompanied by *Prince Henry's Barriers*,
followed on 1st January 1611.   It is a delicate fantasy
of Silenus and his satyrs, fays and elves, Oberon and
his knights ; light in dialogue, and interspersed with a
number of lyrical measures in pleasing variety.   In this
fairy counterpart to the masque of *Queens* Jonson shows
more restraint in the length of the antimasque ; for
elfdom, even to the poet of *The Sad Shepherd*, does not
offer so many learned temptations as the craft of Hecate
and her ugly crew.   The piece, by the dignity of its
lines, in speeches of Arthur, Merlin, and the Lady of
the Lake, marks an advance on Jonson's first attempt
in this kind.   Its personal interest was centred in the
wordless rôle of Prince Henry as Meliadus, a name we
are told he liked to bear in these shows, and of which
Drummond reminds us in the dirge he was called upon
to write so soon thereafter.

In *Love Freed from Ignorance and Folly* and *Love Restored*

---

[1] The theatre had many witch-plays.   One recalls, besides those
referred to, Middleton's *Witch*, Dekker and Ford's *Witch of
Edmonton*, Heywood and Brome's *Late Lancashire Witches*, and
others.   James and his *Demonology* helped the vogue of what to
many, Jonson perhaps included, had the interest of a belief.

—if this be the place and order of these undated
masques—Jonson exhibits two different methods, both
characteristic. The first is a slight piece with an antimasque of Sphinx and the Follies preceding the masque
proper, danced by the Graces and sung by the priests
of the Muses; but it is loaded with commentary explaining the allegorical meaning—a more blatant attempt to
justify the Horatian doctrine of 'profit' than Jonson
generally permitted himself to make. He recovers himself in *Love Restored*, where he makes good his claim
to have created the masque anew, by blending satire
and realism with mythological solemnity, and by asserting the rights of drama as against mere decoration.
Masquerado enters to announce to the Court that all
things are at a stand and that they are like to be disappointed of their entertainment. He is interrupted by
Plutus, disguised as Cupid, who rails at him, declares himself "neither player nor masquer," but the god " whose
deity is here profaned by him," and swears he will have
no more masquing. "How! no masque, no masque?"
cries Robin Goodfellow, rushing in. "No, faith," says
Masquerado. "There is none," adds Plutus insolently,
"nor shall be, sir; does that satisfy you?" and, again,
"Sir, here's no place for them nor you." Robin there-
upon explains what difficulties he met in seeking
entrance to the Palace. Plutus bids him and Masquerado
go packing, and denounces the " prodigality " and " riots "
that are "the ruins of states." "Let them embrace
more frugal pastimes," he cries, with more to the same
effect; which utterances, so niggard and puritanical,
suddenly convince Masquerado that this "reformed
Cupid" is an impostor, and give Robin his revenge in a

speech against the god of money, who steals Love's ensigns and usurps "all those offices in this age of gold which Love himself performed in the golden age." He will bring all where Love is to be found, Plutus meanwhile lamenting "how bitterly the spirit of poverty spouts itself against my weal and felicity." The true Cupid enters in a chariot with the masquers, claims his bow and arrows from Mammon, introduces his ten companions as the ten ornaments or graces of courtly Love, and begins the First Dance. Three short songs complete the literary equipment of the masque. Though *Love Restored* is one of the slightest of Jonson's attempts, and is occasional in purpose, it is one of the easiest for us to reconstruct and enjoy. It is true Jonson, and Jonson at the best. Its dramatic freshness, together with its economy in display, yet without stinginess, was a powerful retort to the Joneses, and even the Daniels, who made carpentry and paint the chief concern. Jonson showed too that it was possible to preserve the character of the antimasque in pure dialogue, without the customary dance.

The death of Prince Henry on 6th November 1612 stopped the customary Christmas festivities, but in February the mourning was interrupted by the marriage of the Princess Elizabeth. Jonson was abroad with young Raleigh, and the honours fell to Campion, with his masque of *The Lords* (14th February 1613), Chapman with his masque of the Middle Temple and Lincoln's Inn (15th February), and Francis Beaumont with his masque of the Inner Temple and Gray's Inn (20th February). We may amuse ourselves by speculating on what Jonson thought of this, and of Campion's coming Entertainment at Caversham House (27th April) and masque at Court (26th December) on the occasion of Lord Somerset's marriage; and how he took the compliment silently offered to his art by his rivals in introducing antimasques of 'twelve Frantics' (in the masque of *The Lords*) or of "baboons attired like fantastical travellers" (in Chapman's). Yet he lost little time, for we find him joining in the Somerset festivities on 29th December with his *Irish Masque* (performed a second time on 3rd January 1614) and an accompanying *Challenge at Tilt*. The first piece is short, perhaps because there was little time for preparation, and, if the text be not at fault, incomplete in its masque form. Novelty was Jonson's best weapon for asserting himself once more, and simple realism again the happiest thrust at the splendours which had been contrived in his absence. So he not only introduces four Irish footmen, but puts the dialogue into the broadest dialect. "For chreeshes sayk, phair ish te king? phich ish he, ant be? show me te shweet faish, quickly" are Pat's opening words to the assembled Court. Jonson offers a sketch of Irish character, of the lower kind, and throws the sordid picture into greater relief by the dignified speech of a "civil gentleman of the nation" and by the dance of his friends. It was a daring compliment to 'King Yamish' and to Irish loyalty. *The Challenge at Tilt* is in Barriers form, and in two parts : in the first, two Cupids engage in a 'flyting,' and in the second they lead their knights, ten in the bride's colours and ten in the bridegroom's, and, after angry words, proceed to tilt, till Hymen bids them cease.

The rivalry of 1613 had stirred Jonson and confirmed him in his endeavour to win for the masque a

higher literary place.   Between January 1615 and
February 1618 he produced no fewer than seven pieces :
Mercury Vindicated from the Alchemists (January 1615);
The Golden Age Restored (January 1616); *Christmas
his Masque* (1616) ; *The Vision of Delight* (January 1617);
Lovers made Men, generally known as the masque of
Lethe[1] (February 1617); *Pleasure Reconciled to Virtue*
(January 1618); and *For the Honour of Wales* (Febru-
ary 1618).   This is the first great group, equalled,
if not surpassed, after an interval of three years, by a
second, between 1621 and 1625, containing these seven
pieces : *News from the New World discovered in the Moon*
(January 1621); *The Metamorphosed Gipsies* (August
1621); *The Augurs* (January 1622); *Time Vindicated to
Himself and to his Honours* (January 1623); *Neptune's
Triumph for the Return of Albion* (for January 1624);
Pan's Anniversary, or The Shepherd's Holiday (?1624);
and *The Fortunate Isles and their Union* (January 1625).
There is then a break of six years, until, with *Love's
Triumph through Callipolis* (January 1631) and *Chloridia*
(February 1631), he completes his work as a masque-
writer.

When Jonson began this remarkable series he had
already clearly formulated his method.   What, therefore,
remains to be said in this chapter will deal mainly with
the modifications which his experience suggested or the
occasion demanded.   His interest was centred in the
antimasque, and more securely now that others had
begun to try their hands.   In *Mercury Vindicated from
the Alchemists* he gives it a stricter form, fixes the
name, and secures his own rights thereto in the stage-

[1] So entitled by Gifford.

directions. The treatment of the prelude is in many ways remarkable — for its dramatic quality, its true relationship to the main masque as a foil, both in motive and in form, its use of mythology and allegory without any suspicion of artificiality, and its satirical freshness. It is something to the credit of the author of *The Alchemist* that for a second time, and in so different a manner, he won success in such a well-worn theme.

The Golden Age Restored is a shorter effort in poetic allegory, relying more on the manner of presentation than on any arresting quality of the style. The antimasque of the Iron Age and the Evils is of the familiar 'heroic' type. *Christmas*, on the other hand, may be called only an antimasque, or a sketch in the vein of antimasque with the masque left out. It was probably part of the ordinary Christmas festivities. Its fun lies in the rôle of Venus as a deaf tire-woman from Pudding-lane, whose vulgar solicitude for the success of her urchin Cupid in his minor part in the show gives opportunity for humorous contrast. Her squabbling entrance, running commentary, and dismissal with the stupid boy who could not speak his lines are all good farce. *The Vision of Delight* takes Jonson back to allegory and his more formal style. He brings small relief in his two antimasques, one of 'Burratines' (puppets) and Pantaloons, another of Phantasms. If we say that the serious part is the better, we do not forget some lines of Phant'sie's :

> And Phant'sie, I tell you, has dreams that have wings,
> And dreams that have honey, and dreams that have stings ;
> Dreams of the maker, and dreams of the teller,
> Dreams of the kitchen, and dreams of the cellar,

> Some that are tall, and some that are dwarfs,
> Some that are haltered, and some that wear scarfs ;
> Some that are proper, and signify o' thing,
> And some another, and some that are nothing.

Learned Ben could have his moments with Mab and be as light-hearted as any.

Lovers made Men,[1] presented at Lord Hay's house in honour of the French ambassador, is, though one of the shortest, so perfect in its form that it may be taken as representative of the Jonsonian masque. It has only one song, the chorus before the Grand Entry ; dialogue and speech take the place of lyrics between the dances of the main masque. Even thus, the musical element was not wanting, for the whole was " sung after the Italian manner, *stylo recitativo,*" under the direction of Nicholas Lanier, who " made both the scene and the music." The motive is the restoring of the joy of life to distressed lovers who think themselves dead to everything. The antimasque shows Mercury receiving " certain imagined ghosts " on the banks of Styx and leading them towards Lethe and the attendant Fates.

> Nay, faint not now, so near the fields of rest.
>   Here no more Furies, no more torments dwell
> Than each hath felt already in his breast ;
>   Who hath been once in love, hath proved his hell.
>
> Up then, and follow this my golden rod,
>   That points you next to agéd Lethe's shore,
> Who pours his waters from his urn abroad,
>   Of which but tasting, you shall faint no more.

Lethe disputes that they are undone, and the Fates deny all record of their death. " Here all their threads are growing ; yet none cut." They only think they are

[1] Or *Lethe.* See *supra,* p. 165 and note.

ghosts. Let them drink of Lethe and forget Love's name and mischief. They drink and "dance forth their antimasque in several gestures, as they lived in love." Then they retire into the grove and come forth changed for the Grand Entry. Cupid greets them to festivity; the 'motions' he would see are

> Not sighs, nor tears, nor wounded hearts,
> Nor flames, nor ghosts ; but airy parts
> Tried and refined as yours have been
> And such they are I glory in.

These passages are here chosen for their explanatory purpose, not because they are the best. There are others, such as Mercury's account of his company to Lethe, of higher power and verse accomplishment, and there are none inferior. Nowhere does Jonson express to such perfection the spirit of masque or show finer appreciation of its form.

Like praise cannot be given to *Pleasure Reconciled to Virtue*, though Jonson tells us that it "pleased the King so well, as he would see it again." This his Majesty did on 17th February, when the antimasque was changed. Nathaniel Brent was probably thinking of the comic part when he wrote, on 10th January, that the masque was so dull that people said the poet should return to his old trade of brickmaking ; [1] for the wit of Comus's bowl-bearer is Pantagruel without the spice, and the two antimasques, the first of men in the shape of bottles and tuns and the second of pygmies, were a risky enterprise. When Hercules dismisses these from the slopes of Atlas, and Mercury and Daedalus assist

---

[1] See *Cal. of State Papers (Dom.)*, 1611–1618, p. 512. Brent was afterwards Warden of Merton College, Oxford.

the masquers in their 'Triumph,' they bring but second-best dialogue and song for our entertainment. The substituted antimasque for the second performance, *For the Honour of Wales*, is contemporary burlesque like the *Irish Masque*, and in dialect. The scene is as before, but Atlas is called Craig-Eriri, and Griffith, Jenkin, Evan, Howell, and other Cambrian absurdities take the place of the Belly-god and his crew. Jonson makes a satirical hit in the second version which helps us to reasons for the alteration, and perhaps to understand his own temper. After an amusing dialogue reducing the courtiers' names to Welsh originals—a joke which James loved to indulge, and which must have been of special relish in the presence of Scots whose patronymics were so explained, as Auchmowtie by plain Welsh "Ap-mouth-wye of Llanmouthwye"—his characters demand that the music and dance shall be Welsh and that no Hercules or other foreign stuff be intro-duced. Evans concludes: "I stand to it there was neither poetries nor architectures nor designs in that belly-god; nor a note of musics about him. Come, bring forth our musics, yow s'all hear the true Pritan strains now, the ancient Welse harp—yow tauke of their Pigmees too, here is a Pigmees of Wales now." Jonson had evidently heard snarls, like Brent's and others that are on record at the expense of the architect, this time, unfortunately, *not* Jones.

We have no more masques by Jonson till 1621.[1]

---

[1] A masque presented by Lord Essex at Coleoverton on 2nd February 1618 has been ascribed to Jonson by Brotanek, mainly, it would appear, because the 'Buz, quoth the blue-fly' catch of *Oberon* is referred to—an argument as much against Jonsonian

His Scottish journey had consumed nearly a year, and he had been amusing himself at Oxford. Absence was not so dangerous to him as at the time of his visit to France, for the Queen had died on 2nd March 1619 and Court festivity was for a time reduced. Four masques are recorded to have been given between that date and January 1621. Three were private—one at the Merchant Taylors' Hall and two at noble houses. Of the masque written for the Prince in January 1620 we have no particulars, beyond some account-book references; but we learn from a letter from Drummond to Jonson, on 17th January 1620, that a masque, recently given at Court, "was not so approved of the King as in former times, and that your absence was regretted." "Such applause," adds Drummond, "hath true worth, even of those who are otherwise not for it."

Jonson is once more in happier mood in *News from the New World discovered in the Moon*. This piece has a strong personal interest, in its allusion to his Scottish experiences and to the break in his literary activities. "Marry, he has been restive, they say, ever since; for we had nothing from him; he has set out nothing." In further gossip, so characteristic of Ben, it tells us that the subject of his next comedy, *The Staple of News*, has already attracted him. "I have hope to erect a Staple for News ere long, whither all shall be brought and thence again vented." The antimasque is a satirical dialogue between two heralds, a printer, a chronicler,

---

authorship as for it; perhaps too because there is a buttery-spirit in it and gibes at Puritans. All things, even the poorest stuff, are possible to great authors, as to some literary critics, but for the present we are not convinced.

and a factor, on the public craving for sensational news. "I'll give anything for a good copy now," says Jonson's (and our) newspaper-man, "be it true or false, so't be news. . . See men's divers opinions! It is the printing of 'em makes 'em news to a great many who will indeed believe nothing but what's in print. For those I do keep my presses and so many pens going, to bring forth wholesome relations, which once in a half-a-score years, as the age grows forgetful, I print over again with a new date, and they are of excellent use." The discussion leads to the importance of the Moon as a new world for the curious; and an amusing account is given of its topography and society, set, of course, to the latitude and fashions of Jonson's London. A group of quaint moon-fowl called Volatees supply the grotesque dance, and then the Grand Entry is announced, played by the masquers, described to the King as "a race of your own, formed, animated, lightened, and heightened by you, who, rapt above the Moon far in speculation of your virtues, have remained there entranced certain hours." This linking up of the antimasque and masque is feeble. It is evidence, though rare in Jonson, that the modern and satirical antimasque had a descriptive tendency, and might, especially in weaker hands, lose its essential character as a foil. Here it seems clear that Jonson began with it, as a first study in a subject which he was planning to treat at greater length, and that the praise of the King, which is the sole motive of the Triumph and the songs between the dances, is no more than a perfunctory addition. The second part, as much as the first, may have led the Court to call for a repetition of the masque in the following February. It is possible that the unusual use of the broken metre in the concluding songs was an effect of Ben's recent familiarity with Scottish verse, and was intended as a compliment to James both as a Scot and as a metrist. The suggestion gains force when we note the intention in the next masque, produced in the same year.

In the autumn the King heard three performances of a new masque, *The Metamorphosed Gipsies*, on his visits to Burleigh, Belvoir, and Windsor. As it appears Jonson made changes for each presentation, and as the printed text is a composite of all, and of inordinate length, we are precluded from judging its construction and balance of parts. Its mood is like its form, a medley of clownage, coarse wit, and lyrical sweetness, the last hardly to be savoured amid the gipsy garlic. The royal taste was at fault, and Jonson, anticipating the wisdom of his cook in *Neptune's Triumph*, took pains to please. As an effort in vulgar realism it cannot compare with the Irish and Welsh masques. There is a touch of Romany here and there, but the compelling purpose is to present the tatterdemalion side of life, with its rough fun, expressed in form reminiscent of Skelton's muse or of *Christ's Kirk on the Green* and its northern kin. Jonson was interested in Skelton, as his experiments in short metres and textual likenesses show, and soon after, in *The Fortunate Isles*, he was to refer to him more directly. It would appear, however, that Scottish influence was not less strong. He was fresh from his visit to Hawthornden, where he had doubtless learned something of the traditional northern talent for verse of the more whimsical and 'midden-fecht' kind. The literary compliment must have stirred the memory of the royal

author of the *Rewlis and Cautelis* and given pleasure,
which later readers, perhaps even his own courtiers,
could not share. Hence, surely, the unusual command
for three performances, and the access of good humour
at Burleigh which prompted James, after a long silence,
to try his hand again at verse. The whole piece is little
more than a tumbled antimasque, with a conclusion, no
less disorderly, in which the gipsies enter metamorphosed
and in rich habits. As we have said, it cannot be tested
by the ordinary rules of masque; and it is right to
recall that Jonson was himself fully conscious of this.
In the Windsor epilogue he says:

> You have beheld (and with delight) their change,
> And how they came transformed may think it strange;
> It being a thing not touched at by our poet:
> Good Ben slept there or else forgot to show it.

So he rides away from critical encounter by saying that
whereas his Ethiopians had been blanched by dipping
in the magic lake, his Gipsies, having smeared themselves with the Court barber's ointment, had made use
of soap and water.

> The power of Poetry can never fail her,
> Assisted by a barber and a tailor.

The ribald song of Cocklorrel amused the King and
brought Jonson an increase in his pension. It was
sung everywhere, and remained a favourite with the later
generations that enjoyed the *Muses' Recreations* and the
Pills to Purge Melancholy.

Though Jonson laughed off his own criticism of the
structure of this masque, he shows in his next, *The
Augurs*, in January and May 1622, that his conscience

is uneasy. When the Groom's question, "What has all this to do with our masque?" is answered by Vangoose in the words already quoted,[1] we read, in the satire of contemporaries, a confession of the poet's own difficulties. His recent restiveness may have made him careless in following his own precepts, or his ingenuity in anti-masque may have outrun his powers of control, but his chief embarrassment lay in another quarter, where Inigo Jones and his artificers were supreme. In this masque there is a significant change in the second part, in the introduction at the close of additional scenic effects and a new set of personages for an effective tableau. The masque proper claims pre-eminence not merely as a picturesque dance but as a theatrical spectacle. There was still room for the antimasque, but it was now to be subservient. Jonson's grumblings in the opening dialogue in the buttery-hatch emphasize rather than excuse the discrepancy between, on the one hand, Urson and his bears, the "straying and deformed Pilgrims," and the entrance of Linus, Orpheus, and their fellow Augurs from their tombs to offer compliments and prophecy to Jacobus Pacificus, and, on the other, the dances of Augurs and Masquers, and the grand finale of Jove and the Senate of the Gods. His uneasiness infects his songs and dialogue in the masque proper. Even the snatches of comic realism—the allegory of Notch and Slug and the Groom, and the broken English of the Dutchman Vangoose—lack the spontaneity of earlier efforts in this kind. The piece fails, not because the non-literary forces were already asserting themselves and giving promise of further inroads, but because

[1] *Supra*, p. 147.

Jonson did not put up the fight to be expected of him.
If, as is likely, its first performance was commanded for
the opening of the new Banqueting-Hall which Jones
had built in place of the older room burnt down on
12th January 1619, Jonson's jealousy may have kept
him from giving of his best as a compliment to the
architectural triumph of his rival.

In the next masque, *Time Vindicated to Himself and to
his Honours,* for which Jones devised three complete
changes in the scene, Jonson makes a fresh effort to
vindicate literature. The antimasque is again an organic
part and the contrasts and climax self-explanatory ; and
the writing is more direct and vivacious. But all
depends on the choice of a subject which allows free
play to his satirical talent. "Good Ben" was not likely
to "sleep" or "forget," when there were contemporary
libellers waiting for the pillory, or Puritans like Wither
to be stripped and whipped. Fame enters followed by
a band of Curious, the Eyed, the Eared, and the
Nosed. She has come from Saturn, or Chronos, or Time
to summon worthy folk to a great spectacle, and her
"hot inquisitors" promise themselves goodly entertainment in a show of all the distempers of the age and
the "several humours of men, as they are swayed by
their affections." Then arrives Chronomastix, *alias*
George Wither, who on hearing what Time has a mind
to do, proclaims :

> The Time ! Lo, I, the man that hate the time,
> That is, that love it not ; and (though in rhyme
> I here do speak it) with this whip you see
> Do lash the time, and am myself lash free.

Yet if he hates the time, he will, on hearing from the

Curious that full liberty is to be allowed them to censure whom they list, "look on Time, and love the same." Fame calls him a "wretched impostor"; he protests against the insult, and, in lines mocking Wither's style, declares his popularity with all, from pudding-wife to lady, and calls forth, by way of first antimasque, a number of Mutes, a quondam justice, a printer in disguise, a schoolmaster, and a soldier—an admiring 'confederacy' of his follies. "Fame, how like you this?" asks Eyes. "These will deify him, to despite you." "'Twill prove but deifying of a pompion," retorts Fame, indifferent. The Curious, disappointed, then ask what show Time will give them, and, on being told that nothing has been promised for *them*, complain they "might have talked of the King—or state—or all the world—censured the Council ere they censure us," and all with licence. "There's difference 'twixt liberty and licence," quoth Fame; but they must have something "monstrous," "a Babel of wild humours," "something that is unlawful—or unreasonable—or impossible."

> *Ears.* We only hunt for novelty, not truth.
> *Fame.* I'll fit you, though the Time faintly permit it.

They have their second antimasque, of Tumblers and Jugglers, brought in by the Cat and Fiddle, and are driven out. Then, on the sudden sounding of "loud music," the scene changes to Heaven, with Saturn and Venus, to whom there enter from below, as it were from the earth, certain Votaries taking the part of Chorus. Fame, doing honour to the King, announces her master's purpose :

Venus hath found out
That Hecate, as she is queen of shades,
Keeps certain glories of the Time obscured,
There for herself alone to gaze upon,
As she did once the fair Endymion.
These Time hath promised at Love's suit to free,
As being fitter to adorn the Age
By you restored on earth, most like his own.

The Masquers are discovered, and the musicians herald
their Entry. The revel of compliment proceeds.
"Good Time, I hope," says Venus, "is ta'en with this."
Then follows a dialogue between Cupid and Sport, to
let the "young bloods" have breathing time before the
next dance. The scene changes to a wood, with discourse
by Diana and Hippolitus, and the whole ends in a Grand
Chorus, in which, for the King's sake, the virtues of
hunting are sung, and, by a pretty figure drawn from
the chase, all are exhorted to follow his example.
Jonson is himself again. He gives unity to the
structure, by making the antimasque lead naturally to
the masque, and the masque to be reminiscent of the
antimasque ; he recovers and strengthens the dramatic
quality which the extended spectacle threatened to
destroy ; he expresses, notwithstanding his satire, and
even there, that courtliness which is of the essence of
masque ; and he translates what was occasional in origin
and for the special purpose of confounding some scurrile
pamphleteers into the general terms of art which later
times can enjoy.

The other three masques of Jonson's second period,
*Neptune's Triumph for the Return of Albion, Pan's
Anniversary, or the Shepherd's Holiday,* and *The Fortunate
Isles and their Union,* present certain bibliographical

N

difficulties. A Quarto of the first gives 1623 as the date of performance, or, as we now know, the intended performance, for it was postponed for a year, on account of some squabbling between the French and Spanish ambassadors. In 1625 it was again held back. In that year (9th January) *The Fortunate Isles* was presented, with the text of the main masque identical (with the exception of some necessary but minor changes) with the text of *Neptune's Triumph*. The stage setting and decorations were also the same. But the first part, with the antimasque, was completely changed. We have no clue to the reason for this, for the Poet's Argument in the first about Charles's journey to Spain with Buckingham (Hippius) might have been excised without loss to the fun of the Cook's views on art (to be rehashed by Lickfinger the master-cook and parcel-poet of next year's *Staple of News*) or of his kitchen antimasque; and it is nowhere inferior to the substituted sketch of Johphiel and Merefool, and the antimasque of Howleglass and his allies. Jonson supplied two introductions, very different in character. The date of *Pan's Anniversary* is uncertain. The second Folio gives 1625 and the inventors as "Inigo Jones, Ben Jonson," in order of evil omen. Some have placed it as early as 1620; others in 1624, by the inconclusive argument that as it was probably a summer performance on the anniversary of the King's birthday or coronation, it could not have been presented in 1625, after James's death in March. Its pastoral setting does not preclude its having been given in winter, and Jones, with a "Fountain of Light" to display, knew as well as his friend Daniel how the smoke of lamps and torches

increased the summer stuffiness of the Banqueting-Hall.
The sole evidence in support of 1620 is a reference
in some accounts to certain characters described as in
the antimasque; but the date is not necessarily more
accurate than the suspected date of the Folio. The
text does not help us to connect it with any other
work, either by its pastoral manner or by the recurrence
of one of its lyrics in a section of *Underwoods* dated
as late as 1635. Its Arcadianism is of the stricter
classical type, as in its flower passage beginning—

> Bring corn-flag, tulips, and Adonis' flower,
> Fair ox-eye, goldy-locks, and columbine.

Its songs have echoes of *The Shepherd's Calendar*. Its
Boeotian and Theban antimasques supply the necessary
foil to the very civil votaries of Pan. But it is a piece
of indifferent power and may properly be joined, in
art, if not by date, with the two masques of James's
last years.

For six years Whitehall amused itself without
Jonson's aid. He was broken in health and wrote
but little for the public theatre. In 1631, however,
he was commanded to present two masques, *Love's
Triumph through Callipolis*, for 9th January, and *Chloridia*:
Rites to Chloris and her Nymphs, for 22nd February.
With these he bade farewell to Court. The two pieces
are closely connected in subject and by occasion, the
first being a compliment by Charles to his Queen, the
second her Majesty's return courtesy to her husband.
In *Love's Triumph through Callipolis* Jonson recovers the
gallantry and courtliness of the masque. It is written
for the honour of the King's Court "and the dignity
of that heroic love and regal respect borne by him to

his unmatchable lady and spouse," and it finds its motive in the Platonism which had coloured English poetry since Spenser, had become a fashion of thought and talk under the second Stuart, and was preparing the way for the heroics of the Restoration. The theme had been much in Jonson's mind, and he had considered it at some length, two years before, in *The New Inn.* In the masque he goes over the same ground and even borrows from himself *verbatim.*[1] Euphemus, a "good character," is sent from heaven to the Court (Callipolis, the "city of Beauty or Goodness") to inform the Queen that in the suburbs were crept in certain "sectaries or depraved lovers," who, though they boasted themselves the followers of Love, knew neither the name nor nature of true passion. Their eccentricities suggest the antimasque—a grotesque dance by "a glorious boasting lover," "a whining ballading lover," "a phantastic umbrageous lover," "a sensual brute lover," and other eight misguided amorists, in four sets of three, each in the "habits of the four prime European nations." Euphemus having defined true love and the Chorus having censed the stage after the departure of the false lovers, the Triumph enters in splendour—fifteen Lovers, including the King, each with his Cupid ; and the spectacle winds to a conclusion, with elaborate scenic changes, dances, visions of the gods, paeans on nuptial love and beauty, and devices of the *impresa* kind dear to the age. The antimasque, it may be noted, is exclusively spectacular, the grotesques "expressing" themselves

---

[1] Cf. the speech of Euphemus with those of Lovel in *The New Inn,* III. ii.

in dance, not by words. In *Chloridia* we have "the celebration of some rites done to the goddess Chloris . . . goddess of the flowers . . ., to be stellified on earth by an absolute decree from Jupiter, who would have the earth to be adorned with stars as well as the heaven." "Upon this hinge," says the preface, "the whole invention moved." The purpose of the first masque, that Love is desire of true union, is declared in the opening song of Zephyrus—

> Heaven of earth shall have no odds,
> But one shall love another.
> Their glories they shall mutual make,
> Earth look on heaven, for heaven's sake,
> Their honours shall be even.

Spring approaches the King and tells him that Cupid, having taken offence at his exclusion " as a child " from the counsels of the gods, had " gone to hell " to set heaven, earth, and hell at variance. This promise of " a chaos of calamity " gives the occasion for the antimasque, which begins with the entrance from the underground of a dwarf, " post from hell," on a curtal, and accompanied by two lackeys. Hell, he announces, is topsyturvy, and if its gates had " been kept with half that strictness as the entry here has been to-night (another thrust at the Lord Chamberlain and the Banqueting-Hall ushers !), Pluto would have had but a cold court and Proserpine a thin presence, though both have a vast territory." Cupid has brought Jealousy and other abominations from hell to trouble the gods, and he is commissioned to raise Tempest and other " infernal spirits " to spite Chloris. These are introduced in the antimasque dance, in no less than eight entries,

with a change of scene at the fourth. But Juno stills
the hubbub. Then Jones's masterpiece, the Bower of
Chloris, is disclosed, and a happy ending is reached
with dance, song, and music, and a changing of scene
and moving of "works" such as had never been seen
before. Jonson made bitter reference to these in his
later *Expostulation*, when he recalled how Fame had
flapped heavenwards and how the Surveyor had
"whirled his whimsies":

> O shows, shows, mighty shows!
> The eloquence of masques! what need of prose,
> Or verse or prose, t'express immortal you?

Thirty years before, Jonson had had the aid of Jones
in his first masque. "So much for the bodily part," he
then said gratefully, "which was of Master Inigo Jones
his design and act." Much had happened since, and
Jonson, while acknowledging the material aid given by
the Surveyor, had striven to secure for Poetry her place
against aggressive spectacle. When masquing time came
round in 1632, Jonson, says the traveller John Pory in
a letter, was "for this time discarded, by reason of the
predominant power of his antagonist Inigo Jones, who,
this time twelvemonth, was angry with him for putting
his own name before his in the title-page." Jonson, ill
and broken, had now to yield in an unequal contest.
But the tragedy to him was that his lesson had not been
taken to heart, and that others would not carry on his
fight. The triumph of the carpenter was already complete, as Shirley's Hippolito tells us in *Love's Cruelty*.[1]
"Are you melancholy? a masque is prepared, and music
to charm Orpheus himself into a stone; numbers presented

---

[1] II. ii. Licensed in 1631.

to your ear that shall speak the soul of the immortal
English Jonson; a scene to take your eye with wonder,
now to see a forest move, and the pride of summer
brought into a walking wood; in the instant, as if the
sea had swallowed up the earth, to see waves capering
about tall ships, Arion upon a rock playing to the
dolphins, the Tritons calling up the sea-nymphs to
dance before you; in the height of this rapture, a
tempest so artificial and sudden in the clouds, with a
general darkness and thunder, so seeming made to
threaten, that you would cry out with the mariners in
the work, you cannot 'scape drowning; in the turning
of an eye, these waters vanish into a heaven; glorious
and angelical shapes presented, the stars distinctly with
their motion and music so enchanting you that you
would wish to be drowned indeed, to dwell in such a
happiness." Jonson's friend is not giving rein to hyperbole in this description of Whitehall's taste in masque
—a half-pennyworth of the immortal English Jonson
to an intolerable deal of scenery. Townsend, Shirley
himself, Carew, and D'Avenant were poor substitutes
for Ben at his worst, and they had no mind to cry up
their wares to the annoyance of the Surveyor. "The
subject and allegory of the masque," says the first, of
his *Tempe Restored*, "with the descriptions and apparatus
of the scenes were invented by Inigo Jones, Surveyor
of His Majesty's Work." With a similar compliment
the second concludes his *Triumph of Peace*. Carew, it is
true, repeats the title-page insult in his *Coelum Britannicum*,
for he had the self-possession of his friend Ben, even to
frankness with *him*, and the King's Sewer was not
beholden to the King's Surveyor; but D'Avenant made

up arrears in these humble words about his *Salmacida Spolia*—" The invention, ornament, scenes, and apparitions, with their descriptions, were made by Inigo Jones, Surveyor-General of his Majesty's works; what was spoken or sung, by William D'Avenant, her Majesty's servant; the subject was set down by them both." Perhaps these poets took fair measure of their deserts. We can imagine what Jonson would have thought had Queen Henrietta been gracious to his efforts as she was to Carew's—" Pour les habits elle n'avait jamais rien vu de si brave."

CHAPTER VI

THE TRAGEDIES: *THE SAD SHEPHERD*

WHEN Meres, in 1598, named Jonson as one of nine poets who were "our best for Tragedy," he offered a compliment which we are not in a position to test, and with which, in the light of the dramatist's later work, we might be loath to concur. Henslowe tells us nothing of these earlier years of dramatic apprenticeship beyond recording the poet's association with Chettle and Porter in a comedy *Hot Anger soon Cold*, and his sketch of the plot of a tragedy, finished by Chapman, which some have associated with the fragment of *Mortimer, his Fall*, recovered posthumously. As this tragedy, as well as the comedy, was not ready for the stage or the printer when, Meres made his survey, we must assume that he based his judgement on work now altogether lost. Jonson himself gives us no aid. In later years he told Drummond that "half of his comedies were not in print," but he never spoke of any tragedies other than *Sejanus* and *Catiline*. That he did not renounce tragedy, after he had found his strength in comedy in 1598, is shown by his collaboration in 1599 in the missing *Page of Plymouth* and *Robert II., King of Scots*, and, as late as 1602, in his preparation of *Richard Crookback* and his

'additions' to *The Spanish Tragedy*. We can understand
his reticence. If he was willing to suppress so much of
his early work in comedy because of its romantic taint
and because of his dislike of collaboration, he had no
less strong reasons after 1598 for refusing to remind his
public of his necessities as a writer or botcher of tragedies.
We may be allowed to doubt whether we should have
had his two Roman plays had that public been more
friendly to his Comic Muse or had he been less sensitive
or of better temper. Tragedy, notwithstanding its
traditional place of honour, was an accident rather than
an essential to Jonson's dramatic career. For which
reason, and without any breach of critical propriety, it
follows comedy and masque in the present account.

Jonson lacked the qualifications required of a writer
of great tragedy, and in this respect he differs from so
many of his age, from Shakespeare downwards, who
have won applause in the two chief dramatic kinds.
We suspect his being conscious of this, and that in so
far as he commended his own efforts his intention was
little more than to counter the rude criticism of contemporaries which he was too proud to endure in silence.
It is absurd to say, with Hazlitt,[1] that his "serious
productions are superior to his comic ones," unless we
merely wish to ruffle the complacency of established
opinion. At best, it is a doubtful compliment to
his achievement in both tragedy and comedy. The
argument that "sense and industry agree better with
the grave and severe, than with the light and gay,"
backed by Jonson's reminder that while others' works

[1] *Lectures on the Dramatic Literature of the Age of Elizabeth*,
1820, p. 165.

were plays his plays were works, is little more than
a brilliant sophism, which becomes less brilliant when
Ben is likened to a diligent mole working in the richest
of soils.   Tragedy, it is true, requires, or may allow,
more solid craftsmanship than comedy, but she requires
something more, some force more spiritual than what
gives the zest to her sister genre.   Coleridge, justly
condemning the "vulgar taste" which makes foolish
comparison between works of different classes, character-
ized *Sejanus* and *Catiline* as successful attempts to relate
"great historical events in the liveliest and most interesting manner," and expressed the wish "that we had
whole volumes of such plays."   This, too, is an indifferent
compliment to Jonson, and cold comfort to us who
expect something more of tragedy—something of the
quality, if not of the accomplishment, of what goes by
that name in the age of Pericles or Elizabeth ; for
description, whether the liveliest or the most in-
dustriously learned, never was and never can be the
mainspring or end of tragedy.   There is a deeper reason
why Jonson had no aptitude for Tragedy.   He could not
shake himself free from his intellectualism, that habit
of measuring everything by theory or scholarship or
logic to the neglect of emotion.   It is seen at work in
his comedies, to the clogging of their movement.   In
his tragedies it is a poor substitute for passion or the
touch of sympathy.   "The truth is," said Milton's
nephew in 1675,[1] perhaps echoing his uncle's opinion,
"*Sejanus* and *Catiline* seem to have in them more of an
artificial and inflate than of a pathetical and naturally

[1] *Theatrum Poetarum Anglicanorum*, by Edward Phillips, ed.
Brydges, 1800, p. 242.

tragic height"—just as Leonard Digges in 1640, in a comparison with Shakespeare,[1] had called the first play "tedious, though well laboured" and the second "irksome." They are cold, at best only rhetorical. Thus the character of Cicero in *Catiline*, to which Jonson devoted the greatest care, is no more than a puppet, delivering himself of interminable speeches which do not explain or help the action and must distract us by their school-room reminiscences. Nor is the excuse valid that Jonson is applying his realistic method in this minute recovery of an old controversy. Something more is necessary in drama, and we need not go to Shakespeare to mark the difference between tragedy and this "mode of relating," even "in the liveliest and most interesting manner." Only once does Jonson show that he could do better work, in his 'additions' to the *Spanish Tragedy*. So unlike are these passages to any in the Roman plays that his authorship has been denied. Coleridge suspected them, because they convey so much more than the mere "relating" he commended in the others, and because of their spiritual kinship to passages in "some one or other of Shakespeare's great pieces."[2] Lamb, earlier, discovered "nothing in the undoubted plays which would authorize us to suppose that he could have supplied the scenes in question," and guessed that the hand was Webster's.[3] And there is Edward Fitzgerald, who thought that Jonson could no more have written the best

---

[1] In the edition of Shakespeare's *Poems*.

[2] *Table Talk*, 5th April 1833.

[3] *Specimens of English Dramatic Poets* (Note to *The Spanish Tragedy*).

scene (III. xii.) " than I who read it, for what else of his is it like ? " [1] We have as yet no conclusive evidence that the five substituted passages [2] are Jonson's or those for which he made himself responsible to Henslowe; but it is no argument against his authorship that they are so unlike *Sejanus* or *Catiline*. *The Case is Altered* or *The Sad Shepherd* is, each in its own way, abnormal. In all three the perplexing element is their romanticism; and in each the dramatist's attitude is different. In the comedy he is leaving his prentice experience behind; in the pastoral he is in the retrospective habit of age, recovering or revising a forgotten mood; in the 'revenge' play, he is committed to no more than a criticism of Kyd's ineffectiveness or reasonably proud of his ability to better the tragedy by its own rule of art. To have acted the part of Hieronimo or written up the scene with the Painter did not make the *Spanish Tragedy* any less a matter for scoffing, as *Every Man in his Humour*, *Cynthia's Revels*, *The Poetaster*, all before 1602, and *Bartholomew Fair*, in 1614, make only too clear. The 'additions,' taken with *The Case* and *The Sad Shepherd*, may justify us in thinking, with some, that Jonson might have achieved a high place in romantic drama. That he did not choose to do so, may show with what deliberation he committed his stage fortunes to a single venture.

There can be no doubt that the later Jonsonian tragedy was reacted on by the experience in comedy, and not to its advantage. Reference has been made to the risks which a comic dramatist, even of Jonson's

---

[1] *Letters and Literary Remains* (1903), III. p. 151.
[2] II. v. 46-97; III. ii. 65-74, xi. 2-50, xii.; IV. iv. 168-217.

power, must accept in his devotion to the humours and
to realism and satire. His success encouraged him
to persist; or, rather, the habit of looking on life in
this way had been so indulged that he had lost the
power of writing in another way. It was as if he had
found a universal method—for tragedy as well as for
comedy; but with this difference, that, whereas in his
comedy he sets up a tyranny for his own control and
as a model of government for the future, in his tragedy
he merely shows, without argument or enthusiasm, and
as it were unconsciously, that the discipline has invaded
his art. There lies the fundamental weakness of his
tragedy, for the humours are a poor substitute for
the human elements of which tragedy is made, and
the elaboration of *milieu*, in a tesselated picture of
character with historical and antiquarian detail—the
Bartholomew Fair method applied to epical Rome
—may become the dullest and most inappropriate
of aids. Jonson's earlier experience in stage-journalism
of the *Page of Plymouth* kind may well have proved
a much more dangerous guide to him in *Sejanus*
and *Catiline* than all Henslowe's tasks of the *Arden
of Feversham* type were to the romanticists in their
full-blown tragedies. It is an indifferent defence
of him to say that, whereas Shakespeare in his
Roman plays is concerned with the interpretation or
creation of character, his purpose is to recover the
life and setting of the ancient city, and that whereas
Shakespeare is content with his Plutarch, he must
have his Sallust and Cicero, and in his *Sejanus*, his Dion
and Suetonius and Velleius Paterculus in addition to
the familiar Tacitus. Perhaps Jonson juggles with all

these as well as any writer, who is both scholar and
dramatist, can, and may be allowed a unique place in
his age for closer attention to historical truth than
was the fashion with other playwrights who accepted
the Sidneian licence to follow their own sweet will.
This distinction seems to underlie Saint-Évremond's
remark to Corneille that Jonson is the Corneille of
England, for it is one of the French dramatist's merits
in that critic's eyes that he is the only author of his
nation who shows a just taste for antiquity.   But Ben's
promise was tragedy; and his historical zeal disappoints
us of the gift.   We miss the transmutation of the
scholar's dross into the gold of tragic passion.   There
is small opportunity for 'pity and terror' in a panorama;
and the audience is not to be blamed for showing
small liking of the pictures, as they pass from roller
to roller.   "Jonson was very learned," says the author
of *Night Thoughts* truly, "as Samson was very strong,
to his own hurt; blind to the nature of tragedy, he
pulled down all antiquity on his head, and buried
himself under it."[1]   In another respect Jonson's tragic
manner is affected by his practice in comedy and
masque.   He relies too much on contrast or foil, a
device of the essence of his conception of these, and
there to be excused even in its most extravagant form.
In tragedy, on the other hand, it must be employed
more sparingly, and with greater respect to experience,
if only because of the complexity and overlapping of
character.   The Othellos and Iagos are not contrasted
personages as the Volpones and their gulls may be
allowed to be.   The neglect of this difference makes

[1] See Johnson, *Life of Young.*

what is tolerable in the one kind but dull artifice in the other; and so we miss both the true picture and the tragic reality. In *Catiline*, for example, in the see-saw characterization of the protagonist and Lentulus, of Cato and Cicero, of Caesar and Antony, of Fulvia and Sempronia, of Cethegus and Curius, there is damnable iteration, to the corruption of tragedy, even if taken at the lower Coleridgean level as a "mode of relating."

The Roman plays have supplied much of the argument for the ill-conceived charge of classicism made against Jonson's art generally. His responsibility for this is not due to any critical pronouncement, for he is more reticent on the theory of tragedy than he is on other matters. It was easy for romantic rivals to call the plays classical, because they had an antique setting and owed, textually, so much to the Latin historians and poets, though no more than his masque-mosaics confess. Yet in some ways Jonson is less a classicist here than in his other writings. On this we call to mind what Dryden says in his *Essay of Dramatic Poesy*. There Crites sums up his argument against the moderns by eulogizing Jonson as the best guide— "Father Ben, dressed in all the ornaments and colours of the ancients." He, "the greatest man of the last age, was willing to give place to them in all things: he was not only a professed imitator of Horace, but a learned plagiary of all the others; you track him everywhere in their snow." Neander, that is Dryden himself, adds that Jonson "borrowed boldly" from the ancients; that "there is scarce a poet or historian among the Roman authors of those times whom he has not translated in *Sejanus* and *Catiline*." But, the critic continues, "he invades authors like a monarch; and what would be theft in other poets, is only victory in him." "With the spoils of these writers he so represents old Rome to us, in its rites, ceremonies, and customs, that if one of their poets had written either of his tragedies, we had seen less of it than in him." So far Jonson's classicism means no more than that he was learned in the classics, and, in Dryden's more generous judgement, that he applied his powers of observation to such good purpose that he transformed mere bookishness into a living picture. Dryden in the same *Essay* calls Jonson the Virgil of our dramatic poets, "the pattern of elaborate writing," which is but an additional compliment to him that he mellowed learning by literary art. Still, this is but shallow justification for calling Jonson a classicist, even if we could forget his breach of the unities and his bold defence. In the opening lines of his preface to *Sejanus* he throws down the gauntlet to the critics. "First, if it be objected that what I publish is no true poem, in the strict laws of time, I confess it." He might have added 'place,' and other matters; but he declines censure by saying: "In the meantime, if in truth of argument, dignity of persons, gravity and height of elocution, fulness and frequency of sentence I have discharged *the other offices of a tragic writer*, let not the absence of these forms be imputed to me." In the words "in the meantime" he refers to his 'Observations' on the *Ars Poetica* which he was about to issue when his library was burnt. We may guess at his line of

defence in the lost book from his jottings in *Discoveries*.
For our purpose it is enough to be reminded that
he had no doubts about the liberties allowable to
English tragedy, as in *Volpone* and elsewhere he did
not hesitate to defy the "strict rigour of comic law."[1]
He confesses himself a rebel when he suggests that
objection may be taken to *Sejanus* for its want of
a "proper chorus, whose habit and moods are such
and so difficult, as not any whom I have seen since the
ancients, no, not they who have most presently affected
laws, have yet come in the way of." Even greater
objections may be taken to what he offers for choruses
in *Catiline*, because they do not arise out of or help the
dramatic development. In the verses at the close of
the fourth act, these mysterious persons tell us that
they know little of Catiline's purpose—

> One while we thought him innocent:
>   And then we accused
> The consul, for his malice spent,
>   And power abused,

—an admission which no self-respecting Greek chorus
could have made or Greek audience tolerated.

If, therefore, Jonson observes classical form but
indifferently, does he hold by the essentials of *decorum*,
τὸ πρέπον, proportion? We may refer to only two
points, his changes in style and setting in the interests
of crude realism, and his lack of restraint. In considering the first we must not allow ourselves to be
forced by the censures of the seventeenth century,
for the taste which condemned the scene of Livia
and Endemus in *Sejanus* or that of Curius and Fulvia

[1] *Volpone*, Dedication.

in *Catiline* as an 'ill-mingle'[1] of farce, or, in Rymer's
more flatulent way, an "interlarding" of "fiddle-
faddle,"[2] was constrained to condemn all blending in
English drama of the serious with the comic, and the
heroic with the familiar and satirical. But we can,
without blindly following, or perhaps misconstruing,
Sidney's doctrine, allow that Jonson's olio, as Dryden
calls it, makes his classical purpose suspect. We
can see how this carrying over from his experience
in the comedy of real life jarred with the traditional
habit of tragedy, and the more rudely in one who
had set his face against English romantic licence.
The notion of Jonson's classical habit had become so
fixed that many did not see how far it was disproved
by the cumulation of exceptions which they freely
named and regretted. When we turn to the second
characteristic, the lack of restraint, we find Jonson's
alienation more marked. It escaped the notice of
the critics of the next age ; not surprisingly, since
they were interested in the ceremonial rather than
the character of classicism. Jonson's great learning
served him both well and ill, but more often ill.
This is so in his comedies. Even the heavier framework of his tragedies is like to buckle under the load.
Passion would have saved him, for whatever be its
intensity, it has measure imposed on it both by art
and human necessity ; but intellect, playing with the
emotions and debauched by scholarship, runs too
libertine a course. Jonson is carried away by his
ingenuity and rhetoric, mistaking these for the tragic

---

[1] *Essay of Dramatic Poesy.*
[2] *A Short View of Tragedy*, 1693, p. 163.

'dignity' and 'gravity' and 'fulness' at which he
aims.[1] This overflowing is more tolerable in his
comedies, where, if the 'story' is slight, the wit may
bubble over like the humours and give entertainment
by its own extravagance. His noble Romans, on the
other hand, cannot be so excused their tiresome
self-possession in talk. Cicero, in the second scene
of the fourth act of *Catiline*, unburdens himself, as if
he were reading his speech against the conspirator,
in screeds from fifty to one hundred lines long; and
we wonder at the strength of memory of the Globe
actor. If it be not a critic's joke to say that Jonson
is but applying his realistic powers in thus presenting
the orator by this flood of eloquence, then either these
powers have failed or realism is sadly out of place.
Cethegus is handled no better, of whom Dryden well
remarked that he said a thousand " extravagant " things
but performed " not one action in the play." [2] Though
Marston was generous enough to say, in prefatory
compliment to *Sejanus*, that

> never English shall, or hath before
> Spoke fuller graced,

he naughtily told the reader of his own *Sophonisba*
(in words already quoted) that "to transcribe authors,
quote authorities, and translate Latin prose orations into
English blank verse hath, in this subject, been the
least aim of my studies." The praise of friends, like
Chapman, Francis Beaumont, and John Fletcher, was
equivocal, though it may have pleased Ben to know
that Minerva had " seen her sacred loom advanced," and
that the plays were caviare to the general.

[1] *Sejanus*, Preface.   [2] *Of Heroic Plays*.

What there is of contemporary defence of Jonsonian tragedy is, after the fashion of the advocate with a bad case, mainly disparagement of others' work, or an attack on Jonson's querulous public. Jonson himself was in angry mood on both occasions, and those who rallied to him in the dedicatory matter in the Folio are less concerned with his art than with his defiance of the mob. In the *Apologetical Dialogue* following *The Poetaster* he frankly says :

> I leave the monsters
> To their own fate. And since the Comic Muse
> Hath proved so ominous to me, I will try
> If Tragedy have a more kind aspect.
> Her favours in my next I will pursue,
> Where, if I prove the pleasure but of one,
> So he judicious be, he shall be alone
> A theatre unto me. . . .
> Leave me ! There's something come into my thought,
> That must and shall be sung, high and aloof,
> Safe from the wolf's black jaw, and the dull ass's hoof.

In 1603 he made good his threat in *Sejanus*, but the clamour against him was not abated. The public "screwed their scurvy jaws and looked awry."[1] He tells us that a "second pen had good share," probably Chapman's, not Shakespeare's[2] as some have thought, but to little purpose with his enemies who chose to scoff at his learned borrowings, "like swine spoiling and rooting up the Muse's gardens." When he published the play in the Folio he excised all his friend's passages and flung fresh speeches of his own for them to nose through. It may be that these passages were the chief cause of Jonson's being haled before the Privy Council

---

[1] William Fennor, 1617, quoted by Gifford.

[2] Shakespeare was one of the actors.

on the charge of "popery and treason." [1] His complete
suppression of them has therefore no significance in his
literary relations with Chapman, who, doubtless, was
grateful, and certainly could not complain of the
chivalrous terms in which Jonson explained his action.
When he came to present *Catiline* in 1611 he was
hardened in his contempt for his audience, and he out-
did himself in ironical wrath. The two prefaces in the
quarto, "To the Reader in Ordinary" and "To the Reader
Extraordinary," are documents without parallel in the
history of the relationship of author and public. To
the first he says:

The Muses forbid that I should restrain your meddling,
whom I see already busy with the title and tricking over the
leaves ; it is your own. I departed with my right when I let it
first abroad ; and now, so secure an interpreter I am of my
chance, that neither praise nor dispraise from you can affect
me. Though you commend the two first acts, with the people,
because they are the worst, and dislike the oration of Cicero,
in regard you read some pieces of it at school and understand
them not yet, I shall find the way to forgive you. Be anything you will be at your own charge. Would I had
deserved but half so well of it in translation as that ought
to deserve of you in judgement, if you have any. I know
you will pretend, whosoever you are, to have that and more ;
but all pretensions are not just claims. The commendation
of good things may fall within a many, the approbation but
in a few, for the most commend out of affection, self-tickling,
an easiness, or imitation ; but men judge only out of knowledge. That is the trying faculty ; and to those works that
will bear a judge nothing is more dangerous than a foolish

---

[1] *Supra*, p. 27.

praise. You will say I shall not have yours therefore ; but rather the contrary, all vexation of censure. If I were not above such molestations now, I had great cause to think unworthily of my studies, or they had so of me. But I leave you to your exercise. Begin.

Then to the second, very briefly :

You I would understand to be the better man, though places in court go otherwise : to you I submit myself and work. Farewell.

There must be few playwrights who rushed a damned play into print in such haste, and pled for it in such blustering manner. It was Ben's way, but he had never before shown such aggressive delight. He backed up his Horatian motto, *His non plebecula gaudet,* with the opinion that he "thought it the best"[1] of his tragedies. Yet he could hardly say he had won in his art half the pleasure he had found in girding at the public he despised. Though tragedy was a ready asylum when comedy proved unkind, it may be that he was attracted by the Roman successes of Shakespeare—*Julius Cæsar* in 1600, and *Antony and Cleopatra* and *Coriolanus,* four and two years, respectively, before *Catiline.* It is at least noteworthy that Jonson comes into closer touch with Shakespeare in the latter's Roman tragedies, perhaps in the textual echo, in the last act of *The Silent Woman,* of Cominius's words, "he lurch'd all swords of the garland" (II ii. 99), but obviously in his censure in *Discoveries* ('De Shakespeare nostrati') of a passage in *Julius Cæsar,* and by his second reference to it in the

---

[1] Dedication to the Earl of Pembroke.

Induction to *The Staple of News*.[1]　It is not unreasonable to see some suggestion of personal rivalry underlying Digges's[2] comparison of *Cæsar* and *Catiline* and his account of the reception of the companion efforts. Jonson's interest in the theatrical market, and for that matter Shakespeare's and others' too, was always keen.　Gosson or Wilson and Chettle had no copyright in *Catiline*, and Shakespeare none in Roman tragedy : the hated public—perhaps less hated than he professed—must be shown what he could do, and what a " true poem " was.　So too in the case of the undated fragment of *Mortimer*.　It would not be surprising to find it connected with Drayton's verse activities, and not a little amusing if Jonson, who had small affection for him either as a poet or as a patcher of plays for Henslowe, were one of the " grammaticasters " who " quarrelled at the title " of *Mortimeriados*.　It would be like Ben to scoff at " the second case " in that title and to consider it his duty, as well as his opportunity, to snatch the subject from its dull Troilus verse or its later ottava rima to the dignity of a stage tragedy.

The tragedies and *The Sad Shepherd* may be described as the two extremes of the Jonsonian gamut.　The defence for giving a brief account of each in one chapter must be, apart from any consideration of space, that both are marked exceptions or sports from the work which was the dramatist's life - concern and is

[1] Jonson's quotation does not tally with the accepted Shakespearian text, but it may represent an early version ; and the alteration may have been the result of the criticism.　(See Lee, *Life of Shakespeare*, 1915, p. 354 *n.*)

[2] *Supra*, p. 188.

accepted as characteristic. They are a kind of supplementary miscellany, showing only an incidental connexion with that work, and, as between themselves, a temporary recovery, in later years, of outgrown or suppressed habit. We might call the pastoral fragment of *The Sad Shepherd* a comedy, and find in it hints of his 'humorous' experiments, or we might link it with his masques in respect of its echoes of faery and pastoralism, its scenic elaboration, or its use of the antimasque device of contrast. Such likenesses are, however, more casual than essential, and they do not allow us to forget that the chief interest of *The Sad Shepherd* lies in its divergence from the Jonsonian canon. So disturbing is this breach to critics who hold comfortably to their theory of a 'classical' Jonson, self-confessed and consistent, that they cannot accept the play as a work of his prime, much less of his old age.[1] None of these dare deny it is his, and none that it has many excellences. They record the exception with some suspicion of regret — so strait is the rule of pigeonhole criticism, and so great is Jonson's responsibility for their interpretation of his quality.

In *The Sad Shepherd* Jonson is romantic, as the drama which he would reform had been and persisted in being, and as his own work had doubtless been before he found his purpose in *The Case is Altered*, or declined the cobbling of tragedies like Kyd's masterpiece. The dramatist notorious for his lack of passion is here passionate, even in love. He lets slip the leashed spaniels of imagination for a free career. He ceases to be satirical, except as Spenser or Milton are, or to

[1] *Infra*, pp. 208 *et seq.*

corrupt simplicity with the shows of learning. He is not
less realistic, perhaps more convincingly so, because
he is more natural. His famous witches of the masques
are theatrical persons compared with Maudlin of the
dimble. Robin Goodfellow, an excellent stage comedian
in *Love Restored*, finds his true self in her famulus Puck-
hairy. It is a new world of fairies and peasants and
merry men of Sherwood, scheming and loving for the
pleasure of the game, moving freely, not as puppets or
book-born things but as Shakespeare's and Fletcher's
people move. Where the play fails, by jars on good
taste or by extravagance, the faults are the vice of its
romantic quality, rarely, if ever, caused by the intrusion
of Jonson's classical mood in alien surroundings.

We are introduced to this new world and new mood
at once. The scene is Sherwood Forest—"a landscape
of forest, hills, valleys, cottages, a castle, a river, pastures,
herds, flocks, all full of country simplicity." Enter
Æglamour [1] distraught by the loss of his love Earine.

> Here she was wont to go! and here! and here!
> Just where those daisies, pinks, and violets grow:
> The world may find the Spring by following her;
> For other print her airy steps ne'er left.
> Her treading would not bend a blade of grass,
> Or shake the downy blow-ball from his stalk!
> But like the soft west wind she shot along,
> And where she went, the flowers took thickest root,
> As she had sowed them with her odorous foot.

This difference in style strikes us more and more as

---

[1] Jonson was probably attracted by the beauty of the name, as
by that of Earine. Shakespeare gives it to Silvia's "agent" in *The
Two Gentlemen of Verona*. Dekker makes fun of it (*Satiromastix*,
l. 1562) and Aubrey borrows it for his *Country Revel*. It is useless to connect the vogue with the romance of the Knight of Artois.

Æglamour indulges his "deep hurt phant'sie" throughout the play, changing from sweet sorrow, recalling Ophelia's notes, to the rage of Tamburlaine or *The Spanish Tragedy*. "I will study some revenge," he says, and later, in the Hieronimo mood, declaims:

> It will be rare, rare, rare
> An exquisite revenge. . . .
> Or I will get some old, old grandam thither,
> Whose rigid foot but dipped into the water
> Shall strike that sharp and sudden cold throughout,
> As it shall lose all virtue ; and those nymphs,
> Those treacherous nymphs pulled in Earine,
> Shall stand curled up like images of ice,
> And never thaw ! mark, never ! a sharp justice !
> Or stay, a better ! when the year's at hottest,
> And that the dog-star foams, and the stream boils,
> And curls, and works, and swells ready to sparkle,
> To fling a fellow with a fever in,
> To set it all on fire, till it burn
> Blue as Scamander 'fore the walls of Troy,
> When Vulcan leaped into him to consume him.

Under the influence of kindly words from Robin Hood, inviting him to join his friends and take "the proffered solace of the Spring," the sputtering anger turns to this :

> A Spring, now she is dead ! of what ? of thorns ?
> Briars, and brambles ? thistles ? burs, and docks ?
> Cold hemlock ? yew ? the mandrake, or the box ?
> These may grow still ; but what can Spring beside ?
> Did not the whole earth sicken when she died ?
> As if there since did fall one drop of dew,
> But what was wept for her ! or any stalk
> Did bear a flower, or any branch a bloom,
> After her wreath was made ! In faith, in faith,
> You do not fair to put these things upon me,
> Which can in no sort be : Earine,
> Who had her very being and her name

With the first knots or buddings of the Spring,
Born with the primrose and the violet,
Or earliest roses blown : when Cupid smiled
And Venus led the Graces out to dance,
And all the flowers and sweets in Nature's lap
Leaped out, and made their solemn conjuration
To last but while she lived !　Do not I know
How the vale withered the same day ? how Dove,
Dean, Eye, and Erewash, Idel, Snite, and Soare
Each broke his urn, and twenty waters more,
That swelled proud Trent, shrunk themselves dry ? that since,
No sun or moon, or other cheerful star,
Looked out of heaven, but all the cope was dark,
As it were hung so for her exequies ?
And not a voice or sound to ring her knell,
But of that dismal pair, the scritching owl,
And buzzing hornet ?　Hark ! hark ! hark ! the foul
Bird ! how she flutters with her wicker wings !
Peace ! you shall hear her scritch.

These extracts are from the first act. One does not require
to read much to gust the unexpected romantic flavour.
Even the images which are grotesque or inappropriate—
as when he would hug her corpse and "eat her kisses,
suck off her drowned flesh"—are of romantic birth, the
mad hyperboles of the 'revenge' play and its passionate
kin.

The fragment is, in the second place, exceptional
on account of its pastoralism.　Jonson had meddled
occasionally in peasant matters, and most formally in
his masques, but nowhere had he so confidently accepted
the Virgilian motto, which is prefixed to this play in
the Folio, *Nec erubuit silvas habitare Thalia.*[1]　The form
had attracted him, for though he was wont to gibe at
the *Pastor Fido* and even at the English *Arcadia*, as his
comedies and his *Discoveries* make clear, he had made

[1] *Ecl.* VI. ii.

experiment in a piece called *The May Lord*, and had
expressed his intention to compose a pastoral or fisher
play.[1] It is also on record that he admired *The
Faithful Shepherdess*,[2] and that one of his favourite
snatches for 'repetition' was a pastoral dialogue about
singing.[3] If, as we shall ask the reader to consider,
there is some connexion between *The Sad Shepherd* and
the lost *May Lord*, we have a hint of an abiding
interest in pastoral and of an ambition to try his hand
with the best. Drummond's remark, when speaking of
The May Lord, that "contrary to all other pastorals, he
bringeth the clowns making mirth and foolish sports,"
argues a consciousness on Jonson's part that, as in his
comedies, in his masques, and indeed in nearly all his
work, there was opportunity for his reforming talent.
This leads us to a third point in the exceptional character
of the play.

Though Jonson carries over much of the machinery
of the traditional pastoral, rehandles the commonplaces
about the honest and loving qualities of true shepherds,
and, on occasion, when he seems to forget the pastoral
artifice, recovers himself, as Milton does (and nowhere
better than in his *Epitaphium Damonis*) by direct touches
of country life, he makes no pretence to preserve the
stricter Italian or English conventions of the form.
Indeed, his romantic mood is so aggressive, that were the
rest of his record obliterated he would be classed with
the extreme brethren of the 'mixed' English style who
disturbed Sidney and his critical following. He blends
the pastoral, as the ancients knew it, with the plain
experience of the village, the artificial with the real, the

---

[1] *Discoveries*, xvi.   [2] *Ib.* xii.   [3] *Ib.* v.

real with the supernatural, Pan with Sylvan, shepherd-lovers with merry-men of the Forest, curial English with the dialect of clowns. This riot in contrast may be in part the effect of Jonson's practice in comedy and masque, but it is better explained as a direct reaction against the classical habit by which these were controlled, as a simple thrust for freedom by his long dormant romanticism rather than as a degenerate falling away from his 'classicism.' If the incongruity is, as Swinburne would have us call it, " a pure barbarism, a positive solecism in composition," let us so conclude after comparison with work in the same kind, and after noting what it professes to be. Jonson saw that pure pastoral, which might be tedious in masque, must be intolerable in the theatre. He could feel little satisfaction in the love formalities of Arcadia. He shrank from the sentimental, and, apparently with a side-glance at the author of *The Queen's Arcadia* and *Hymen's Triumph*, made easy fun of the " Ah ! and O !" of the whimpering pastoral of the day.

Jonson accepts, openly, his part as rebel. He will have mirth as fitting pastoral ; his Muse must spin and weave the wool of " mere English flocks," worthy to match " those of Sicily or Greece " ; the scene will be Sherwood, and his play " a tale of Robin Hood " as well as of love-lorn shepherds. We need not press the contrast between the pastoral and sylvan elements, or look upon Jonson's anglicizing of the setting as a novelty in English-made pastoral and his chief claim to originality. The essence of his 'exception' is that he mixed together such different material, and that so much of that material was romantic.

In yet another way, the most important of all, *The Sad Shepherd* stands apart from the rest of Jonson's work. It has a richer poetic quality than he usually allowed his 'laboured' pen, and it is, as a whole, the most spontaneous of his writings. He had written before of Queen Mab and her folk, but not as in these lines :

> There, in the stocks of trees, white fays do dwell,
> And span-long elves, that dance about a pool,
> With each a little changeling in their arms !
> The airy spirits play with falling stars,
> And mount the sphere of fire to kiss the moon ! [1]

In this mood he is nearer Shakespeare, and by his promise of picturesque freedom no distant kinsman of certain poets of his ancestral North. His good spirits help him dramatically too, if we may judge his plot-making in a fragment; and his satire is both rarer and mellower. His attack on the Puritans, the "sourer sort" who "call ours Pagan pastimes," [2] has the dignity of the counter-protests in *The Shepherd's Calendar* and *Lycidas*. He has given us little in this vein, but he has given us enough to show what he might have done had his critical 'humours' been less overpowering. If unstinted praise be out of question, because of occasional pedantry, overdrawn reminiscence of classical verse, and indifferent lyrical power (when compared, say, with Fletcher's), depreciation such as Swinburne's, because of "incongruous contrast," is hardly just. But unexpected amends are made at the close of the modern poet's critique. "No work of Ben Jonson's is more amusing and agreeable to read, as none is more graceful in expression and more excellent in simplicity of style."

[1] II. viii.   [2] I. iv.

Two bibliographical problems are of interest; the one, whether the play was completed, the other, whether it was written early or late. As there is little evidence of the ordinary kind, external or internal, opinion must rest mainly on aesthetic grounds. The closing lines of the third act do not convey the impression of a sudden break, by accident or editorial carelessness, in a completed text. Nothing can be deduced from Gifford's grouping of the 'Arguments' of the three acts in front of the play, for in the original each precedes its act and may have been written after or before the composition of the act, or inserted when the three acts or the whole play were finished. Nor are the naming of one Reuben, "a devout hermit" among the *dramatis personae* and the absence of all reference to him in the extant text convincing evidence one way or other, though the fact that he is named last in the list, is called 'The Reconciler,' and is placed in a group by himself, may imply that he was not to play his part till near the close. The fragment shows that five acts were planned, but there is no proof that five acts were written and some reasonable suspicion that they were not written. In which case, Waldron's "continuation" of 1783 runs small risk of the indignity of comparison with Jonson's part. A further contention that we could not have had a prologue if the whole had not once existed is merely plausible, for a prologue of the descriptive kind is little more than an 'argument' to an act.

On the question of date, there is most to be said for the contention that the play belongs to Jonson's closing years. The main objection urged by those who decline to consider it as work of Jonson's age is that it

could not have been written by an old man, in miserable
health, that it is too youthful in sentiment and too
vigorous and free to be contemporaneous with his later
efforts in humorous comedy and certainly with his
'dotages.' There is little in this view, as many well-
known cases will show, and it might be countered by
saying that the divergence from the poet's life-tenor was
but a natural reaction or breaking-out in old age of
youthful habit that had been rigorously suppressed.
There are indications in Jonson's later years of dis-
satisfaction, which may have impelled him to forsake
the difficult path of his own making as readily as when
in his prime he turned from it to tragedy and masque
and other things. While we allow the possibility that
the inception and even the composition belong to his
middle (or early) period, we are not less certain that the
play was the direct concern of his old age. On the other
hand, too much may be made of the opening line of the
Prologue—

> He that hath feasted you these forty years ;

for the Elizabethan 'forty' had no numerical value, and
may be here as indefinite as in a host of examples in
Shakespeare, or in our 'forty winks.' At the same time,
the intensive purpose of the numeral indicates that
between Jonson's stage apprenticeship and his offering
of *The Sad Shepherd* a *considerable* period of time had
elapsed. The admission that his audience,

> with patience harkening more and more,
> At length have grown up to him,

and the protest in the last line against the contemning
of those "that are known artificers" show that the

P

date cannot be early and that 'forty' must not be
interpreted too literally. There may or may not be
some significance in the lines of Meliboeus in Falkland's
Eclogue in *Jonsonus Virbius* :

> Not long before his death, our woods he meant
> To visit, and descend from Thames to Trent.
> Mete with thy elegy his pastoral,
> And rise as much as he vouchsafed to fall.

We seem to be forced to conclude, if these refer to
The Sad Shepherd, that he had written it before his visit
to the scene. The Northern dialect, taken in connexion
with its appearance in the masques, suggests a date
posterior to the poet's visit to Scotland. The reference
to the drowned lands of Lincolnshire [1] cannot well be
earlier than 1613, but the disaster may have supplied
a figure in the thirties just as well. If there is more
than an accidental likeness between Æglamour's eulogy
of his lost love [2] and a passage in Goffe's *Careless
Shepherdess*,[3] *The Sad Shepherd* must be dated very late,
whether it be borrowed from or be the borrower. Goffe
died in 1629, and his play was produced at Salisbury
Court Theatre in that year. Assuming therefore (what
is by no means outside debate) that the two passages
are related, we are forced to conclude that either Jonson
recollected, perhaps subconsciously, what he had heard
on the stage, or that Goffe had had access to Jonson's
unacted text ; and further, that the transference (unless
we make the additional assumption that *The Careless
Shepherdess* too had lain long in manuscript) was not
made long before or long after 1629.

Some contributory aid to the theory, if not to the

---

[1] II. vii.   [2] I. i.   [3] V. vii.

proof, of a late date is offered in the record of the lost pastoral, *The May Lord*. When Jonson was in Scotland he gave Drummond some particulars of that play. "He hath a pastoral entitled *The May Lord*," says the latter. "His own name is Alkin, Ethra the Countess of Bedford's, Mogibell Overbury, the old Countess of Suffolk an enchantress; other names are given to Somerset's Lady, Pembroke, the Countess of Rutland, Lady Wroth. In his first story Alkin cometh in mending his broken pipe. Contrary to all other pastorals, he bringeth the clowns making mirth and foolish sports."[1] Though Alkin and an enchantress appear in *The Sad Shepherd*, and the remark about the clownage recalls the critical protest of the Prologue against

> an heresy of late let fall,
> That mirth by no means fits a Pastoral,

there are too many differences in the description of *The May Lord* to allow us to identify it with the piece in question. Some have suggested that *The May Lord* was lost in the fire which destroyed Jonson's library and is referred to in the "parcels of a play" in his *Execration upon Vulcan*. One writer is convinced that it was not a play but a series of eclogues.[2] From the clues supplied by the names of Overbury and Somerset's Lady we may fix the date of the lost pastoral about 1613. We are therefore compelled to date *The Sad Shepherd* as the later, for while we may believe that the poet substituted for the direct personalities of an earlier version a more poetical and general treatment, we

[1] *Convers.* xvi.
[2] Mr. W. W. Greg in his edition in Bang's *Materialien*, xv. This is disputed by M. Castelain in his *Ben Jonson*, p. 473 *n*.

cannot imagine his pursuing the opposite course by reducing the freer conception to the narrower and more particular. On the whole, it seems best to assume that, *The May Lord* having been destroyed and its 'occasional' interest being spent, Jonson took pleasure in recovering, whether from memory or from manuscript that had been laid aside, what appeared to be of more permanent value. In this way we can think of *The Sad Shepherd* as a recasting of *The May Lord*, but with such differences as give it the place of an independent work. As so much is left to speculation, is it too foolish to assume that the critical doctrine in the second half of the prologue was the major cause of the old man's continued interest in pastoral ; that his thoughts on mixed pastoral and the " Ah ! and O ! " mannerism of Daniel and others still clamoured for expression ? We may allow that the gibes first took form when his rival's work was fresh. They would not have lost their point when Jonson made a second attempt. So too in certain tricks of style, which argue the prentice rather than the journeyman's hand, as—

> For simple loves, and sampled lives beside (I. v.)
>
> As doth the vauting hart his venting hind (II. i.)
>
> Green-bellied snakes, blue fire-drakes in the sky (II. viii.)
>
> I long to be at the sport, and to report it (*ib.*),

we may have patches of an early text imbedded in the new. The piece is certainly not an old man's work, if by that we mean that old men *must* deliver themselves of dotages ; but there is no reason for denying that it was the concern of Jonson in his closing years and that he then left it in the form in which it remains.

CHAPTER VII

THE POEMS

JONSON'S admirers hesitate when they come to consider his quality as a poet. His studied realism, his satire, his critical habit, his aggressive pedantry seem to deny him, almost of necessity, what comes freely to so many, even of inferior talent, in the Great Age. We can never think of him as we think of Shakespeare and Fletcher. If the concert-room occasionally reminds us of his song *To Celia* and the anthologies of the epitaph on the Countess of Pembroke, we like to qualify our admiration by giving half the credit of the one to an ancient Greek and perhaps all the honour of the other to a minor English contemporary. It seems so useless to look for the lyrical note and the abandon of the poet in the analyst and scholar. Popular opinion has never had any illusions about the Winged Horse as a Jonsonian symbol. It thinks of steadily driven furrows in heavy soil, of obedience to the critical flick and call. It expects no Hippocrene to start under this laboured hoof, and, though allowing that in the scholar's cabbage-patch springs may break forth and that Helicon itself is often dry, is so convinced of the security of Jonson's art against such accidents, that when these occur it expresses its surprise with a farmerly touch of annoyance.

The Ingenious Hand who will give us Ben's 'Compleat Muse' is yet to seek. The poet made only a partial attempt to bring his pieces together when the novel idea of publishing his *Works* took shape in the Folio of 1616. He then presented two separate sections of verse, entitled *Epigrams* and *The Forest*. The first, indeed, was licensed in 1612, but circumstances delayed its issue, and the sheets were incorporated in the Folio. In the Second Folio, issued posthumously in 1640, there was added a third, with the title of *Underwoods*, which Jonson had given (in the form *Underwood*) to his "lesser poems of later growth." The three books taken together contain two hundred and fifty poems; to which we must add the pieces printed separately in the Folios, or imbedded in the plays and masques and in the dedicatory verse of other men's books, or drawn from odd sources, or now only extant in their titles. The whole is a very miscellaneous collection of short pieces, offered as examples of all the familiar kinds of minor poetry—epigram, memorial, epithalamy, epistle, panegyric, and dedication, descriptive and satirical sketches, didactic and devotional passages, topsyturvy fun, full-dress translation, lyric. No system by subject, form, or date is attempted, and Jonson makes this clear in the choice of his general titles. For the term 'epigram' he disclaims the restricted modern sense of a short poem working up to and closing with a witty, satirical, or ingenious turn, showing that love of 'point' which finds a parallel in the English treatment of the Italian sonnet. He addresses "My mere English Censurer" thus:

> To thee, my way in Epigrams seems new,
> When both it is the old way and the true.
> Thou sayest that cannot be ; for thou hast seen
> Davis and Weever, and the best have been,
> And mine come nothing like.[1]

He reverts to the "old way," the *epigramme à la grecque*, disparaged by French writers of the seventeenth century as colourless, and allows himself what latitude he may under the rules that the piece should be short and should deal with a single idea, chosen freely from the full range of human interest. He enters two caveats ; first, against confounding epigram with 'narration,' as Harrington and Owen had done,[2] and secondly, perhaps more strongly than his own practice warrants, against the Roman and modern limitation of the epigram to a thing

> bold, licentious, full of gall,
> Wormwood and sulphur, sharp, and toothed withal.[3]

It must not

> Become a petulant thing, hurl ink, and wit,
> As madmen stones, not caring whom they hit.[4]

It may be satirical, even "sulphurous," for satire or anger may deserve expression as well as any other of the poet's moods ; but it must not be denied its rights in every other vein. An epigram is in essence occasional, and a book of epigrams is a true miscellany ; and Jonson claims no more for his than that they are a garland or posy of short reflections, or an anthology, as Meleager and Cephalas and Planudes had understood their business as collectors. In a book of Jonsonian epigrams we may therefore expect to find many things which by present-

---

[1] *Epigr.* XVIII.   [2] *Convers.* i. and xii.
[3] *Epigr.* II.   [4] *Ib.*

day usage would be ruled out. This conception both of the individual poem and of the gathering together is the key to Jonson's method in his later books of verse and the explanation of their titles. In *Underwoods, consisting of Divers Poems,* he tells the reader : "With the same leave the ancients called that kind of body *Sylva,* or "Ὕλη, in which there were works of divers nature and matter congested ; as the multitude call timber-trees promiscuously growing a Wood or Forest : so am I bold to entitle these lesser poems of later growth by this of *Underwood,* out of the analogy they hold to the Forest in my former book, and no otherwise." A Latin version of this passage, plainly Jonson's original of his editor's English, appears in the posthumous prose-book named on the title-page *Timber or Discoveries* and elsewhere *Explorata or Discoveries.* If, as we believe,[1] the title *Timber* is the editor's devising, it is at once a pretty courtesy to Jonson's tree-figure and a just description of the medley of critical wisdom in that much misunderstood work.

As each of the three collections of verse is so mixed in character, and as pieces in one have their analogues in the others and in the scattered writings, it is better to take the whole as a single miscellany. We shall thus make a better survey, and see more clearly where Jonson's likings lie and in what kind he is most successful. We must not read too much into Drummond's gossip of the poet's favourite pieces for "repetition." Authors are notoriously unreliable in self-criticism, and the holiday frolic at Hawthornden must have given greater prominence to some poems than even Jonson

[1] See *infra,* p. 251.

himself would have allowed had he had his public in
mind. So we pass by such verses as those on Gout,[1] or on
the Countess of Bedford's grant of a buck [2] (one of the
pieces he repeated from memory), and satirical exercises
like the lines on the Court Pucelle which he read to
his host; but we note with satisfaction, and for later
comment, that he approved his "Musical Strife" (beginning "Come with our voices let us war"), "Drink to me
only with thine eyes," the festive "Swell me a bowl
with lusty wine," from *The Poetaster*, and "For Love's
sake kiss me once again," from *The Celebration of Charis*.
We should like to think that this vein, amatory and
bacchanal, is the true Jonson whom the humorist
and fighting critic hides from us, and that it was
more than their swinging metre that kept them in his
affection.

Jonson is at his best in his *Epigrams* when he keeps
closest to the original conception, when the epigram is
truly epigraphic, an inscription on something, a saying
deserving record on the temple-front or altar of the
poet's memory ; concise, with a touch of ceremony, but
convincing. It may be on a person, dead or living, or
on a mood ; in one place an epitaph or congratulation,
in another a snatch of song. It is chiselled work, brief
in compass, often a restoration rather than an adaptation
of old models in motive and phrase, restrained and
orderly in its expression, drawn as a cameo or panel is,
not wantonly as the graffiti of free passion. In a word,
it is classical in origin and nature, and always at its
best when frankest in confessing that tradition. Jonson's
classical habit was admirably suited for this work ; but

---

[1] *Epigr.* XVIII.   [2] *Ib.* LXXXIV.

at the same time, as already shown, he never sacrificed individuality.

No form, the sonnet alone excepted, has attracted more attention from all manner of poets than the epitaph; and none, the sonnet again excepted, has supplied a more summary test for separating the good poets from the crowd of indifferent or bad. Nash remarked in 1589: "Epitaphers and position poets we have more than a good many, that swarm like crows to a dead carcass, but fly, like swallows in the winter, from any continuate subject of wit."[1] He would have admitted, had he lived to read what Jonson could offer, that one poet at least who did not write an epic, and was not likely to have succeeded had he tried, had on occasion done surpassing well as a "position poet." That others thought so of Jonson, in his own day and later, is shown by the ascription to him of pieces by both predecessors and successors, and only, it would appear, because they were good and worthy of his reputation. The pseudo-Jonson like the pseudo-Chaucer is no small compliment to the real poet, though the workmanship be inferior. Even in the present day we persist in speaking of the famous lines on the Countess of Pembroke ("Underneath this sable hearse") as his, though the attribution as late as *The Spectator*[2] was to an "uncertain author," and is now convincingly in favour of William Browne. Fortunately we possess others which help us to excuse the mistaken judgement on the Pembroke poem.

The memorial verses on 'My first daughter'[3] and

[1] Preface to Greene's *Menaphon*.   [2] No. 323.
[3] *Epigr.* XXII.

'My first son'[1] show the difficulties of adjusting the claims of Art and intimate sorrow. We do not suspect the mourner; but the artist, by insisting overmuch, perhaps as an effect of his own feelings, spoils the impression he would give. When we select these lines as among the best—

> Rest in soft peace, and asked, say here doth lie
> Ben Jonson his best piece of poetry—

we commend the ingenuity of the conceit, but little else. Jonson is happier when kinship or deep affection is not involved and he can survey his object at greater distance. Perhaps this is true of all epitaphers; for the exercise of Jonson's "cool art" and his sense of proportion it was a first condition. Hence, without doubt, the success of the Pembroke piece, which, if not Jonson's, remains to us typically Jonsonian. We see him at his best in the lines on Salathiel Pavy,[2] one of the Children of the Chapel who played in his *Cynthia's Revels* and *Poetaster*. The conceit about the Fates' mistaking the youth for an old man, which is transferred from Martial,[3] the metrical and rhyme ingenuity, in a word everything that confesses the literary and scholarly character of the writer harmonizes with the sentiment and brings no suspicion of affectation. It is, notwithstanding its greater length, a memorial epigram in the best sense of the term, satisfying all traditional claims, and having sufficient 'point' and pathos to commend itself to the modern reader. He is less successful in the shorter piece *Elizabeth L. H.*, whose surname the poet, in affection, withholds from us. In the *Epitaph on the Lady Jane*

---

[1] *Epigr.* XLV.　　　[2] *Ib.* CXX.　　　[3] x. 53.

we have, on the other hand, only the colder and more professional side of Jonson's art; and in a longer piece, *To Jane, Marchioness of Winchester* (probably the same lady), also written late, we see more clearly where Jonson's peril lay. Only mixed praise can be given to those longer poems which Jonson called Elegies, in the vaguer usage of the title, as practised by Donne and many of his contemporaries, and continued and defended later by Shenstone. The shortest and best of these, beginning—

> Though beauty be the mark of praise,
>   And yours of whom I sing be such,
>   As not the world can praise too much,
> Yet is't your virtue now to raise—

is pleasing, and produces, in the fifth stave:

> His falling temples you have reared,
>   The withered garlands ta'en away;
>   His altars kept from the decay
> That envy wished and nature feared.[1]

This form, used again in stanzas of eight lines in *Catiline*,[2] recalls *In Memoriam*; but Tennyson, whom some would make a debtor to our poet, protested against the charge.[3] The verse is found before Jonson's time, in certain paraphrases of the *Psalms* about the middle of the sixteenth century, and it is described in Puttenham (chap. xi.). Francis Davison has it; so too, after Jonson, have George Sandys and Lord Herbert of Cherbury. Neither Ben nor Tennyson were originators, but each made it his own and had his following. The elaborate Pindaric Ode on the death of Sir H. Morison,

---

[1] *Underwoods*, XXXIX.   [2] Act II.
[3] *Life*, I. p. 306.

with its compliments to Sir Lucius Cary, the bosom-friend of the deceased, will be referred to later in this chapter. His most elaborate elegy is *Eupheme*, in ten sections (incomplete), on the Lady Venetia Digby ; but, with the exception of the compliment—

> All that was good or great with me she weaved
> And set it forth ; the rest were cobwebs fine,
> Spun out in name of some of the old Nine,
> To hang a window, or make dark the room,
> Till, swept away, they were cancelled with a broom,

and the interpolated counsel to her three sons—

> Boast not these titles of your ancestors,
> Brave youths, they're their possessions, none of yours :
> When your own virtues equalled have their names,
> 'Twill be but fair to lean upon their fames,

there is little to justify Aubrey's opinion that Ben "hath made her live in poetry"[1] or added to his fame in the attempt. The strongly religious cast of the last section is noted as rare in Jonson's work.[2] If the poem will be remembered, it will be for the gruesome sketch, in a recovered fragment of the series, of the worms ("my rivals") "tasting" her tender body and nibbling a cross on her breast and an epitaph on her cold forehead—as nastily absurd as the picture of Earine's corpse in *The Sad Shepherd*,[3] and hardly paralleled in the most morbid mood of the Metaphysicals. Some of the less repellent, if more enigmatic, fancy of that school discovers itself in a strange parcel of elegies in *Underwoods*, but the critic, having found that one of these, "To make the doubt clear that no woman's true,"[4] is no other than

[1] *Lives*, ii. 231.   [2] *Infra*, p. 237.
[3] *Supra*, p. 204.   [4] *Underwoods*, LVIII.

Donne's *Expostulation*, may find excuse for suspecting that not all, or much of, the remainder may be Jonson's, and turn with some relief to another in the same volume, named *An Elegy*.[1] There the poet, escaping from a style mainly reminiscent and decadent, gives a hint of that simpler metaphysical quality and that transfused melody which changed the old 'common metre' exercises to the magic of Caroline song :

> Fair friend, 'tis true your beauties move
>   My heart to a respect,
> Too little to be paid with love,
>   Too great for your neglect . . .

And to these the critic will add the verses, "Oh, do not wanton with those eyes," or, better still, those in dedication of Warre's *Touchstone of Truth* (1630)—the lateness is significant, if they are indeed Jonson's—

> Truth is the trial of itself,
>   And needs no other touch ;
> And purer than the purest gold,
>   Refine it ne'er so much. . . .

It is an easy transition from elegies of this kind to the lyrics and songs on which Jonson's second chief claim as a poet is based.   The Jonson of the anthologies presents no difficulties to readers who know no more than "Drink to me only with thine eyes" and one or two others.   They cannot praise them overmuch.   Only when they take a wider view of his art is it brought home to them how rare such successes are.   Not even the best of these lyrical pieces are truly spontaneous. Jonson refines and adjusts.   Rarely, if indeed ever,

---

[1] *Underwoods*, XL.

is he possessed by compelling song. He has no passion,
and scarcely needs to tell us "why I write not of
love"; how the god

> Into my rhymes could ne'er be got
> By any art ;[1]

at least, he has no great fervours. Yet the result in
his best pieces is more or less satisfactory, though his
art may be derivative even to plain plagiarism of motive
and words, or may be conventional. In the well-known
lines of one of his two songs *To Celia* ("Drink to me
only with thine eyes") we see how, as it were by
sheer artistic intelligence rather than by personal feeling,
he conveys the impression of lyrical ease and directness.
It is an old tale now that these lines are transferred
from the Epistles of Philostratus the Athenian. They
are, however, something more than a happy translation,
and they help us to understand what Dryden meant
by saying that "what would be theft in other poets
is only victory" in Jonson ; or Carew's reminder that
there is no robbery

> if the rich spoils so torn
> From conquer'd authors be as trophies worn.[2]

The most noteworthy fact is not the poet's pious following of the old text, as for example in his third quatrain
rendering the Sophist's πέπομφά σοι στέφανον ῥόδων,
οὐ σὲ τιμῶν, καὶ τοῦτο μὲν γάρ, ἀλλ᾽ αὐτοῖς τι
χαριζόμενος τοῖς ῥόδοις, ἵνα μὴ μαρανθῇ, but that
the whole is gathered from the prose of four separate
letters. We have here some pretty evidence for consideration by our theorists on lyrical verse, on 'heat,'

---

[1] *Forest*, I.   [2] *To Ben Jonson.*

and 'first impression,' and the linnet-will to sing. To
some the discovery of borrowing is vexing. The
dramatist Cumberland, with a literary sense even duller
than that of his famous grandfather, saw nothing but
" a parcel of unnatural far-fetched conceits, more calcu-
lated to disgust a man of Jonson's classical taste, than
to put him upon the humble task of copying them," and
added petulantly that the poem " taken from this
despicable sophist is now become a very popular song." [1]
But the poem is not what the pedants would take it to
be. That it is a mosaic in translation is no more than
a curious fact for the entertainment of commentators—a
fact which not all of them might have known or suspected.
The perfection of the poem is its own—its unity, its
melody, its fresh appeal. Its conceits are not bookish,
or is its sentiment formal. If it surprise us, it is not as
the paradox of Jonson's laboured art, but as the triumph.
Though he may often, when working in the same way,
show no more than the excellences of an academic
exercise, it is something to the credit of his method
and craft that on occasion he succeeds so well. The
page's song in *The Silent Woman*, " Still to be neat,
still to be drest," is another borrowing, from the
anonymous *Semper munditias, semper, Basilissa, decores,*
persistently ascribed in error to the French Latinist
Bonnefons, one of Jonson's favourite obscurities. The song
in the *Forest* " That women are but men's shadows " is
another, which, notwithstanding Drummond's anecdote,[2]
is now known to be carried over from some Latin
verses by Barthelemi Aneau, the sixteenth century

[1] *The Observer*, No. 74.
[2] *Convers.* xiv.

Anulus of Gruter's French *Deliciae*.[1] Volpone's song
to Celia (III. vi.), which appears also in *The Forest* (v.),
with an extension beginning "Kiss me sweet; the wary
lover" (VI.), is open challenge to Catullus in one of his
best-known passages. We misjudge Jonson if we put
these happy lines to the test of translation. He adapts
to his own ends and builds in, partly of necessity, partly
in compliment, pieces of the ancient fabric which he
would preserve for English use. Or it may be that a
lively memory is the prompter, unconsciously, of the
theft; for seldom, as in the other song to Celia, do we
think of Jonson with the original at his elbow. Fair
criticism will not condemn this traffic in other men's
fancies. Extravagance, as in the second part of Volpone's
song in *The Forest*, is rare; and it is acceptable even
there. If it is not Catullus, it is at least Jonson in
happy mood.

In the larger body of lyrical work which may be
called original, Jonson is less successful. In the plays
and masques there are none surpassing the two songs
already referred to, but one or two may be named.
The well-known song by Hesperus in *Cynthia's Revels*
(V. iii.), "Queen and huntress, chaste and fair," is an
excellent example in that more formal genre in which
the personal note is weak and the literary interest only
partial. We hardly require the stage direction 'Music
accompanied,' for the words are resonant of horn and
theorbo and win half their effect by the orchestral
suggestion. So too is the earlier echo song in the same
play (I. i.), with its direct reference to the music, its
variety of line, and its onomatopoeia; and Hedon's song

[1] See *Notes and Queries*, III. viii. 187.

'The Kiss' (IV. i.) with its *fioriture* in word and rhythm. There is a like suggestion in the tripping measure of the Songs of Crispinus and Hermogenes in *The Poetaster* (II. i.), and in Albius's "Wake! our mirth begins to die," with the part song following (IV. iii.) ; but Jonson's favourite bacchanal snatch in the same play, "Swell me a bowl with lusty wine" (III. i.), is of clearer literary pretence. The other songs in the plays call for little or no remark. Two of the best are in later pieces, "Do but look on her eyes, they do light," in *The Devil is an Ass* (II. ii.), and Karolin's song, "Though I am young and cannot tell," in *The Sad Shepherd* (I. v.), but they show the crippling of his powers. The masques yield little of merit ; but the catch in *Oberon*, beginning—

> Buz, quoth the blue flie ;
> Hum, quoth the bee ;

has the abandon of Shakespeare's faery, and the songs in *Pan's Anniversary*, "Of Pan we sing, the best of singers, Pan," and the others remind us of Spenser, and "O, how came, Love," in *Love Restored*, of more than one Elizabethan paean.

In Jonson's books of verse the most elaborate effort is one in *Underwoods*, called *A Celebration of Charis* : *in ten lyric Pieces*. Gathered together perhaps as late as 1624, just before his health began to break, it shows him in a light amatory mood which he rarely allowed himself to indulge. It has a freshness which compels the fifty-year-old poet to an expression of his own surprise, and just enough of classical reminiscence to enhance its quality and to show us, as in the case of the Celia songs, but with less textual closeness, the happy effect of this stimulus. The ten pieces are in varied form, and appear to be a final grouping of poems written or sketched at different times. The description of Charis in the "Discourse with Cupid" (v.) has clear verbal and metrical kinship with the *Elegy*, numbered XXXVI. in the same book; the seventh part, "For Love's sake, kiss me once again," was, with some variations, noted by Drummond in the *Conversations* as one of Jonson's favourites for repetition; and two of the stanzas of "Her Triumph" are given *verbatim* by Wittipol in *The Devil is an Ass* (II. ii.). The seventh part is perhaps the best in the set. There is no evidence to show that Charis has a more personal interest than the Delias and Ideas of Elizabethan homage. The name probably had, apart from its familiar sense, some association in Jonson's mind with his admired Bonnefons, to whose *Pancharis* he refers in an Ode in *Underwoods*.[1]

In another division of his verse, the Odes, Jonson is on the whole less good than in the epitaphs and lyrics. Their kinship with *Charis* is at once suggested by the revel in metrical variety, as an escape from stanzas grown too familiar, and as an occasional relaxation from the couplet mode which Jonson himself had done so much to fix, and secondly, by the lyrical quality shown and sometimes unexpectedly sustained. Though Jonson once, and for the first time in English, bent this erratic form to stricter Pindaric shape,[2] he was attracted as Cowley and later libertines were by the freedom which it offered. The indulgence is not strange, even had Jonson been more of a formalist than he was.

[1] XLVI.　　　[2] *Infra*, p. 229.

He could say at times, as he said in his epigram to Lord
Newcastle on his fencing,

> I hate such measured—give me mettled—fire,
> That trembles in the blaze, but then mounts higher
> A quick and dazzling motion.[1]

With the ode we may associate the epithalamy,
more disciplined, still following, rather haltingly,
Spenserian tradition, and chosen for that larger
orchestral opportunity which the lute-melody of the
song could not give.

The *Epode* (*Forest*, XI.) shows us glimpses of Jonson
at his best, notwithstanding its didactic cast. It
sustains, on the whole, the metrical ease of the
opening—

> Not to know vice at all, and keep true state,
>   Is virtue and not Fate ;
> Next to that virtue, is to know vice well
>   And her black spite expel ;

and in one passage at least, in its brief for "chaste
love," reaches the higher ground of poetry—

> It is a golden chain let down from Heaven,
>   Whose links are bright and even,
> That falls like sleep on lovers, and combines
>   The soft and sweetest minds
> In equal knots.

The birthday *Ode to Sir William Sidney* (*Forest*, XIV.),
is merely a *tour de force* in stanzas built up with lines
of extravagant variety, occasionally recalling (it may
be intentionally) in the swish of the movement, and
in phrasing like—

> And some do drink, and some do dance,

---

[1] *Underwoods*, LXXXIX.

the northern verse-frolic of *Christ's Kirk on the Green*
and its kin. The *Ode to Lord Desmond* (*Underwoods*,
XLIV.) shows the fuller "rage" of the English
"hard-mouth'd horse," as Cowley called the "Pin-
darique Pegasus,"[1] and, like another following it,
beginning "High-spirited friend," has only an experimental interest; and other two, loosely called Odes,
one in couplets (*ib.* XLVI.) and another in stanzas on
the Queen's Birthday, 1630 (*ib.* LXXXV.), hardly
deserve mention. There is more to be said of the
Pindaric Ode on the Death of Sir H. Morison, otherwise entitled "To the Immortal Memory and friendship of that Noble Pair, Sir Lucius Cary and Sir
H. Morison" (*ib.* LXXXVIII.). Here the interest is
mainly formal, in scholarly protest—to be repeated
later by Congreve and Gray, and as ineffectually—
against the disorderly imitations of Pindar by English
poets. The arrangement of strophe, antistrophe, and
epode is maintained throughout with due recognition
of the antitheses required in the treatment of the
motive and with strict metrical parallelism. We feel,
however, as we do to some extent in Gray, that
English does not affect the Greek fashion with an
easy grace, and that in English memorial verse its
ceremony becomes mere theatrical pretence. When
we find the last line of an antistrophe—

> And there he lives with memory, and Ben,

and the first of the next epode—

> Jonson, who sung this of him, ere he went,

and encounter this impossible couplet—

---

[1] *The Resurrection.*

To separate these twi-
Lights, the Dioscuri,

we feel that the poet fails, almost discreditably. The
metrical difficulties react hurtfully on the treatment
of the subject, and we may amuse ourselves by
thinking that it was some such exercise as this that
prompted Ben to write his *Fit of Rhyme against Rhyme*.
The straining of the form forces the poet to "metaphysical excess." Scott thought ill of the verses for
this reason, and pointed a comparison between the
Shakespearian statue and the Jonsonian monster.
"We have often to marvel how his conceptions
could have occurred to any human being." [1] The late
Mr. Palgrave met this criticism by allotting to the
stanza, "It is not growing like a tree," one of the
three places reserved for Jonson in the *Golden Treasury*.[2]
Tennyson liked these lines too; but we feel that
Jonson, though declining the "thousand liberties"
which Cowley fairly claimed for the entertainment of
his readers, indulges figures "unusual and bold, even
to temerity, and such as [one] durst not have to do
withal in any other kind of poetry" [3]—or in this. In
the *Ode to Himself* (*Underwoods*, XLI.), of which a portion
appears in the *Apologetical Dialogue* at the close of *The
Poetaster*, the irregularly-lined stanzas convey, more
happily, the rush and swell of anger at critic-fools and
a strumpet stage. Indeed, of all Jonson's odes the
Pindaric shows itself least suited not only to seventeenth-
century art but to his own talent. He may have
been attracted by the experiments of Ronsard. He

---

[1] *Life of Dryden*, i. p. 10.   [2] P. 77.
[3] Cowley, Preface to *Works* (1668).

told Drummond that the French poet's "best pieces" were his *Odes*.[1] But his knowledge of the form was direct, not an echo like that of John Southern, who had claimed, in 1584, that

> never man before
> Now in England knew Pindar's string,[2]

and had been snubbed by Puttenham[3] for his second-hand "braggery." Jonson did not try again to carve his odes to the pattern of Pindar.

In the three epithalamies—one at the end of *Hymenæi*, another concluding *The Hue and Cry after Cupid*, and a third, written as late as 1633, as an independent piece in honour of Mr. Hierome Weston and Lady Francis Stewart—there is, as might be expected, a veneer of Spenserian tradition, but the differences show more plainly. The difficult and artificial form, far from hiding the idiosyncrasies of each poet, rather compels them forth; and if Jonson's experiments suffer by comparison with the *Epithalamion* and *Prothalamion* —the perfected music of Colin's Dirge in the *Shepherd's Calendar*[4]—it is not because Jonson is not at his best. Rich imagination and passion, and that processional quality which gives Spenser's verses the movement of a triumph, combining in a single and increasing effect the shouting and blare and flaunting with orderly and solemn march, are not within reach of Jonson. Scholarly conceits, with exhortation and unpoetic details of the procedure at "Venus' vigil," are a poor substitute for the colour and stir of the Spenserian ode. Jonson cannot divest himself of his realism, and

---

[1] *Discoveries*, iv.   [2] *Pandora.*   [3] Ch. xxii.
[4] 'November.'

realism, even if there is no thought of immortality
for the verse, is least in place on such occasions.   His
inability to keep up the promise of his opening lines—
a blight upon all his poetry, even in his shortest pieces
—is here plain palsy.   The more ambitious *Epithalamion*
is his feeblest.   His best, the ode at the close of *The
Hue and Cry after Cupid*, might have been accepted
more thankfully had not Spenser set the standard.
In so far as it is an imitation, it misses the essentials
and hardly achieves a mannerism.

Of Jonson's remaining poems—the greater part of
the whole—no arrangement by group is satisfactory,
whether on grounds of matter, treatment, or technique.
A large number may be described as panegyrical, rang-
ing from snatches to epistles, in praise of friends, or in
compliment to Great Ones or to literary contemporaries.
They are rich in biographical and critical interest, but
only rarely poetical.   The most elaborate, and perhaps
the best, of the more personal pieces, *To Master Colby*, is
really a social satire, in the vein of Juvenal, for the good
youth is urged to show his goodness by forsaking a
vicious London for the battlefield.   He begins, in
words which sound strangely intimate in the twentieth
century—

> Wake, friend, from forth thy lethargy ! the drum
> Beats brave and loud in Europe, and bids come
> All that dare rouse : or are but loth to quit
> Their vicious ease, and be o'erwhelmed with it,

but in a long middle section he says many bitter things
about luxurious fashions, greed of money, and the
whoredom of society, sometimes in lines which Dryden
has not bettered, as these :

> To do't with cloth, or stuffs, lust's name might merit ;
> With velvet, plush, and tissues, it is spirit.

Of the shorter pieces, his friend Roe and his family claim the largest number : all are in a more solemn key, and one or two remind us of Jonson's art in epitaph. His compliments are successful for the same reason, that he is direct and has, or assumes, a genuineness which is so often wanting in Donne's. The latter so involves the simple intention in subtleties that the reader, if not the recipient, may incline to think that the poet is paying his greatest compliment to his own ingenuity. Jonson's addresses to Great Ones, to the two kings and their queens, to nobles like Dorset, to Lady Rutland and other Court ladies, are better than the generality of ceremonious verse. Nor do the verses to James and Charles refute what has been said of Ben's being no courtier, for if the praise here, as in the masques, seems extravagant to us, it is more measured than was the practice of his age ; and, in the case of the former especially, there is the touch of personal regard, the sympathy in scholarship, and the dislike of Puritanism (witness the prologue and epilogue in *Bartholomew Fair*) and other matters which relieve it from the charge of unreality. Even in his distress he approaches Charles with a quip about the "*poet's-evil*, poverty," and with no beggar-like calling on heaven for blessings. One piece *To Penshurst* has attracted attention as an address to a *place*, and as exceptional in Jonson and the literature of his time in respect of its natural description and its interest in country life. It does not, however, give, as some have imagined, a hint of the outlook which we find even in poets before the days of *The Tales of the Hall*, and *The Task*, unless we allow to

these no more than may be claimed by any writer, however classical or artificial, in the setting forth of the
facts of external nature and in their decorative use. The
poem is a panegyric of the Sidney family. The glories
of the "ancient pile," the rich hospitality, all the gentle
ways of Penshurst, are but ancillary to and expressive
of the main theme of personal eulogy. If Jonson speaks
of "the purpled pheasant with the speckled side"
and "the painted partridge"—which the most formal
poetaster may observe and so describe—he shows how
little he has of the later mood by the confession that the
one is "to crown thy open table" and that the other
"for thy mess is willing to be killed." Something more
might be said of his sympathy with Nature in the
lines to Sir Robert Wroth, "How blest art thou, canst
love the country, Wroth" (*Forest*, III.), in which the poet
interests himself in "lowing herds," the "loud stag," the
"apple-harvest," and "mowed meadows," and, rather
riskily, in his favourite partridge and hare :

> In autumn, at the partridge mak'st a flight,
>   And giv'st the gladder guests the sight ;
> And in the winter, hunt'st the flying hare,
>   More for thy exercise than fare.

The terms of the compliment to Sir Robert's sportsman-
ship hardly excuse Ben from a very trencherly love of
fur and feather. As in the Penshurst poem, the purpose
is to proclaim the contentment of his friend in his
retirement from city hubbub. "Thy peace is made," he
says towards the end, when, done with the decorative
opening, he praises Sir Robert's disentanglement from
the worries of soldiering, advocacy, and money-making.
In truth, the whole is a clear reminiscence of Horace,

and one has only to compare it with the *Beatus ille qui procul negotiis* of the Odes and with Jonson's own favourite translation ("Happy is he, that from all business clear") to see that the scholar keeps to the beaten track of literary tradition. Jonson's attitude to Nature is frankly Roman. Nature is welcomed for the pleasure of repose which it brings; the hills and woods are invoked as silent sympathizers with the poet in his misfortunes and in his fits of malaise; and it is not all Nature or Nature herself, but only this or that countryside or quiet spot which he welcomes as a companion for a time. The lines dedicated to literary and artistic friends are of greater interest, and of some critical value. Among those selected for compliment are Bacon (*Und.* LXX.), The Beaumonts, Francis and Sir John (*Epigr.* LV., *Und.* XIII.), Breton (*Und.* XXIII.), Brome (*Und.* XXVIII.), William Browne (*Und.* XVIII.), Camden (*Epigr.* XIV.), Chapman(*Und.*XX.), Donne (*Epigr.* XXIII.,XCVI.), Drayton (*Und.* XVI.), Thomas May (*Und.* XXI.), Overbury (*Epigr.* CXIII.), Selden (*Und.* XXXI.), Shakespeare (Lines prefixed to the first Folio (1623) and *Und.* XII.), Sylvester (*Epigr.* CXXXII.), the actor Alleyn (*Epigr.* LXXXIX.), and Ferrabosco, his musical collaborator in some of his masques (*Epigr.* CXXX., CXXXI.). But the verses are rarely poetical and they are often hobbling; yet they carry some pretty courtesies.[1] The most elaborate are "A Vision of the Muses of his friend Michael Drayton," in which he describes the poet's works *seriatim* with a fine enthusiasm, and the address "To the Memory of my beloved Master William Shakespeare, and what he has left us," the *locus* of "Soul of the age!", "Or sporting Kyd, or

---

[1] Though some of the 'conceits' are stale.

Marlowe's mighty line," "small Latin and less Greek,"
"insolent Greece or haughty Rome," "He was not of an
age, but for all time," "Sweet Swan of Avon"—lines and
phrases which so many know and not quite so many
associate with Jonson, as they do some of the apparently
less favourable dicta of *Discoveries* and the *Conversations*.
We forget the compliment—

> Yet must I not give Nature all ; thy art,
> My gentle Shakespeare, must enjoy a part.
>
> .   .   .   .
>
> For a good poet's made, as well as born.
> And such wert thou !

but remember Drummond's brief report of Ben's opinion,
"that Shakespeare wanted art." [1]

More or less outside the groups already discussed,
but with overlappings which make precise separation
impossible, lie scattered epistles, a few didactic and
devotional pieces, epigrams of the short satirical pattern,
burlesques, and translations. In the epistles of the
more ceremonious kind, like those to the Countess of
Rutland (*For.* XII.) or to Lady Aubigny (*ib.* XIII.),
Jonson writes in a lumbering manner, with now and
then a rhetorical ecstasy. He is more at ease with a
literary subject, as in his epistle to John Selden ; lighter
still in places in the Drayton and Colby pieces, already
referred to ; perhaps best, both for the form's sake, as we
understand it through the perspective of the eighteenth
century, and as an expression of Jonson's idiosyncrasy
and power, in snatches of the lines to Lord Dorset
(*Und.* XXX.), "To one that asked to be sealed of the
Tribe of Ben" (*ib.* LXVI.), or "Inviting a Friend to

[1] See *infra*, p. 267.

Supper" (*Epigr.* CI.). But in none of these things is Jonson a Horace or a Pope. He is denied the suavity and formal ease of the great masters. His satire is too heavy-handed, and in reference to himself he is inclined, as ever, to protest too much. He tells more than one friend how much he loves the truth, and to Selden, in particular, he says, that, being suspected of overpraising some, he will "turn a sharper eye upon himself."

Though Jonson is strongly didactic, it is hard to find anything worth remembering which would give him place as a didactic poet. His best in this kind are embedded in his greater works, but we can pick out one, and only one, minor and self-contained piece which has any individual merit. This is the justly praised 'Not to know vice at all, and keep true state," already mentioned in connexion with the *Odes.* He has left little religious verse, though he lacked neither the power of writing it well nor the mood of piety. In his address *To Heaven* (*For.* xv.) he begins, *more suo*, by a protest against misconception of his venture :

> Good and great God ! can I not think of Thee,
> But it must straight my melancholy be ?
> Is it interpreted in me disease,
> That, laden with sins, I seek for ease ?

He disclaims "the breath of discontent" or—

> that these prayers be
> For weariness of life, not love of Thee.

He seems conscious of general surprise at his effort as a writer of Noble Numbers, and at once assumes an attitude of defence. Yet it must be admitted that his protesting manner does less harm to the expression of his piety than it often does in other personal concerns.

It certainly does not disturb the metrical ease of the
poem. A like facility, joined with a simplicity of treatment rather unusual, characterizes the other pieces, *The
Sinner's Sacrifice*, with its three hymns, and the greater
part of the ninth section of *Eupheme*. Though he
indulged this pious mood, he did so with characteristic
reserve. He had none of the mystical or ecstatic
experience which moulded the verse of Southwell and
Herbert, or Habington, Crashaw, and Vaughan, and
perhaps little of the simpler reverence of his 'son,' the
vicar of Dean Prior. His bluff intellectualism denied
him all finesse in emotion, here as elsewhere in his
work. He was, says Drummond in his summing up,
"for any religion, as being versed in both."[1] It is
significant that in praising Southwell's *Burning Babe*—
"so he had written that piece of his, he would have
been content to destroy many of his"[2]—he chose a
poem which by its simplicity of sentiment and style is
exceptional amid the Jesuit's prodigal fancies. He
took religion honestly enough, but in a workaday way,
without any zeal for Laudian beauties of holiness; and
he exerted no influence, such as can be claimed for
Donne, on the growth of that strange twin enthusiasm
of the century for the secular Muse of the Hesperides
and her saintly sister of Noble Numbers.

In another, but more usual, mood Jonson threw off
a large number of satirical snatches in epigrammatic
form, not always happy in their wit or in their verse.
Some of the personalities in which he indulges have
a biographical value; and some of the topics which
occur most frequently bear directly on his literary

---

[1] *Convers.* xix.   [2] *Ib.* xii.

relationships.   For example, he writes three on 'Play-wright,' one on 'Poet-Ape,' which, since Chalmers's silly suggestion that Shakespeare is glanced at, has innocently encouraged the Shakonian heresy, and another on 'Proule'—all on the same subject, the plagiarism by indifferent authors of other men's ideas and work, and of his own in particular; and in another, "To a weak Gamester in Poetry," he ridicules under a metaphor from the forgotten game of primero, the provoking vanity of his imitators.   On spies he writes:

> Spies, you are lights in state, but of base stuff,
> Who, when you've burnt yourselves down to the snuff,
> Stink, and are thrown away.   End fair enough.

He has others, of greater length than the epigram allowed, which exhibit a lighter side of his muse, such as *A Fit of Rhyme against Rhyme* (*Und.* XLVIII.); *To Master John Burgess* (*ib.* LXXVI.), in Skeltonical doggerel; a parody of Wither's "Shall I wasting in despair"—

> Shall I my affections slack
> 'Cause I see a woman's black;

some laboured experiments of the 'nonsense' kind, with rhymes as daring as any in *Hudibras*; and the scatological *Voyage* (*Epigr.* CXXXIII.).   Happily for his reputation, Jonson seldom dipped his quill in sewage, as he does in this last intolerable piece.   He is some-times rude or coarse, as modern taste interprets the matter, but in nearly every case only in passing, not blatantly and of purpose as in this *Voyage*.   In this respect he is no monster among contemporaries; and he does not show half the fondness of which Pope gives

proof. It may or may not be something for extenua-
tion that the piece is a burlesque, that the violent
mingling of quasi-romance (with its tags of "Now, lord-
ings, listen well," "It was the day, what time the
powerful Moon," and the like) and the unsavoury
details of the riverside is but the realist's or parodist's
fun. Jonson may have been coarser by nature than
Swift was; and he may not have Swift's excuse, that
for the deeper disgrace of a victim one may sacrifice
an innate fastidiousness; but no fair-minded reader
can endorse Swinburne's hysterical glossing of Scott's
innocent remark that Ben often used "the language of
scavengers and nightmen." Like all writers, greater
and smaller, and of other times as well as Ben's free-
spoken age, he claims to range at will, but he never
leaves the impression of morbid indelicacy. He is as
little a coprologist as he is a sensualist, and of his being
the latter Swinburne would not suspect him. "I have
loathed the use of such foul and unwashed bawdry as
is now made the food of the scene," he says fairly in
the Dedication to *Volpone*.

A streak of burlesque relieves the tragic theme of
An Execration upon Vulcan.[1] This piece which appeared
"with divers epigrams" in a separate quarto in 1640
has been remembered chiefly for its record of the works,
finished and unfinished, which perished with his library;
but it is more than an antiquarian document. It is one
of the best examples of Jonson's invective, written in a
serio-comic vein, and in better humour than might be
expected of him under such cruel provocation. In
quizzical anger he addresses the "lame Lord of Fire"—

---

[1] *Underwoods*, LXII.

"your Flameship"—and, in suggesting to him how he could have made a nobler "feast of fire," insinuates some criticism of his own work and of that of others. If there was no "scurril paper" in his desk, no treason, heresy, imposture, or blasphemy—or (let us note) no branding of the times or "lewd self-boasting rhymes" —"then why this fire?" when there is the Talmud and the Koran,

> The Tristrams, Lancelots, Turpins, and the Peers,
> All the mad Rolands and sweet Olivers

—all the medieval stuff of romance for which he had small affection, to make "a meal for Vulcan to lick up"? It was bad taste in the god

> to devour
> So many my years' labours in an hour.

The reader who turns to this body of verse with the conviction that Jonson *cannot* prove himself a poet may find little in this survey to compel a more generous view; and he will be satisfied that aggressiveness, intellectualism, ponderous scholarship, and devotion to theory supply an adequate explanation. He will not trouble himself that these vices are not forbidden to poets, or that some of the greatest have won reputation in spite of them. He will say that it is a question of degree, and that Jonson is too strongly shackled. Successes like the lines to Celia have the unexpectedness of an oasis, welcome indeed, not because it is greener than other groves, but only because it lies in the wide desert: that they are the exceptions which

[1] *Supra*, pp. 41-42.

throw the general failure into stronger relief. He may go further and say that these successes are not so complete as they should be, as if some of the desert sand had blown in and choked the wells of imagination. No one need quarrel with this judgement. But it is by no means clear that, because this verse falls so far short, Jonson lacked, as it were constitutionally, qualities essential to the making of a poet. In his happier, if rarer, moments, he is too strong a rival of the best in richness of fancy and vivacity of phrase to be classed with the mediocrities who never surpass his lower levels. Our disappointment is less that he did not do better than that he denied himself, or was denied, a fuller experience. "One cannot say he wanted wit," remarks Dryden, "but rather that he was frugal of it."

Jonson's verse presents us with a paradox, for hardly without exception, and certainly in the very best, the fallings away betray a lack of that self-reliance which is necessary to lyrical art. Here the most self-assertive of writers, is, as of a sudden, in a transformed mood. He seems to be thinking of the 'other man,' what he has said or what he may say, not, as in his other work, meeting him with the conviction of superiority, measuring his powers with him, capping his good things, and improving his own. This attitude was necessarily disastrous, even if he had had more of the poet's passion, and more sustained energy.

His lack of this continuing power is only too clear. We cannot think of his writing an epic, and we have no regrets that he did not tempt the "weak gamester in poetry"[1] to rival him in that vein. If we allow

[1] *Epigr.* CXII.

that he showed the Carolines how well they were on the way to their imperishable lyric, can we say that he ever reveals their sustained perfection of technique, much less that crescendo by which they move to a completed close? His failure is the effect of his derivative habit of mind. His astonishing memory and his scholarly experience gives him a repository of ideas from which he draws at will and on which he is tempted more and more to rely. Sometimes he is content merely to translate, and then his critical talent, which the selection reveals, helps him best. When, however, he is attracted by the opportunity of a modern analogy, or of 'metaphysical' elaboration, he loses the momentum which he has when he keeps close to his original. Even in translation, especially in mosaic-work like the better known of his Celia songs, he soon begins to flag and stumble; while in lines like those on Margaret Ratcliffe (*Epigr.* XL.) he will pass from a first stanza, which we can praise without being distracted by its artifice, to a second so inferior that it cannot be excused as a *tour de force.*

Another limitation is not less serious, that even in his best passages he is interested only in 'literary' values, that, with all his art in transferring or transforming the good things of classical or humanist thought, he seldom gives that spiritual suggestion which in master-verse lies behind the magic of phrase and rhythm. That magic is too often with him merely the legerdemain of style, ingenious, sometimes elegant, but a conjurer's rather than a magician's mystery. This is not surprising when we consider the evidence which he himself and later critical antiquaries [1] have offered on

---

[1] As Mr. Charles Crawford in *Collectanea*, I. and II.

his method. Drummond records that "he wrote all his first in prose, for so his Master Camden had learned him." [1] That he often did so can be easily shown in the plays and in the poems, as for example in his deliberate working over of passages from *Discoveries* in *The Staple of News.* It is always a study in expression, a turning and returning of phrases, interest in the medium at the expense of poetic sincerity. This is shown even more strikingly in his borrowings from himself, sometimes without alterations, at others with studied editing : as, in the first kind, *To True Soldiers* (*Epigr.* CVIII.), repeated at the close of *The Poetaster* ; the Catullan " Come, my Celia, let us prove " (*Forest*, V.), in *Volpone* (III. vi.) ; the song in *The Devil is an Ass* (II. ii.), given, with a first stanza as eke, in ' Her Triumph' in *A Celebration of Charis* (iv.) ; or, in the second, in the phrase and rhyme identities in *His Discourse with Cupid,* another section of the last piece, and the elegy in *Underwoods* (XXXVI.), or in the likeness of parts of the *Epistle to Sir Edward Sackville* (*Und.* XXX.) and of the *Elegy* (*ib.* LXI.) to passages in *The New Inn.* The extent of these copyings is of less importance than the fact that they are dictated by literary sense rather than by poetic faculty, that they are matters of taste, editorial toying, craftsman-pride, rather than what used to be called, in Shakespeare's case, ' recurrences ' and ' fervours,' the restatement of deepset opinion and favourite image, and the expression, half-unconsciously, in a form which, though familiar, is still fresh because it is final.

Jonson prided himself on his zeal in refashioning,

---

[1] *Convers.* XV. Even if we read " first " as " first poems," the evidence holds. See *infra,* p. 262.

whether in direct translation or in minor borrowings. When Drummond says, in his concluding summary, that "above all he excelleth in a translation," he may be hinting at his happy acquisitiveness rather than his ceremonious Englishing of Latin texts. If Drummond's meaning is to be taken more literally, then his critical wisdom is at once suspect. No one, not even of Whalley's party, would judge Jonson by his rendering of the *Ars Poetica* and three of the *Odes* of Horace, or by his snippets from Martial and Petronius. In these, and especially in the first, he set a model of "metaphrastic severity" which did some harm in his own age and the next, and may have encouraged some collateral absurdities not yet discredited with us. Chapman speaks not too strongly in his preface to his Homer when he says:

> so the brake
> That those translators stick in, that affect
>   Their word-for-word traductions (where they lose
> The free grace of their natural dialect
>   And shame their authors with a forced gloss)
>   I laugh to see.

Dryden passes the first reputable censure [1] on Jonson for his turning an author word by word and line by line, as a pedantry proceeding from "superstition, blind and jealous" and in direct defiance of Horace himself. Johnson condemns Ben's "absurd labour of construing into rhyme," and contrasts it with Dryden's happy mean between that "closeness" which "best preserved an author's sense" and that "freedom" which "best exhibited his spirit." [2] To Scott the translations are

---

[1] Preface to *Ovid's Epistles*.
[2] *The Idler*, No. 69.

"jaw-breaking":[1] while to Swinburne Jonson's method is as "exceptionally abominable, as his genius, when working on its own proper and original lines, is exceptionally admirable."[2] An occasional happy turn cannot save Jonson from the shame of this, for lines 14-18 of the *Ars Poetica*:

> In grave beginnings, and great things profest,
> Ye have ofttimes, that may o'ershine the rest,
> A scarlet piece or two stitched in : when or
> Diana's grove, or altar, with the bor-
> D'ring circles of swift waters that entwine
> The pleasant grounds, or when the river Rhine
> Or rainbow is described.

Such verse is not representative of the translating talent of the age of North and Florio and Holland, or to be excused with Sandys's in its strictest mood or Stanyhurst's in its wildest eccentricity. In confessed translation he must be denied the compliment which Dryden passed on his exploits in plagiarism. He is never less like a monarch when seizing this Horatian territory for English, though, to his credit, he never again comes so perilously near the dull ingenuity of a mere auctioneer of other men's words.

The general failure of his efforts as a poet is in part the effect of his theoretical prejudices on verse technique. No one dare say, with the finer passages in memory, that Jonson had a bad ear, or was indifferent to the nicer values of words, but few will fail to see that he worked under difficulties of his own making, and either could not or would not move freely. He had

---

[1] *Life of Dryden, u.s.* i. 427.
[2] *A Study of Ben Jonson*, p. 111.

some ambition to be a prosodist, in the practical way
he tried to be a grammarian. We learn that he had
fixed opinions on the couplet, on stanzas (and especially
Spenser's), on the sonnet, a form which he, unlike so
many contemporaries, studiously declined (he "cursed"
Petrarch for this folly, among others with which he had
afflicted the Muse in England), on long verse and the
Alexandrine, on the English hexameter, on the relation
of "sense" to "colour and accent," and on Donne's "not
keeping" of the last. Had he given us a treatise on
these things he must have outdistanced all the amateurs
in the science from Gascoigne and James VI. and won
the title of our first prosodist; just as, we may well
believe, he surpassed the Webbes and Puttenhams on
the theory of poetry in the burned essay (with Donne
as Criticus) which he prepared as commentary to
his unfortunate translation of Horace. But the Best
for Prosody and the Best for Poetics is not, as
Meres Secundus must admit, the Best for Poesy.
Though Jonson has written some tolerable blank
verse, but only when he allows rhetoric to supple
its constitutional stiffness, though he has dealt
competently and sometimes happily with the couplet,
and though in lyric he has on occasion, but never with
sustained brilliance, taken his place with the best, he
compels us in a general estimate to reckon against him his
long tale of undistinguished work. We share Cowley's
regret when "a vast heap of stones or rubbish" is
thought "a better monument than a little tomb of
marble."[1]   Cowley suspected the "indiscretion of
friends" and "the avarice of some stationers." Un-

[1] Preface to *Miscellanies* (1668).

fortunately Jonson himself is not without responsibility
for the recovery, when the pride of collecting his *Works*
was upon him, of so much of this strange miscellany—
"the ripest of my studies!"

CHAPTER VIII

SPOLIA OPIMA

JONSON'S debt to the past, especially in textual borrowings from classical writers, has never been in doubt. Contemporaries, in unfriendly mood, found the charge of plagiarism easy to drive home, and Jonson himself by his confessions and not less by his protests encouraged criticism. Dryden with characteristic insight and good humour transformed the censure into the magnificent compliment that "what would be theft in other poets is only victory in him." Later readers have sometimes thought this praise exaggerated—the more scholarly cavilling at times at the way the old material is turned to account, and, with the less scholarly, at his taste in working over his sketches of English life with such learned detail. It is so hard to escape from his dear Greeks and Romans, and his not less dear Humanists; and this may be boring in the comedy of London streets, in masque and love-poem, and in occasional verse. Now and then we detect him in unblushing translation from obscurities like Philostratus, Bonnefons, or Anulus, but we accept his endless reminders of more familiar masters as the natural speech of one who knew his ancients surpassingly well, loved

them, and could not forget what he read. Reasonable
critics allow that, notwithstanding all his pedantries and
schoolmasterly repetitions, he shows a spontaneity which
some greater poets lack in their moments of learned
reminiscence. Nor do we forget how Jonson protested
against blind devotion to antiquity and how he prided
himself on his freedom in dealing with its rules and
forms.

We may decline to test this spontaneity too narrowly,
or ask ourselves how it stands in relation to what
we know of Jonson's 'laboured' style. We may say
that 'slowness' does not prevent his being original, as
we say that a mind richly stored with instance and
analogy may yet be strongly individual. We are not
disconcerted when a poet borrows, even without acknowledgement, or when in our ignorance we are deceived.
To this attitude there may be no objection in general,
but in the case of Jonson, and in his more strikingly
than in any other in the whole range of our literature,
some qualification must be made. Indeed, when we
consider the evidence which the industry or luck of the
literary antiquaries has gathered together in late years,
we question whether this attitude is not altogether
wrong in direction. It is always easy to say hard things
about parallel-hunting and other activities of our *Quellen-*
gentry and critical Gothamists ; and some writers, keener
in attacking these follies than in defending Jonson, have
passed by the evidence in this case as just another
impertinence of the study. A brief examination will
show that in revising our views of Jonson's method
no dishonour is done to his pride of place. It always
remains possible to the reader who is unconcerned with

the why and how of Jonson's borrowing to say frankly
with Rymer : "Nor can I be displeased with honest Ben
when he rather chooses to borrow a melon of his
neighbour than to treat us with a pumpion of his own
growth." [1]

The interest of the problem centres in his *Discoveries*,
a prose miscellany issued posthumously in the second
volume of the 1640 Folio (but dated separately 1641),
probably under the direction of Jonson's friend Sir
Kenelm Digby. The book is known by several titles,
of unequal authority ; *Explorata or Discoveries* (or simply
Discoveries, as in the page-headings), which is clearly
Jonson's choice, and the most satisfactory ; *Timber*,
inserted in the title-page, and there only, presumably
by the editor, with the purpose of linking up the book
in a figurative way with *The Forest* and *Underwoods* ;
and *Sylva*, erroneously applied by some on the strength
of the "Υλη passage printed on the back of the title and
transferred by the editor from its appropriate place in
the true 'Sylva' or *Forest*. These Discoveries, as the sub-
title tells us in words which we have no reason to doubt
were taken from Jonson's manuscript, are "made upon
men and matter, as they have flowed out of his daily
readings, or had their reflux to his peculiar notion of
the times," and deal, in one hundred and thirty-seven
sections of varying length, with matters of practical
interest in conduct, politics, and literature, but chiefly
with the last on its theoretical side. The book makes
no pretence to system. The notes were apparently
made at different times, as passages, memorable and
provocative, were encountered in his reading. It is

[1] *Tragedies of the Last Age*, Edition of 1692, p. 143.

possible that the earlier were destroyed with his library,
and that some were recovered by recollection or modified
in their application.   Digby appears to have done little,
if anything, to throw the connected passages together.
What grouping there is, especially of the remarks on
style towards the end of the book, is self-explanatory.
Each series of paragraphs on a single topic was obviously
written by Jonson in sequence as he proceeded with his
reading.   The Latin headings seem to be his own.

The collection has been, in recent years, the subject
of much controversy, more or less irrelevant.   For a
long time after its publication, it attracted little notice
even in critical quarters where Jonson's work was
appreciated.   Dryden refers to it two or three times in
the *Essay of Dramatic Poesy*; Pope twice in the preface
to his edition of Shakespeare, but only for its testimony
to the blotting of lines, which he mentions again in the
Epistle to Augustus [1], and to Ben's personal regard for
his great rival.   The neo-classicists generally remained
indifferent to a text so rich in material for the making
of their critical mosaics, and it was not till late in the
nineteenth century, and somewhat unexpectedly, that it
found in an eminent poet a student and panegyrist.   We
should like to hear, in some 'Imaginary Conversation,'
honest Ben's opinion of Swinburne's eulogy, which left
hardly more than two thirds of an elaborate essay for
the whole tale of plays, masques, and verse.   The
strange disproportion is not an effect of that tangential
fervour which so often sets the poet-critic shouting
about the stupidity of other critics, but in defence of
a pronouncement that "a single leaf of his *Discoveries*

[1] Line 279.

is worth all his lyrics, tragedies, elegies, and epigrams
together."[1] So the "golden little book" found, though
late, many friends for its own sake, as was just and
proper, and with these some, who, not less properly,
were impressed by its value as an *apologia*. Above all,
it was to them Jonson's own, as original as his comedies,
however much he had borrowed in it as in them. Then
came Dryasdust to vex the Swinburnians by showing
that one patch here and another there were not mere
coincidences in critical wisdom but literal translations
from well-known Latin writers; and these detective
activities were so successful, that by 1906 there was
little left to Jonson. But the antiquaries, humanly proud
of their quest, were as far out in placing this book as were
the ecstatic persons who saw nothing but "fresh and
vigorous spontaneity."[2] Let us face the facts and get
a truer perspective of the book, and at the same time
confirm its importance.

The extent of Jonson's borrowing, as traced so far,
may be roughly indicated by saying that he draws
from over thirty authors, and from some at considerable length. From classical writers, from Aristotle to
the Latins of the Silver Age, he takes most, and in
particular from the two Senecas and Quintilian. The
last heads the list with no less than twenty-five extracts
or adaptations; the younger Seneca makes a close
second with twenty-one, and the elder follows with
eleven. The younger Pliny, Plutarch, and Horace
yield four passages; the rest, including Cicero, Plautus,
Juvenal, Apuleius, Vitruvius, with a dozen others, are
quoted occasionally. There are Humanists too, among

[1] *A Study, u.s.* p. 124.   [2] *Ib.* p. 130.

them Vives, Erasmus, Justus Lipsius, J. C. Scaliger,[1] and D. Heinsius, the first the source of at least nine topics, discussed in three main passages, the last of at least five of considerable length. In four places Jonson draws from Machiavelli, and in at least four from Bacon.

It would be easy to say that this range of indebtedness, extensive as it is, is to be expected in Jonson, and might be paralleled by the crowded reminiscence in a single comedy. He has his rights, by Dryden's decree, as an invader. Closer inspection, however, puts a different complexion on the purpose of the conveyance. Here it is not merely 'invasion,' for spoils and trophies; it is annexation of the most thorough-going kind. In some cases paragraphs are taken over bodily in close verbal translation; in others, and often when the younger Seneca is at his elbow, the original is 'telescoped,' not as in a précis, but by the 'cutting' of sentences after the stage manner, or as in his treatment of the letters of Philostratus when he built up his lines *To Celia*; in a third pattern he disperses the original sentences and reorders them with little or no internal change; and in a fourth he adapts his quotations, by the alteration of names or by excision, but without any material interference with the words, to some modern instance, in order to illustrate, "their reflux to his peculiar notion of the times." Four-fifths of the book have been accounted for in this way and the remaining fifth may yet have some of its secrets torn from it. The reader who is interested in examin-

---

[1] Mr. Percy Simpson has added the younger ('J. J.'), among others, to the list of creditors (*Mod. Lang. Rev.* 1907, p. 201).

ing the proofs of this extensive borrowing must turn to
the editors[1]: here there is only space for a sample or
two. "I am not of that opinion," says Jonson, in the
critical section towards the end (§ 130), "to conclude
a poet's liberty within the narrow limits of laws, which
either the grammarians or philosophers prescribe. For,
before they found out those laws, there were many
excellent poets that fulfilled them: amongst whom
none more perfect than Sophocles, who lived a little
before Aristotle. Which of the Greeklings durst ever
give precepts to Demosthenes? or to Pericles, whom
the age surnamed Heavenly, because he seemed to
thunder and lighten with his language? or to
Alcibiades? . . ." There is nothing in this to make us
suspect that it is not a jotting of Jonson's own. The
use of the first person and of the term Greeklings and
one or two other touches would disarm that suspicion,
if it had arisen. Yet what says Daniel Heinsius in his
tract on tragedy? "Neque in ea sum opinione, ut ad
eas quas grammatici praescribunt, aut philosophi
angustias, poetae libertatem esse revocandam arbitrer.
Cum praesertim ante observationes has summi in
tragoedia extiterint poetae. Nemo enim postea ad
majestatem Sophocleam, meo quidem animo, accessit,
quem non paucis annis ante Aristotelem, philosophorum
regem fato suo functum satis constat. Verum idem
aliis in artibus quoque usu venit. Nam quis Graeculorum
unquam qui dicendi traderent praecepta, ad divinam et
fatalem vim Demosthenis accessit, qui plerisque multo
est antiquior? Nec Pericles ante eum, quem Olympium
dixere, quod tonare ac fulgurare videretur, neque

[1] Especially to M. Maurice Castelain, in his edition, Paris [1906].

Alcibiades. . . ."[1] When Swinburne quotes "I cannot think Nature is so spent and decayed that she can bring forth nothing worth her former years. She is always the same, like herself; and when she collects her strength, is abler still. Men are decayed, and studies: she is not,"[2] and remarks "how grand is this," we turn to a page of Vives. If the last sentence, of which Swinburne says, "Jonson never wrote a finer verse than that, and very probably he never observed that it was a verse,"[3] is not in Vives, it arises easily out of the borrowed observations. "There is a distinct streak," says Swinburne again,[4] "of what is usually understood as Machiavellism in the remark, that when a prince governs his people 'so as they have still need of his administration (for that is his art) he shall ever make and hold them faithful.'"[5] Undoubtedly, when we read the very words in the tenth chapter of *The Prince*, that thus is it done, so that the people may have "bisogno dello stato di lui, e sempre poi gli saranno fedeli." In another place[6] we are told that the hundred-and-fourth section "De sibi molestis" is worthy of Epictetus or Aurelius, and that its second sentence is an "awkward and affected Latinism," Ben being often blind to the fact that what "makes very good Latin may make very bad English." Excusably, let it be said, when he is translating closely from Seneca's letters to Lucilius (No. cxv.). Or again, when we are referred to the "fine passage" in which Jonson shows his hatred of indolence—"It is a false quarrel against nature that she helps understanding but

---

[1] *De Trag. Constit.* i.   [2] *Discov.* § 20.
[3] *A Study, u.s.* p. 132.   [4] *Ib.* p. 152.   [5] *Discov.* § 90.
[6] *A Study, u.s.* p. 163.

in a few (§ 117)"—we find we are reading, as plainly as
English can guide us, Quintilian's words on this *falsa
querela* in the opening chapter of the *De Institutione
Oratoria.* If the Swinburnians must yield these outlying
trenches, they dig themselves in again, confident that in
their inner positions they can defy further raids. It is a
reasonable confidence that the antiquaries will never
think of suspecting the autobiographical and personal
passages. Yet even in these there is no security. The
section on Memory (§ 56) is described as a "touch of
mental autobiography, not less interesting than curious,"
and the critic adds, "Had Shakespeare but left us the
like !"[1] Jonson's initial reference to Seneca the elder
as the possessor of a miraculous memory is treated as
a mere allusion and the main part of the passage
beginning with "I myself" is accepted as Jonsonian
memoir. But we find that the "I" is no other than
the Rhetorician himself, that, though an adapted phrase
like "till I was past forty" suggests the autobiographic,
the whole is even in its more intimate places a deliberate
extract from the first book of the *Controversia.* So, too,
another suspected fragment of autobiography,[2] *Otium
studiorum* (§ 68), with its "I have known a man," is
carried over from the preface to the same book of the
elder Seneca : just as the well-known passage on
poverty in *De bonis et malis* (§ 100), beginning "At last
they upbraided my poverty ; I confess she is my
domestic," is no other than the "Idem mihi etiam
paupertatem opprobravit, &c." of the eighteenth
chapter of the *Apologia* of Apuleius. The familiar
loci on Shakespeare and Bacon are of exceptional

[1] *A Study, u.s.* p. 137.   [2] *Ib.* p. 147.

interest. The first, *De Shakespeare nostrati* (§ 64), has all
the appearance of direct impression. With the exception of the phrase " sufflaminandus erat," which is quoted
as a saying of Augustus, there is nothing to suggest
that Jonson is not making a first-hand sketch. There
is an immediate touch in the reference to the players
and their gossip of Shakespeare, in Jonson's "male-
volent speech" and his defence of it to posterity,
in his honouring of his rival "on this side idolatry,"
in the criticism of Caesar's "ridiculous" line. Yet
the quoted words of Augustus help us to discover
that the famous passage is a conveyance of some
remarks by the elder Seneca, in the preface to the
fourth book of the *Controversia*, and that the censure—
all question of its personal and critical importance
apart—is an ingenious adaptation of a literary model.
This is clearly shown not only in the number of
borrowed 'points,' but in their sequence throughout
the passage. If the opening remark on the blotting of
lines is in itself too free to be called a copy of Seneca's
initial "tanta erat illi velocitas orationis, ut vitium
fieret," what shall we say of these, among other
identities—"in sua potestate habebat ingenium" for
"his wit was in his own power," "saepe incidebat in
ea quae derisum effugere non possent" for "many
times he fell into those things could not escape
laughter," or, better still, "redimebat tamen vitia
virtutibus et persaepe plus habebat quod laudares quam
cui ignosceres" for the closing words, "But he redeemed
his vices with his virtues. There was ever more in him
to be praised than to be pardoned"? There can be
no quarrelling with these facts. Though Mr. Saintsbury

makes amiable fun of the antiquaries in their discovery
of *Discoveries*,[1] there can be no controversy about the
Controversia in this passage. The Senecan debt is here
too clear, and is not to be dismissed as an occasional
borrowing of phrase, like "insolent Greece or haughty
Rome," also from Seneca and also in application to
Shakespeare, in the familiar verses in *Underwoods*.[2]
In the second personal criticism, that on Bacon (§ 71),
we have a similar problem; and again the source
is the *Controversia* (iii. 2). The Lord of Verulam is
Severus Cassius *redivivus*, as the elder Seneca found
him. "Oratio eius erat valens, culta, ingeniosis plena
sententiis"; "nulla pars erat, quae non sua virtute
staret, nihil in quo auditor sine damno aliud ageret,"
as in Bacon's case his hearers could not cough without
loss; "nemo magis in sua potestate habuit audientium
affectus," or "no man had their affections more in his
power"; "nemo non illo dicente timebat ne desineret,"
or "the fear of every man that heard him was lest
he should make an end"; "quamdiu citra jocos se
continebat, censoria oratio erat," or, as Jonson says of
the noble speaker, with the intimate touch "in my
time," "his language (where he could spare or pass
by a jest) was nobly censorious."

Facts such as these at once compel us to revise
the criticism which denies Jonson's indebtedness or
which brushes it aside as unimportant. We are dealing
neither with a brazen-faced plagiary nor with the
compiler of a commonplace-book. The collection is,
with all its confusion, too methodical for the latter, and
it is too extensive in its borrowings to be fraudulently

---

[1] *Hist. of Criticism*, ii. 204.   [2] No. XII.

passed off by any middleman in letters as his own.
It is true the passages thus closely related to previous
writings differ much in character: some are mere
apophthegms, jotted down as one would a motto for a
chapter or a legend for a carving over a fireplace;
some, which have deluded us by their personal and
contemporary touches, are no more than illustration
of a habit, common to most of us, of identifying a
friend's likeness in an old portrait or finding a use
for the thrust of an old phrase in a new set of
circumstances; some are quoted for their intrinsic
value to one who can appraise the good things of art
and promises himself the pleasure of refashioning
them in worthy English; some are selected for their
suggestiveness to an alert critic of life and letters, for
their aid to an intended, and it may be systematic,
commentary on the things nearest the poet's heart.
The last are the most important and supply the key to
Jonson's main purpose. They were chosen not merely
because they echoed his own views or discovered these
for him, but because they were material to be worked
up in later essays or incidentally in other work, even
in drama (as we know), when opportunity offered. If
a point was worth enforcing or a theory worth enlarging
it was all the better of corroboration, especially to a
classicist such as Jonson, and it was not less desirable,
when the argument was extant in perfect form, that it
should be boldly transferred. It is possible that in the
essays which he did not complete, or are lost, some
of the obviousness of this indebtedness would have
been blurred; and it is evident from the care which
he bestowed on the translating and on the eking and

touching-up to contemporary ends, and not least by
his repeating of himself, that all these things had
grown into the fibre of his work and had become,
as by nature, Jonsonian. If they are copies, they are
also "invasions" in the full sense of Dryden's compliment. The book has a strangely double character of
unoriginality and originality, and has therefore been
misunderstood by extremists, who, choosing one point
of view or another and taking up the cudgels for or
against Jonson's credit, have missed his purpose.

Nothing is clearer than that *Discoveries* is, as has
been already hinted, something more than a record,
in commonplace-book fashion, of other men's sayings
confirming Jonson in his artistic and critical faith. Had
this not been so, there is no reason why he should not,
and many reasons why he should, have copied out
the extracts in the original Latin and Italian. The
pains taken in translating, re-ordering, and adapting
each section suggests more than a mere relishing of
good opinion. That he had something else in view is
shown in two chief ways : the one formal, as an exercise
in the choice of words and turn of phrase, to the
achieving of a precise yet rhythmical prose [1] and the
justifying of his contempt for the "well-conceited
wittiness" of Euphuism [2]; the other, material and critical,
for argument to be developed and systematized elsewhere.
The latter is perhaps the more obvious. It is the high
seriousness of the book which attracts Swinburne. It
is so wise on many things of the critic's business, that

---

[1] Cf. "That vital, judicious, and most practicable language of
Benjamin Jonson's Poems," Bolton, *Hypercritica*.

[2] See *Cynthia's Revels*, V. iii. ; also *Every Man out of his Humour*,
V. vii.

we deeply lament the loss of the completed critical
statement, and would surrender a play or two and all
the verse for the burnt treatise on Poetics, with Donne
as one of the interlocutors. This material lies apart,
for separate use in the professional exposition of a
Jonsonian *Ars Poetica* ; it could not be expressed to any
extent in the body of drama or verse, except in the
off-hand way of the apostrophe to Poetry in the first
version of *Every Man in his Humour*, which Jonson's
dramatic instinct ultimately cancelled. The formal
interest of the book, if not obvious till the antiquaries
had taken the matter in hand, is now of first importance
to the study of Jonson's method. We might have overlooked the fact that his English renderings show more
than ordinary fastidiousness, had it not been brought
home to us that he had a further purpose for these carefully prepared notes.

Jonson, it will be recalled, told Drummond, when
giving him his "opinion of verses," "that he wrote
all his first in prose, for so his master Camden had
learned him."[1] If by "his first" we are to understand
the verse of his apprenticeship, the confession means no
more than that he continued a school method, still
familiar, of "versifying' prose selections in class-reading,
perhaps from the young Ben's own essays. In these
exercises he would be more interested in the "colours
or accent " as against the "sense " than he professed to
Drummond in later years. But the passage has generally
been interpreted in a more general way, that he had
always been in the habit of preparing a prose draft first,
and had afterwards recast it. In any case, and especially

---

[1] *Supra*, p. 244.

when the final form is verse, the work must lack spontaneity; it will be "laboured," though not necessarily
in the cruel sense applied to Jonson's by some of his
contemporaries, or to Dryden's by the author of *The
Rehearsal.*[1] The result must be the sole test; yet our
interest in the matter is that Jonson's procedure is
artistic in intention. If he chose to say so little about
the getting of his materials for his workshop, this only
shows more clearly what value he placed on the fashioning. To condemn him for stealing so carefully from
the ancients is both an irrelevance and an anachronism
in criticism; and to hint at intentional concealment of
his 'thefts' is, as his practice in the masques and elsewhere makes clear, and as Langbaine testifies in his
contrast of him with Dryden,[2] nothing less than unjust.
The condemnation also imposes upon *Discoveries* a purpose of publicity which its author never intended.

There are many proofs of the purpose for which
the collection was so carefully compiled by Jonson.
The argument acquires its force quickly by the cumulation of instances[3]; but here only an indication of the
method can be given, for Jonson's assimilation of his
translations, in his plays, prefatory matter, and verse,
is so extensive and subtle that many passages would
have to be quoted at length. Let two examples, one in
verse and one in prose, suffice. When Jonson puts

---

[1] See Bayes's account of his 'rules' in Act I.

[2] 'Dryden,' in the *Account of the English Dramatic Poets.*

[3] The reader whose judgement is still in suspense will be satisfied
after reading the detailed evidence of M. Castelain, in the Appendix
to his edition, and of Mr. Charles Crawford, in his *Collectanea*, I.
and II., who first pointed out the debt of the Address in *The
Alchemist* (see *infra*, p. 264).

into the mouth of Pennyboy Senior, in *The Staple of News*
(III. ii.), the harangue beginning—

> Who can endure to see
> The fury of men's gullets and their groins?

he not only has his notes on "Amor nummi" before
him,[1] but he does nothing more than convey in verse what
he had already conveyed from the younger Seneca.
Ideas and expression are the same. A few verbal
changes are made through metrical necessity or for
improvement. That some of the sentences and phrases
are given in different order, even when repeated *verbatim*,
but proves how closely the dramatist is editing himself. Only the more foolish of unfriendly critics will
describe the changes as an attempt to "cool the scent
of [his] own fox-like thefts."[2] Even more striking,
because less necessary in prose, is the mosaic address
'To the Reader' prefixed to the quarto edition of *The
Alchemist*. Its relationship to *Discoveries* has always
been clear, but few who have seen the likeness have
cared to examine Jonson's device in detail. It is
surely one of the most remarkable examples of editorial
zigzag to be found in English literature, perhaps in any
other. If the reader will turn to §§ 63 and 65 (notes 9
and 10) of *Discoveries*, he will find that he has all the
material, even the very words, of Jonson's critical onslaught in the Address to the Reader in *The Alchemist*.
When Gifford "retrieved" that Preface he called it a
'spirited composition," doubtless picturing to himself
Ben's throwing it off for an unworthy age, as *he* hurled
his gibes at Jonson's critics. Let us allow the spirit,

---

[1] *Discov.* (§ 101).   [2] *Discov.* § 68, *n.* 8.

but let us recognize the studied effort in polishing and *composing* the periods of Quintilian.[1]

Several problems of more general literary interest follow in the wake of this general consideration of Jonson's indebtedness. We select two for brief statement by way of conclusion to this chapter. The first deals with his "censures" of great contemporaries, especially of Shakespeare and Bacon. His attitude to Shakespeare has been treated as an outrage and has brought him more abuse than all his own failures. He was, as he tells us, pilloried for it in his own day ; and the bald record by the gossip of Hawthornden that his "censure" was "that Shakespeare wanted art" fixed a critical tradition which has survived the noisy protests of Gifford. Yet when we calmly examine what Jonson actually wrote, and what he himself said of it, we may wonder at the long tale of misconstruction. Jonson has many references to Shakespeare. These fall naturally into three groups. In the first they are incidental and of the allusive kind, passing touches on Caliban and Doll Tearsheet, on *Pericles* and *Julius Cæsar*, or, as in the Prologue to *Every Man in his Humour*, on his rival's practice in three or four different plays—a few perhaps personal or querulous, but the most with a purely critical purpose. In the second we have formal eulogy, in the lines for the portrait of the First Folio, and the longer poem "To the Memory of my Beloved" in the same volume.[2] The third group contains the more informal and intimate observations

---

[1] *Inst. Orat.* II. xi. xii.

[2] The Dedicatory matter there has been finally excluded from the Jonsonian canon.

preserved in the *Conversations* (such as the comment on
the sea-coast of Bohemia in *The Winter's Tale*, § xii.),
in *Discoveries*, and in the anecdote reported by Sir
Nicholas L'Estrange, or in another, associated with
Hales of Eton by Tate, Gildon, and Rowe.   In neither
the second nor the third group—and these alone are
of importance—is there any ill-considered or ungenerous
expression, though Dryden, in an unhappy moment,
spoke of the second as "an insolent, sparing, and
invidious panegyric, where good nature, the most god-
like commendation of a man, is only attributed to your
person, and denied to your writings."[1]   Indeed, there
is praise enough, even for the greatest of poets; but,
because it is conjoined with honest comment of a
critical kind clearly intended to explain and enforce
the admiration, it has been taken for cavilling and
proof of unfriendliness and insincerity.   For this Ben's
subtlety in verse-conceit, not less than his critical
finesse, is to some extent responsible.   The opening of
the longer poem,

> To draw no envy, Shakespeare, on thy name,

might be called unfortunate.   The reference to "peers"
and to the outshining of Lyly, Kyd, and Marlowe, and
the compliment with the qualification of "small
Latin and less Greek" are easily misunderstood;
and meanings have been wrested from words like
"censure" and "wanted art" which neither Jonson
nor the English of his day could allow.   Yet there is
nothing more remarkable in Jonson's judgement—the
precursor of all our Shakespearian criticism, wise and

---

[1] *Essay on Satire.*

foolish—than its generosity. We must measure that generosity by the wide difference in the critic's outlook. What man, from Longinus downwards, with Jonson's scholarly prepossessions, with the theorist's views on the rules and labours of Art and the active reformer's consciousness of the mistakes of his age, with a domineering and aggressive way with opponents, has adjusted himself so to the understanding and praising of work in many ways so alien to his taste and practice? Has not Jonson, while commending Shakespeare's natural genius, also praised (*pace* Drummond and the repeaters of his crude phrase) his art?

> Yet must I not give Nature all: thy Art,
>> My gentle Shakespeare, must enjoy a part.
> For though the poet's matter Nature be,
>> His Art doth give the fashion : and that he
> Who casts to write a living line must sweat
>> (Such as thine are) and strike the second heat
> Upon the Muses' anvil ; turn the same
>> (And himself with it) that he thinks to frame ;
> Or for the laurel he may gain a scorn ;
>> For a good poet's made, as well as born.

And so there was no malevolence in his too famous retort about the blotting of lines, whatever the players and later critics have thought ; as there was none of the insolence of lesser fry like Cowley who would not shirk from showing how the blotting should be done.[1] Jonson by his "candour" has been harder upon himself than upon the friend whom he loved, and whose memory he honoured "this side idolatry." His last sentence in the note in *Discoveries* has proved even more unfortunate : "There was ever more in him to be praised than to be

---

[1] See *supra*, p. 247.

pardoned." On this Swinburne says, "It needs the utmost possible exertion of charity, the most generous exercise of justice, to forgive [this] final phrase of preposterous patronage and considerate condescension." [1] What would not this critic have said, to the confusion of charity and justice, had he suspected that the phrase was a plain conveyance from the elder Seneca? But we are here concerned with Jonson, not Jonson's critic, and less concerned with the validity or impropriety of Jonson's judgement than with his intention in thus laying hold of other men's phrases about other men. Nothing helps us better to see the dominance of the literary 'humour' in Jonson, or better hints at that divergence between 'laboured' and 'flowing' style and explains what is truly 'classical' in Jonson's talent. Do we doubt that these characterizations had an accidental origin, that in his wide reading Jonson encountered passages which served with sudden conviction as sketches of his friends and their work? As Haterius or Cassius Severus, so Shakespeare or Bacon. Or need we doubt that he was tempted, as we have already hinted, to offer what was at best only an illustration as an identity and perfected opinion; that, though he may have started with definite views of his own, he was induced, as it were, by the compliment of Seneca's agreement, not only to adopt the ancient parallel, but to borrow details of which he had not thought, or which, taken by themselves, he might not have been willing to acknowledge, either in substance or expression? It may surprise us that a writer so self-possessed as Jonson was willing to make the exchange, and to quote so freely, whether

[1] *A Study, u.s.* p. 140.

in the order of his original or in a mosaic of his own
making—even though we allow that the notes have a
private character and might have been recast in the
essays which he had in view : just as it may surprise
some to find that the conceits in the lines facing the
Droeshout portrait in the First Folio Shakespeare are so
hackneyed and the last of them strongly reminiscent
of the verse inscription for Du Bartas's picture in
Sylvester ; or that the phrase " insolent Greece or
haughty Rome" applied in the passage on Bacon from
Seneca appears in the eulogy of Shakespeare ; or that in
that eulogy he thought it worth while to seek a foot-
hold in the ingenuities of some verses by Basse.[1] Yet
all these reflections help us little, if we overlook the
fact that Jonson's interest was primarily and mainly
formal. Realist though he was at times, when the
special purpose of his drama demanded, and at others
provokingly academic, he had always the artist's sense
and care of language. He tasted words and phrases as
a connoisseur ; and it is not too much to say that in his
critical portraiture the first suggestion, as well as the
shaping forth, was mainly literary. Was it not the
imperial phrase, " Haterius noster sufflaminandus est "—
the "noster" and "sufflaminandus" — which pleased
Ben for its own sake, then called up the contemporary
association, and set him a-work to see how far and how
well the rest of Seneca's words could be turned to
account ; just as in another place in the same author the
" censoria oratio" of Severus Cassius inspired his picture
of Bacon. In most, if not all, of these derived or adapted
passages the 'literary' interest transcends the critical

[1] Ed. 1893, p. 115.

and personal : in those which he took over bodily it is
not hard to see that he was attracted by the manner of
his original as much as by its matter, and that he found
his task accordingly.   For this reason he ran more
than the ordinary risks in adapted criticism of the
' Shakespeare ' and ' Bacon ' kind, by forcing the analogy
from considerations which were artistic rather than
exegetic.   These might supply some excuse for him,
were excuse necessary ; but the author of what is
perhaps the most generous and sincere tribute to a
friend's greatness needs no defence.   Our " charity "
and straining after " justice " would be " preposterous
patronage " and " condescension."

The second point is Jonson's relationship to Bacon,
not merely as shown by his praise in the three sections
of *Discoveries* (§§ 71-73), but by his general indebtedness,
in matter and form, in that book and elsewhere.   The
evidence has now been marshalled so fully [1] that it
is here unnecessary to illustrate Jonson's intimate
knowledge of the *De Augmentis*, the *Essays*, and the
Promus.   The deliberate extracts in *Discoveries* by no
means sum up his obligations.   Bacon's influence is
everywhere, in turn of phrase, in the " colour " of the
reflections on men and matters, in the exposition of
literary theory, and in the general habit of the book.
Jonson says " he may be named and stand as the mark and
$\dot{\alpha}\kappa\mu\dot{\eta}$ of our language " (§ 72), and he is thinking not less
of Bacon's art than of his wisdom.   The argument in the
Advancement of Learning against " affectionate study of
eloquence and copy [2] of speech " was after Jonson's heart

[1] By Mr. C. Crawford in his chapter on ' The Bacon-Shakespeare
Question ' in *Collectanea* II.   [2] Copiousness, *u.s.*

and may have helped him to formulate his own views. Bacon's writing had the precision, the 'decorum,' the care which he prized as the gift of the classical spirit. " No man ever spake more neatly, more pressly, more weightily, or suffered less emptiness, less idleness, in what he uttered" (§ 71). With Jonson this did not rest merely as a critical conviction. It was a lesson to be applied in the practice of his art; and so *Discoveries*, even in its incomplete sections, is a set of Essays in the strictest Baconian sense. It is immaterial that the book as we know it is in disorder : each part declares by its self-discipline what the finished work would have been. If Jonson is severe on those who "turn over all books" and write "without choice," and condemns "all the essayists, even their master Montaigne" (§ 65, *n.* 6), he is not thinking of Bacon as one of these. For they " in all they write confess still what books they have read last, and therein their own folly so much, that they bring it to the stake raw and undigested ; not that the place did need it neither, but that they thought themselves furnished, and would vent it" (*ib.*). A book of essays may be a miscellany of topics, but no single essay must be miscellaneous and 'undigested.' Discursiveness, as indulged by the great Frenchman, was to Jonson flat contradiction of the whole art. *Montani nostri sufflaminandi sunt.*

CHAPTER IX

INFLUENCE

ONE is tempted to conclude that because Jonson produced so much and in such diverse kinds, and because he was in close personal and literary touch with so many contemporaries, he must have impressed himself upon the fashion of letters then and for some time to come. One assumes, too, that his influence must have been positive, that he won something more than the notoriety which comes to the man who picks his own quarrel and fights it with spirit to the end. For Jonson, least of all our writers, made a lottery of art; he reasoned out his purpose and applied himself to it with a care, sometimes, it is true, painfully laboured; he had, if any man had, the personal momentum which can coerce an indifferent or hostile public. Yet experience tells us how little the most masterful talent may affect the main current of literature; how mere weight, even if imposed without Jonson's bluster, may be no more than a passing embarrassment to one period and may be forgotten by the next. Jonson's case has been to some a favourite illustration how energy and strong personality may be ineffectual in moulding taste or in securing fame. It is said that it has fallen out with him as he deserved, that

272

he was a ruffler, that he resists our better acquaintance as he resisted the goodwill of so many in his day, that he stands condemned by his own angry confessions of failure, and that if he is worthy of a place in the record of English Men of Letters, it is not because he is entertaining or inspiring or even readable as other writers are, and some learned and argumentative persons can be, but only for professional and 'grammarian' reasons. We do not require to be sealed of the Tribe of Gifford to protest that this limitation is too partisan, or to say that all the dislike of the early seventeenth century of an undisciplined Jonson and his over-disciplined art does not exclude the possibility of his having exerted considerable influence, even upon the most unfriendly. If to some Jonson is an egotist and, by consequence, sterile, to others the completeness of his literary character conveys a contrary lesson. Perhaps both are right.

Rarely, if ever, has criticism of Jonson been impersonal, in the way we speak of Spenser or Shakespeare. It is the man hardly less than the writer who provokes controversy in his lifetime and excuses indifference in ours; and Jonson himself might have found it difficult to decide between his dictatorship and his cared-for 'Works' as the final test for posterity. The familiar parallel with his great namesake of the eighteenth century is still useful. Ben's 'honesty' and hatred of cant, his magisterial manner, his 'bearishness' and good heart, his 'solidity,' his conservatism, his conviviality, his bodily habit and ill-health call the Doctor to mind with astonishing accuracy, notwithstanding some fundamental differences — nowhere clearer than in the comparison of the temper of the *Ode to Himself* with that of the *Letter to Lord Chesterfield*. The true significance, however, does not lie in the identity of the pictorial details, but in the suggestion of a strong personal influence, which is only indirectly literary, which gives little hint of a discipleship such as Chaucer or Spenser inspired, which, in spite of Jonson's individual learning, comes from the salon rather than the study. It is Father Ben and his circle, as it is the Great Cham and his. Even now we confirm them in these domestic privileges, to the forgetting of their Alchemists and Princes of Abyssinia.

Though Jonson had no Boswell to recover for us the setting, or, let us rather say, the atmosphere which his personality partly created for its activities, he drew forth from contemporaries a remarkable record of opinion and reminiscence, which, though a miscellany, goes far to make good the loss. Indeed, of few of our older writers has so much gossip been preserved ; and its range and enthusiasm so overtop what comes from petty jealousy or is mere curiosity about a man who has forced himself before the public, that some good people must revise their views of Jonson's isolation. It was no mere text-book Morose who ruled it so at the Apollo, and was the chosen of the Tribe of Ben and a memory for wit and good-fellowship to so many. Fuller's anecdote of the wit-combats between the Spanish great-galleon and the English man-of-war may have encouraged, through no fault of the teller, this fiction of Jonsonian heaviness. The figure is easily pushed to suggest learned arrogance, slowness, and other qualities unwelcome at a tavern feast. A second story, from gossip through Tate, Gildon, and Rowe, backed up by some notes by

Drummond, of Jonson's habit of girding at Shakespeare's poor acquaintance with the ancients, has convinced many that our poet was a very troublesome guest. In both tales he is unfortunately pitted against Shakespeare, a situation of great risk to any one even then, but there is sufficient evidence that he held throughout his prime the undisputed place of symposiarch of English Letters. If the honour of inaugurating our first literary club belongs in strictness to Sir Walter Raleigh, let us remember that Jonson was one of the wits who, with Shakespeare (so runs the tradition) and fellow poets, antiquaries like Cotton and Selden, men of affairs, and others, made the venture at the Mermaid in Bread Street, Cheapside, a success, and that the renewing of these glories in the Apollo Room at the 'Devil and St. Dunstan' near Temple Bar[1] was Jonson's personal triumph. One likes to think that it was his fondness for criticizing his neighbours that helped to give the meetings at both houses their zest and to establish their literary character. Long before the Mermaid and 'Devil,' literature had found refuge in the taverns of London, and in Jonson's younger days there must have been few 'Centaurs' or 'Porpentines' in which a gadding Dromio could not have had a poet, in uninspired mood, for companion. But as the craft of letters grew in numbers and power, so that unconsciously facetious persons likened its haunts to nests of singing birds, and as the poetic thirst for sack did not abate, and would not, there came, as Raleigh was quick to see, an

---

[1] The Swan at Charing Cross, with one Ralph as host, also supplied Ben with good canary ; and he was known at the Mitre and elsewhere.

opportunity for professional good-fellowship, when the solitary might have something better than Boar's Head converse with wenches and Sir John's noisy friends. If Ben was tedious, even insolent to better poets, he may well be forgiven for keeping so many irritabilities in good countenance with each other and setting their tongues wagging to better purpose.

What these occasions meant to the inner circle of London wits has been memorably told by Francis Beaumont in a "Letter to Ben Jonson, written [1] before he and Master Fletcher came to London, with two . . . comedies then not finished which deferred their merry meetings at the Mermaid." It is honest compliment, confessing that the delights of the country, even at Grace-Dieu, had grown stale. In his longing to return he seems to recite all the articles of the Mermaid faith, good-fellowship, brilliant conversation, personal devotion, —all to be confirmed, nearly thirty years later, by the younger wits of the Apollo. His resolve that he will finish the work in hand before joining in again—strangely prudential in one of that rollicking company — has a significance which we do not miss, but which some have exaggerated and thought to find excuse for in the verse of Ben's 'sons' Marmion and Herrick. When Careless, in *A Fine Companion*, enters drunk, and is asked by Æmilia if he comes from the Apollo, he replies—

> From the heaven
> Of my delight, where the boon Delphic god
> Drinks sack, and keeps his Bacchanalias,
> And has his incense, and his altars smoking,
> And speaks in sparkling prophecies ; thence do I come !

---

[1] Probably as early as 1606 or 1607.

> My brains perfumed with the rich Indian vapour,
> And heightened with conceits, from tempting beauties,
> From dainty music, and poetic strains,
> From bowls of nectar, and ambrosiac dishes,
> From witty varlets, fine companions,
> And from a mighty continent of pleasure,
> Sails thy brave Careless.[1]

Æmilia may have had her doubts. But we are not Æmilias, and must not misjudge the clearest testimony. Though Bacchus, by indefeasible right, ruled the feast at the Devil and had for cellarer the ever‑famous Simon Wadloe — Jonson's "Simon the king,"[2] and the original of Squire Western's favourite song—all was to the honour of Apollo and the Muses.

If Marmion's "mighty continent of pleasure" sounds hyperbolical, there is Herrick, the brightest youth of the company, to tell us that Caecuban was not the full measure of their frolic.

> Ah Ben !
> Say how or when
> Shall we, thy guests,
> Meet at those lyric feasts,
> Made at the *Sun*,
> The *Dog*, the triple *Tun* ?
> Where we such clusters had,
> As made us nobly wild, not mad ;
> And yet each verse of thine
> Outdid the meat, outdid the frolic wine.

> My Ben !
> Or come again,
> Or send to us
> Thy wit's great overplus ;
> But teach us yet
> Wisely to husband it,
> Lest we that talent spend ;

---

[1] II. iv. [2] *The Staple of News*, II. i.

And having once brought to an end
That precious stock,—the store
Of such a wit the world should have no more.[1]

Or better still, in the mellowed bacchanal "To live merrily and to trust to good verses," written in 'banishment' at Dean Prior, does he help us to understand the subtler meaning of this comradeship with Ben and his 'sons.' Though "the golden pomp is come," as it had to the poets at Grace-Dieu, he will toast Ben's favourite 'ancients' in turn and swear that "only numbers sweet" survive life's wreckage. If, like his 'father,' he loved canary and could with Beaumont find no offence in being called "The Son of Beer,"[2] it was for no Fat Knight reasons, but to

present
My genius with a fuller blandishment.[3]

Or, best of all, Ben himself, in his *Leges Convivales* for the conduct of their festivity, cut in gold letters in marble over the chimneypiece in the club-room at the 'Devil.' The sum of these twenty-four rules, in concise Latin (too long to quote, much less translate) is this: good company—no fools and dullards, but 'learned' and jovial, and women-friends on occasion; good wine from "Old Sim, the king of skinkers"; good talk, "contests rather of books than of wine," avoiding solemn topics and quarrel, and undisturbed by the reading of dull poems. There is to be moderation in all things, in cups and in frolic (no ragging or breaking of glass): "neminem reum pocula faciunto." Fare must be simple;

---

[1] *An Ode for him.*   [2] *The Welcome to Sack*, l. 87.
[3] *Ib.* ll. 55-56.

and no unbidden fiddlers must intrude,[1] though for
variety the feast may end with dance and song. The
secrets of the symposia shall be respected : the drawers
shall be all eyes but silent, and the guests under threat
of expulsion for blabbing. What 'moderation' meant
to Jonson and his friends is undetermined, but there is
discipline enough, and of wit promise enough, to convince us that the praises of the Apollo were no mere
memories of good sack. Later topers might say,

> Thus to the place where Jonson sat we climb,
> Leaning on the same rail that guided him,[2]

and roll down as uninspired as when they came in.
And we may doubt that, when, long after, Dr. Johnson
made merry in the same room with Mrs. Lennox and
some friends,[3] till at five in the morning his face
"shone with meridian splendour," the ghosts of Simon's
company would feel that they had been outdone.
They might have shivered at the Doctor's libations of
lemonade, hot apple-pie, and tea, and found him and
the authoress of *Harriot Stuart* too formal. When, in
1783, the Doctor—"like his namesake Old Ben," says
Boswell—drew up the rules for his club at the Essex
Head, he helped us to a pretty contrast in human
documents, of two very human men.

Jonson's personal authority was not confined to
his chairmanship at the Apollo. The meetings there
were the corporate and formal homage (if formal be the
word) of men who honoured him not only as *arbiter*

[1] Cf. *Convers.* xvii. : "The best banquets were those where
they mistered no musicians to chase time."

[2] *The Hind and the Panther Transversed*, by Prior and Montagu.

[3] December 1750.

bibendi and grand master of revels. They called him
'Father,' and liked to call themselves 'Sons of
Ben.' They were 'sealed' of the 'Tribe of Ben.' This
spontaneous expression of respect, perhaps unique in
our literary annals, must not be misunderstood. The
'Tribe of Ben' was no more a 'school' or professional
coterie than the Areopagus had been in the preceding
generation. Howell, as devoted as any of the party,
could not claim to be literary, though he could
interest himself in offering a 'plot' for Ben's consideration (and, as it happened, just the kind that Jonson
would *not* meddle with), or write a rhyming letter when
sending a book desired by Ben,[1] or add five dull couplets
to a miscellany of posthumous praise. Youths like
George Morley, later Duppa's successor in the see of
Winchester, whom Waller rescued from arrest because
he was "one of Jonson's sons,"[2] were impressed by the
senior's learning. Though Herrick owed more, pro-
fessionally, than any, it was not altogether the critic who
spoke in him when he referred to the bad reception of
The Alchemist; any more than the rioting of Cleveland,
Carew, and Randolph, when *The New Inn* was damned,
was purely a protest in the interest of good letters.
There were others, like Sir Francis Stewart, sea-captain
and member of the Mermaid 'sodality,' to whom Jonson
dedicated his *Silent Woman*, and Dick Martin, to whom
The Poetaster was addressed, Recorder of London and
good fellow at many a "convivium philosophicum" at
the Mitre (Inigo's haunt) and elsewhere, whose chief

---

[1] *Familiar Letters, u.s.* p. 276.

[2] Johnson, *Life of Waller.* Waller told Aubrey that "he was
not acquainted" with Ben (ii. 275.)

fame is that he "died of a symposiac excess with his
fellow wits."[1] It was a large company this 'Tribe of
Ben,' larger indeed than the record of those actually
'sealed' would show. Of those who made profession
the greater number were not literary ; and of those
writers who did not there were many who in virtue of
their friendship and literary intercourse were as truly
of the fellowship, though the compliment could never
suggest that the work of these, whether we name
Donne or Beaumont or Drummond or twenty others,
was Jonsonian in quality. If Jonson was, as Saint-
Évremond told his great countryman, "le Corneille
d'Angleterre," it was as the acknowledged president of
literary society rather than as the spiritual director of
its moods.[2] He himself clears up the matter for us in
*An Epistle, answering to one that asked to be sealed of
the Tribe of Ben.*[3] He first rules out the inadmissible
persons :

> Let those that merely talk, and never think,
> That live in the wild anarchy of drink,
> Subject to quarrel only ; or else such
> As make it their proficiency how much
> They've glutted in and lechered out that week,
> That never yet did friend or friendship seek,
> But for a sealing : let these men protest.

With those who cannot "speak well" of others, dead or
living, he will have "no portion." "I study other
friendships." Prattle on politics and intrigue he abjures,
though it lose him credit with "the animated porcelain
of the Court" and his "frail pitcher" (even Jones must
have smiled !) run the risk of being "jostled" by the

---

[1] Aubrey, *Lives*, ii. 49.   [2] *Œuvres* (ed. 1725), iii. p. 49.
[3] *Underwoods*, LXVI. (? c. 1620–1625).

"coarser sort of earthen jars." We need not therefore
be in doubt as to the meaning of the reciprocal compliment conveyed in this giving and taking of the Seal.
There is no literary implication in 'son of Ben' as
there is in 'limb of Fletcher,' and in being of the Tribe
no such intimation of discipleship as the text-book tradition would suggest.

There is, however, another kind of evidence, which
hints at something more than the simpler delights
of acquaintance—the *Commendatory Verses* prefixed to
the plays, private testimony like that by Clarendon or
at second-hand through the *Conversations*, and, above
all, *Jonsonus Virbius*. We pass over the testimonials to
three of the comedies and the two tragedies, by Chapman,
Donne, Francis Beaumont, John Fletcher, and James
Shirley, among others. The compliments, which are
repeated at greater length in the *Virbius*, have little
prospective critical interest. Even Beaumont's "all I
have to flow from thee" is not unsuspect, or Shirley's
calling Ben "the poet's king," on the revival of *The
Alchemist* after his death. Clarendon's eulogy [1] is strictly
personal. He "owed all the little he knew and the
little good that was in him to the friendships and
conversation he had still been used to, of the most
excellent men in their several kinds," and to Jonson
among others named. Ben's name "can never be forgotten," for he "reformed the stage" and was useful as
a disciplinarian ("judgement to order and govern fancy,
rather than excess of fancy"); but chiefly because "his
conversation was very good." For a like reason Jonson
attracted the less sympathetic Drummond, to whose

[1] *Life*, ed. 1827, i. 34.

notes we are indebted for so much information about the poet's life, his circle, and his opinions. If its innuendoes on Jonson's uncomfortable manner, breaking out at the close into such bitter censure as that "he was a contemner and scorner of others," are indifferent witness to the poet's qualifications in conversation, they at least show that it was on these grounds that he made his strong appeal to many contemporaries. Something more, however, is disclosed in the *Jonsonus Virbius* which Brian Duppa had been collecting for over a year before Ben's death, and which he published under that title, suggested by Lord Falkland, early in 1638. When Howell sent his verse-contribution to the editor, "upon the solicitation of Sir Thomas Hawkins," he wrote: "It is a well-becoming and very worthy work you are about, not to suffer Mr. Ben Jonson to go so silently to his grave, or rot so suddenly"[1]—a sad confession that a power so founded on personality could not long survive. The book was a resurrection, as the title reminds us, but it took over thirty leeches to perform the job, as against single-handed Aesculapius for Hippolytus. As a literary operation it was not without chance of success, from the ardour of all the encomiasts and not less from their youth; for youth gives better warrant that the influence of the master will be continued as a living purpose. Yet the contributors were perhaps too young; Buckhurst was a boy of sixteen, many were in their twenties, and perhaps not more than half-a-dozen were above thirty-five. Also, only a small number had any experience of setting out their enthusiasms in literary form; for, though there

---

[1] *Familiar Letters, u.s.* p. 332.

were dramatists such as May, Cartwright, Mayne,
Rutter, Marmion, and even Ford, poets of later repute
such as Habington, Waller, and Cleveland, with writers
like Felltham, there was heavy ballast of rhymers, made
up of titled persons, clergymen, soldiers, college fellows,
and Templars. Westminster had its share; at least
five of the contributors were of Ben's old school. All,
"friends of the Muses," claimed to "revive" the
memory of their friend; they repeated what had been
often said of his work and much that he had said
himself; they commemorated, and only faintly suggested
that posterity would follow the pattern they admired.
What is most remarkable throughout this miscellany is
the uniformity or rather the identity of praise, which
would seem to show that what is not a rehandling of
Jonson's written pronouncements on his work had
grown to a common opinion in the conversations of the
circle. It reads like a record of the compliments
required and given at the Apollo or at "solemn feasts"
in the poet's lodging. Much of it is on the defensive,
combating the unfriendly commonplaces about Jonson's
borrowings, his heavy style and excessive learning, his
slowness in composition, his playhouse unpopularity,
even his "thirst." The libellers are met squarely, are
sometimes countered with thrusts at their incompetence,
sometimes reasoned with that they may see how they
have misunderstood one whom "choicer judges" hold
worthy to be "read as classic in [his] life." [1] The Virbians
lay stress on other characteristics : on Jonson's judgement
in selecting, his "wit" and "art," his learning and
"solidity," the "solemn measures of his wit,"

---

[1] *Jonsonus Virbius* (Cartwright).

> beyond a gaudy show
> Of boards and canvas, wrought by Inigo,[1]

his refining of poesy and his power of language, his
reformation of a "prostituted stage," his "ethic lectures"
in his comedies as well as his art in writing what "could
be acted," the realism of "his all-resembling pen," his
"copious Muse," and the "valour of his pen" — all
mingled with apostrophe, which the Chaucerians could
not have bettered, to the "poet of princes, prince of
poets" (West), the "king of English poetry" (May), the
"mirror of poets, mirror of our age" (Waller), "the
wonder of a learned age" (Cleveland), the "great soul
of numbers" (Cartwright). Much of this praise may be
described in the modest words of one of the company,
"'Tis noise we utter"[2] and "a task above our skill";[3]
but some of it comes from reputable pens and is by no
means negligible either as criticism or verse. It is all
very interesting as a monument of devotion, personal
throughout even to such intimacies as that the stage
"was bed-rid by thy age," that "slow are substantial
bodies," or that Jonson created the "book" of nature
a "work" of art; also interesting because it supplied
ready-made to later criticism some of its dicta concerning the dramatist.

Though Jonson was acknowledged by so many as the
master-force of his age, it is not difficult to see that
contemporary opinion commended him less for offering
a new literary gospel, whether by counsel or in his
practice, than for confirming them in the process of change
to which they were half-consciously committed. It is

---

[1] *Jonsonus Virbius* (Richard West).   [2] *Ib.* (John Vernon).
[3] *Ib.* (R Brideoake).

not playing with paradox to say that this force, with all its protest and fight and roughness, succeeded because it was really passive, or that a literary purpose which appears to be expressed and accepted on strong personal grounds succeeded because it was so impersonal. We have an incurable habit, not always bad in its effects, of tracing descents and founding 'schools' in literary history. We assume an 'influence' for Jonson because he shouted so loudly and was acclaimed so loudly, for-getting that the moving fashion of literature is less often controlled by the noisy and spectacular talents.

The problem resolves itself into one of representative character rather than of domination. It has a parallel in the contemporary case of Donne, who, since Hurd's day, has been linked with Jonson as the moulder of the poetry of the mid-seventeenth century. Both stand for reaction against the Renaissance in the Italian guise affected by the Spenserians—the one, as father of the Metaphysical Poets, countering the formal splendours with the subtleties, if not the asceticism, of the medieval spirit, and the conventions with the hurried intimacies of passion, the other, of the 'learned sock,' offering relief from disordered luxuriance by a reasonable use of classical discipline and 'good sense.' It is easy to see that no single-handed effort of Donne or Jonson could have diverted the national literature from the Spenserian and Shakespearian channels in which it had been flowing so strongly. As long as Elizabethan poetry retained its vigour of imagination, no excuse was necessary for its luxuriance or its conventions ; and no protest came except from the thin voice of academic criticism. But when the force began to fail, the poets

themselves felt the overweight of the Italian tradition,
and, joining half-unconsciously with the opposition of
the 'grammarians,' set about to throw it off. History
tells us of many tentative efforts to revolt, but it was
Donne and Jonson who first made the issue clear, the
one seeking to recover the direct touch of passion, the
other the direct touch of life, and both the free exercise
of intellect as against the revel of sense. With Donne
it was the rigid formalism of the Italianate manner,
the loveless loves of the sonneteers, which provoked him
to indulge the whims of intellect and feeling and to
express them in the most disorderly verse; with Jonson
it was this Petrarch, whom he "cursed" for putting
English poetry in the "tyrant's bed,"[1] and the amorists,
with all their affectations, who sent him to a world
of simpler moods and scrupulous habit, and gave him
pleasure in being crabbed or rough — "they can hit
nothing but smooth cheeks : they cannot express roughness or gravity"[2]—that he might rouse the Muse to
the realities of art. It was perhaps not obvious to the
age how this disorder and roughness made for classicism
and was a cure for the perilous facility of the older poets,
or why two writers so essentially classical in training
and outlook chose this way of attack upon the
Spenserians. Doubtless, the continuing, though reduced,
strength of the Petrarchan tradition forced the contrast;
as it was the violence of the contrast which readily
suggested to Jonson's opponents their 'libels' about his
harshness, pedantry, and heaviness. These faults struck
contemporaries the more forcibly because they were
committed by a writer of acknowledged power, and

[1] *Convers.* iv.   [2] *Discov.* 110.

partly because Jonson made a point of drawing attention to his method. Criticism took its cue from his attitude, and has always been strongly personal, whether friendly or severe. Yet Jonson was much less a deviser of new doctrine than an explainer of changes which were afoot. When some of his age spoke of the suddenness and violence of his 'reform' they were only confessing that they had not realized how things were shaping. They are more to be excused than we, with the long perspective of our literature behind us, in looking upon him as an innovator. The process would have gone on had there been no Jonsonian criticism to track out its course; as it was going on freely in Donne and others. This does not commit us to the other extreme that had there been no Jonson the result would have been much the same. But the caveat is proper, especially in a problem of 'classical' influence, when we think what criticism would have proved, say, to Collins's credit as a romantic leader, had his *Ode on the Popular Superstitions of the Highlands* been published, as it might have been, forty years earlier than it was. So, if we retain the epithet of original for Jonson and assume an 'influence' for him, we mean that his originality lies in his clear-sighted sympathy rather than his egotistic love of novelty, in his being the first to interpret the classical longing in the practice of letters; and that his influence was provocative and intensive rather than absolute, general rather than direct and personal. This is not to say that he had no following, even in mannerism. Herrick and Shadwell would show that he had 'sons' in a closer sense than is conveyed in the compliment of his friends of the Apollo. Yet it is remarkable how

few there are to claim direct descent, or how seldom
the partial likenesses are more than the mark of literary
race. Even the echoes of style, the phrases remembered
and recast, are rarer than in many a poet on whom the
public eye was never fixed as it was on Jonson.

If there is a presumption against the view that there
is no Jonsonian discipleship in the sense that there is a
Spenserian, the proofs would be looked for in comedy,
masque, and lyric, in which the poet worked with such
complete and admired effect. In comedy, especially,
the evidence of direct contact might be expected. We
are not, of course, concerned with pilfering like that
of Shirley, or of Dryden in his first play *The Wild
Gallant* (I. iii.), where Trice plays tables with himself,
as Carlo has his "drunken dialogue" with the two
cups in *Every Man out of his Humour* (IV. iv.), or with
frank adaptations like that of *The Alchemist* in F. Gentleman's *Tobacconist* in 1771. There is the usual crowd of
minors eager to acknowledge their kinship, most of
them in poor copies of 'humour,' plot, play-title,
character-names, or language, or merely in prologue
greetings—one or two, like Wilson and Brome, showing
how far intelligent imitation could go. There is the
vogue of the plays in the seventeenth century, in close
rivalry with Fletcher's and Shakespeare's, and the
effect of that vogue on the playwrights' practice, as a
corrective to Restoration habit. There is the persistent
reference in all quarters to some of the striking characters, occasionally, as in *The Anatomy of Melancholy*,
in aid of professional argument. There is the significance of the protest by Shadwell — that caricature of
'mountain-belly' and humours—that if the Jonsonian

U

lesson was then like to be lost, it had hitherto been
accepted.   And yet all this profession of following
is strangely superficial and unreal; a cribbing of
mannerisms and devices, with little or no critical appreciation of the deeper process which Jonson and his
contemporaries were expressing; with these, as with
Jonson himself, the indulging of the 'superior' pleasure
of correction.   The truth is there was little to copy.
Hints about time, place, plot-making, and other matters
of classical technique could not be translated into the
practice of a 'school,' and these were not Jonson's only.
Even his treatment of the Humours, the most arresting
part of his work in contemporary eyes, was tonic in
intention and not for the setting up of a pattern [1]; and
the poorer sort of imitators who took it in the latter
way, and in their blind devotion made comedy no better
than the "cable-hatband" stuff of Jonson's protest, only
show how poor is their claim to have been influenced by
his art.   At our distance direct influence of this kind
counts for little in comparison with what Jonson did to
define and guide the shaping forces which a declining
romanticism was setting free.   If we can fix on anything
which may be said to have affected seventeenth century
drama, it is the combination of satire (but a partial
drawing on Jonson's great reserves) with the zeal for
domestic realism.   For what is the Comedy of Manners
but Jonsonian in type, differing from that type mainly
by its throwing out the grittier elements in Jonson's
exemplars, their learning, their satirical excess, and, in its

---

[1] Though some would call the Jonsonian gull, Ben's triumph in
characterization, the father of the best in that kind—even of Sir
Andrew Aguecheek.

Restoration phase, their ethical sanity? Indeed, we may honour Jonson as much by thinking of him as a founder of the Comedy of Manners as the exponent of the Comedy of Humours.

We must speak in like terms of Jonson's masques, perhaps the most original of all his efforts. Their occasional character, their extreme artificiality, their limited range, the uncertainty of courtly fashion, *and* the Master Surveyor, are a very strong argument against any later effects which are not minor and of a technical kind : only their literary quality, which Jonson made his first concern, was likely to attract, if not the writers for the popular stage, some younger poets. So Mr. Gosse has remarked that "it is very strange that no writer upon the poetry of that age has noticed what an extraordinary influence the masques of Ben Jonson had upon Herrick."[1] He is thinking of Herrick's "fairy-fancies" and Jonson's mood in the masque of *Queens* and *Oberon.* This suggestion is not unreasonable, if it mean only that the young Herrick, in 1610, in the first flush of piety, had his thoughts of Queen Mab quickened by Ben's success. For there is nothing in the three Oberon poems to show a textual indebtedness of the loosest kind ; and it is hardly fair to a poet of Herrick's quality to assume he required Ben's introduction to "her Mabship" and the groves "tinseld with twilight," or was oblivious of what Spenser and Shakespeare had done, or what in Drayton and Browne and others down to his friend Simeon Steward was a common diploma-subject for adventures in verse. Besides, there was jovial Dick Corbet, bishop to be, Jonson's and Herrick's

[1] *Seventeenth Century Studies,* p. 117.

companion, who loved a fairy next his glass, who was known for his "romantic fancies," who dabbled in verse and produced his best in his *Fairies' Farewell*. Why not he, or another, or nobody in particular, for this setting of the fashion in fairy frolic?

Some have tried to see Jonson's influence at its strongest in the seventeenth century lyric. Mistaken views about the tradition of the 'Tribe of Ben,' the 'paternity' allowed by so many poets in this vein, the haunting timbre of "Drink to me only" and others in Cavalier song have helped easily to this conclusion. "He that loves a rosy cheek" or "Ask me no more where Jove bestows" makes Carew at once a debtor in some critical ledgers; even Herbert must do homage to Jonson as well as Donne; and Milton, to many since Godwin's day, draws as much inspiration from the formal beauties of the masques and odes as from Ben's learning and moral force. These half-truths seem to become whole-truths when all the borrowings of word and turn, which no one will dispute, are gathered up, when the parallel-mongers have taken toll of Herrick, the master 'lyrick,' and when others of a broader critical spirit are impressed by the family likeness of the *Night Piece to Julia* to the Second Song in the masque of *The Metamorphosed Gipsies*. Yet, when all is collected and pigeon-holed, it is a poor body of evidence of direct influence, and neither better nor worse than might be claimed for any one of a score of poets chosen at random. Jonson has no textual authority such as the less dogmatic Donne had over contemporaries, even over Jonson himself, or as Spenser had to a greater degree in his own day and later; and that he was better

"understood" than Donne was no security to himself
against the fate he foresaw for his friend's reputation
(*Convers.* xii.), notwithstanding his opinion that Donne
was "the first poet in the world in some things"
(*ib.* vii.). His verse was not accepted as a style-book
of metre, word, or phrasing, certainly not as a storehouse
of imaginative suggestion. But it helped the purpose
of the time by the emphasis which it laid on two
things, by pointing the way to Classicism as an escape
from a tired Petrarchism, and, partly in corollary to
this, by setting an example of considered and precise
craftsmanship. In neither case was a strict following
likely or even possible. Herrick is an example. All his
confessed devotion, his Jonsonian echoes, his delight in
tasting word and phrase, his belief that (as Ben put it)
"words borrowed of antiquity do lend a kind of majesty
to style,"[1] which Spenser, Shakespeare, Milton, and others
held—all this counts for little on the credit side. For
he rarely shows that superfine sense of the "colours" of
words and phrases which is Herrick's. His have a
bookish propriety, whereas Herrick's, though borrowed,
are convincing because they are inevitable, grown out
of as well as grown into the sensuous imagination of
the poet. The learned Jonson is spectacular, external,
English in his classicism; the parson of Dean Prior is
a true pagan, accepting the conventions of the past
only because of his spiritual sympathy with it. An
art expressing such a mood takes its guidance from
immediate predecessors only in a very incidental way. Of
metrical 'influence,' too, the same may be said. Waller,
who praised Jonson for many things, but is silent on his

[1] *Discov.* 119 *b.*

verse, best proves his claim to be "first in the list of refiners"[1] by the fact that he helped the ten-syllabled couplet to recover the 'flow' which it had lost in the rocks and eddies of Jonson's and Donne's manner; and Cowley is in his happiest verse—as in his lines on the death of Crashaw—but preparing for Dryden at the expense of Jonson. The religious lyric, the crown of the seventeenth century Muse, shows Donne's hand, not Jonson's, in the fashioning. Ben's comment on South-well is good self-criticism,[2] but it is without effect on his art. We might expect that in some kinds of lyrical work he would have profited by his comradeship at Whitehall and at the Apollo with the best musicians of the most musical age in English annals. If his happiest pieces forbid our saying that he had a poor ear, it may still be fair to think of his achieving these by a critical nicety in adjustment rather than by emotional necessity. At its best, or at its worst, his verse had little effect on poetic taste, though he in-terested some poets of later times and of the most diverse kinds.

What has been said is not to be interpreted as a denial that Jonson exerted influence in any of these directions, even in technique, but as a warning against the easy conclusions to which his strong personality, the acknowledgements by the Tribe, and his place in controversy in his own day and long afterwards have encouraged the good people who make literary history but the tracking of X in Y's snow. We are on safer ground when we turn from the narrower matters of

[1] Francis Atterbury's Preface to *The Second Part of the Poems*, 1690.   [2] See *supra*, p. 238.

text and expression to the general effect of Jonson's
critical attitude. To do so implies neither exaggeration
of his originality in framing rules or in expounding
them in his practice, nor contradiction of what has been
said about his being an expresser rather than the creator
of seventeenth century classicism. He said little that
Sidney and the Elizabethan critics had not said or hinted
at, or drew little from the ancient rhetoricians or from
their Italian and Dutch expositors that was novel or
alien to the changing taste of his time. But we may
claim for him that he is the protagonist in that
movement, not so much by awakening of contemporaries to an understanding of what the critical
doctrine involved, as by enforcing by his own example
a respect for more orderly and precise craftsmanship.
It is rather futile to argue whether Jonson was a
transformed or arrested romanticist or a classicist born
out of his time. He shows both sides, as all strong
writers do, and as his age certainly did, if somewhat
erratically ; and all his classicism does not exclude his
being at first, and remaining to the last, sympathetic with
the romantic spirit. We might even say that he was
not fully alive to the change which was already shaping.
The essential matter is that he, whether romanticist or
classicist by nature, fixed upon the faults of a decadent
romanticism, and offered a cure, as Spenser himself
might have done had he seen what Spenserianism and
the other -isms of the early seventeenth century had
brought in their train. He invited the attention of his
age to classical tradition not primarily because it was
older or different from what was in repute, but because
its sentiment and discipline provided for the immediate

necessities of English. No one knew better the individual merit of that tradition, yet few have been franker in maintaining that its true value was of the spirit and not of the letter. If *Sejanus* and *Catiline* seem to testify against this, it is perhaps because they are spectacular fakes, and are neither great in themselves nor characteristic of what all agree to consider his best work. "I know nothing can conduce more to letters," he says in a passage, partly adapted from Vives, "than to examine the writings of the Ancients, and not to rest in their sole authority or take all upon trust from them. . . . For to all the observations of the Ancients we have our own experience, which, if we will use and apply, we have better means to pronounce. It is true they opened the gates, and made the way that went before us; but as guides, not commanders."[1] He has no partisan interests in any *Querelle*, such as set many learned fools by the ears towards the close of the century. Unfortunately, some in his day thought or pretended to think he had, and made easy points about his pedantry, plagiarism, and dull artificiality, and in the hubbub of personalities drove all to a false issue. There was no difficulty in proving what Jonson was not; and his angry retorts, sometimes overstating his views to counter his opponents' excesses, but clinched their argument. Even men who were themselves half-consciously moving towards the 'classical' position, shouted with the die-hards against this Latinist and doctrinaire. It is doubtful whether many, then or later, understood Jonson's position. Dryden did, notwithstanding some hard things assumed by him rather for argument's sake and to help the

[1] *Discov.* 21.

dialogue of the *Essay*, as when he says, "I presume he loved their [the Ancients'] fashion, when he wore their clothes." But Dryden's critical sanity lets him see how sane Ben also was, and for what he really fought: nowhere more clearly than in the full-dress 'Examen' of the *Silent Woman* in the same *Essay*, and when he reasons out the matter of the Unities. He accepts these as Ben accepts his lessons from the Ancients, not because they are ancient or French but because of their essential and *immediate* value. We may say, without risking foolish reflections as to whether Dryden would have been different from what he is had there been no Jonson, that he found himself by the grace of Jonson. There lies Jonson's true influence, through Dryden to Dryden's age, not to be sought in textual cribbings and affectations of his manner, even in Dryden himself, but in the growth of a general critical temper. It is an influence too vague for the parallel-mongers who like to search for Herrick's echoings or Shadwell's copyings of 'humours'; too obscure to others who see Jonson only as a militant and extravagant classicist. We leave the first to their police tasks in the petty-sessions of criticism. The others, when they know Jonson and the seventeenth century better, will find that he is no follower of strange gods or a forcer of English conscience.

Yet we take poor measure of Jonson's claim, if we only say that his direct influence on the craft of letters is negligible, and that he merely encouraged it in a venture to which it was committed. Somehow we feel that it was his interest in critical speculation which directed him to the problems in his work as playwright and poet; that he did not proceed in the opposite

direction, from experience to theory. He was first
and always the critic and enquirer—*Tamquam explorator*,
or *Percunctator*, or *Perscrutator*, as in his mottoes—not
less strongly attracted than his 'rhetorical' predecessors
were by the philosophical aspects of literature ; and
he was the least likely of any to turn from these even
in the most crowded years of popular work. In that
work, in the text of his comedies, in the addresses to
his readers in the quarto editions offered for their
sixpences, he cannot away from the things which they
cannot care for or understand. In his *Epigrams* and
other poems he is often in the same mood ; as he appears
to have been at Hawthornden in the intervals of personal
gossip, story-telling, and drinking of healths. His views
on this or that poet's verses are not impressionist, but
explanatory of his systematized convictions. He meets
Campion and Daniel with an essay on prosodic principles,[1]
and supplements his translation of the *Ars Poetica* by a
dialogue on poetry, with Donne in the rôle of Criticus—
neither, alas ! extant to show in what good humour he
was with himself and his subjects. Great as is our loss
of these—and there are few other losses for which we
find it so hard to forgive the execrated Vulcan and all
the pastry-cooks and landladies of London—there is in
what we have ample evidence of his dominating critical
'humour.' When Dr. Johnson, in a phrase less cheap
than it has come to be in our time, called Dryden the
"father of English criticism," he was neither ignorant
of Ben's claims nor willing to underrate them. The
reflections in *Discoveries*, which he must have commended, are perhaps only "a few hints," when compared

[1] *Convers.* i.

with the "regular treatise" of Ben's successor, but these
are not the sum of the material on which the judgement
must be based. Johnson's compliment to the *Essay* is
enhanced by his recollections of the scattered aphorisms
throughout the rest of Dryden's work, but no parallel
aid is allowed to *Discoveries* from Ben's prefaces and
innumerable asides. By naming Webbe and Puttenham
in the same sentence with him, as early contributors
from whom "something might be learned," Johnson is
apparently unconscious of the wide difference between
these rhetorical gentry and the author of *Discoveries*,
wider by far, in spirit, knowledge, and expression, than
between Jonson and Dryden at his best. In the whole
group of Elizabethan critics, interesting as they are for
themselves and in the history of literary ideas, there is
little more than good kneading of the rhetorical dough.
Jonson is no such bakerly critic. When he borrows,
he borrows only because his 'authorities' confirm his
independent judgement. He is not a mere retailer
of tradition; nor is he an enforcer of rules till he
has convinced himself of their sanction and of their
contemporary relevance. On the other hand, when
we compare him with Dryden, we can say without
exaggeration, and with all his faults in mind, that
he holds his own by his critical touch and sanity of
judgement, and opens up a field of study which the
other did not choose to enter. If the honour of Father
or Founder is to go to any man, it must be to
him who, possessing the critic's faculty and the valour
to exercise it, was the first to endeavour to relate
practice to principle and to give Criticism her individual
place.

Let us welcome for objection to this comment on Johnson's honouring of Dryden, that he was thinking of Dryden's happier judgements—of Ben among many— and that there is nothing in our author to suggest what we generally understand by literary criticism, from the *Lives of the Poets* to *The Spirit of the Age* and its successors. The statement is a half‑truth which, like all half‑truths, brings its own answer, to the disclosing of what is perhaps Jonson's strongest claim upon posterity. Probably none saw, and none could be expected to see, that in the conflict of devotion and animosity which the dictator had inspired he had put into their hand, and they through him had begun to use, a new instrument which was to change the methods of the literary workshop. For he, as no one before in England, was sensitive to the finesse of the form and spirit of literature, and taught, while insisting on the value of experience and of the rules which it had framed, that the book itself—its purpose and individual manner—was the business of sound criticism. In a word, he is the first to show that directness and personal touch in the art of appreciation which is the mark of the later literary essay and which some have not traced farther back than Dryden. We have but to glance at what passed for this before, in the two centuries between the first eulogists of Chaucer and the crowd of praising and snarling pedants of Jonson's youth, to see that there is a change, or promise of change, in the literary attitude. We allow Jonson some credit on the side of theory, though not without a grudge that he is pilfering or at best dressing up old opinion ; but we do not look for any hint in his

practice of that difference in outlook and manner which
distinguishes modern criticism from the 'censures' of the
traditional rhetoric. Yet the hints are clear, if we have
patience with his liking for ancient models and with
his intoxicate learning. In one respect his claim is
beyond doubt, that he is the first to attempt the literary
'portrait' in English. His sketches of Shakespeare
and Bacon and others, incomplete though they are,
show a quality which we associate with no earlier
writer, but which we accept as peculiarly modern. It
is of little moment whether we can prove that Dryden
and his successors owed much or nothing to him for
the 'individual' art of their more elaborate 'examens'
and essays. In these matters Jonson is not unconsciously expressing a general change in the habit
of criticism, as we have said he expresses the general
change in the poetic habit of the seventeenth century.
Nowhere is he more deliberate, less tied to tradition
or contemporary fashion. The weakness of so much
of his larger effort is that it is occasional, that circumstance turns him to comedy or tragedy or masque or
verse, arranges his plan, and guides his invention. In
his critical sketches he seems to be free to enjoy and
to convey the direct and intimate impression, though he
is describing his English friends in language borrowed
straight from his admired Seneca. Puck has never made
better sport with a reputation or with its expositors
than when the virtue of original style was found in
trifles which had been condemned as unoriginal in
everything except 'malevolence.' It is all to the good
for it brings us nearer to the true Jonson, to the critical
Jonson who was more than a mere academic or law-

giver.   We may wish that he had ventured farther.   Yet
he did enough to secure abiding respect for this part of
his work, when the rest, more laboured, of his age
and *not* for all time, may be esteemed only as "matter
of antiquity."

INDEX

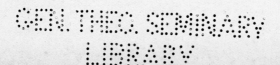
GEN. THEO. SEMINARY
LIBRARY

THE END

Printed by R. & R. Clark, Limited, *Edinburgh*.

GEN. THEO. SEMINARY
LIBRARY

BY THE SAME AUTHOR

Extra Crown 8vo. **8s. 6d.** *net.*

SCOTTISH LITERATURE
CHARACTER AND INFLUENCE

BY

G. GREGORY SMITH

THE ten essays or chapters in *Scottish Literature* are offered as a critical study of the general characteristics of Scottish Literature and of the influences which it exerted on others. They deal with a number of questions of historical and present-day interest: among others, the antiquarian habit of Northern Literature, foreign influences, the absence of drama, the problem of prose and of dialect, the contributions to the Romantic Movement and to critical journalism, the Northern Augustans, Burns, Scott, and the Moderns. The book is not a history, though it handles details in support of its argument, and, while restating some which are familiar to readers of Scottish Literature, offers others which may be allowed to be new or set in another light and in fresh relationships. The author's purpose is to give, for the first time, a general impression of the habit and process of the literature.

LONDON: MACMILLAN AND CO., LTD.

𝕰nglish 𝕸en of 𝕷etters

NEW SERIES

Crown 8vo.   Gilt tops.   Flat backs.   3s. net each.

MATTHEW ARNOLD.   By HERBERT W. PAUL.

JANE AUSTEN.   By F. WARRE CORNISH.

SIR THOMAS BROWNE.   By EDMUND GOSSE.

BROWNING.   By G. K. CHESTERTON.

FANNY BURNEY.   By AUSTIN DOBSON.

CRABBE.   By ALFRED AINGER.

MARIA EDGEWORTH.   By the Hon. EMILY LAWLESS.

GEORGE ELIOT.   By Sir LESLIE STEPHEN, K.C.B.

EDWARD FITZGERALD.   By A. C. BENSON.

HAZLITT.   By the Rt. Hon. AUGUSTINE BIRRELL.

HOBBES.   By Sir LESLIE STEPHEN, K.C.B.

BEN JONSON.   By G. GREGORY SMITH.

ANDREW MARVELL.   By the Rt. Hon. AUGUSTINE BIRRELL.

THOMAS MOORE.   By STEPHEN GWYNN.

WILLIAM MORRIS.   By ALFRED NOYES.

WALTER PATER.   By A. C. BENSON.

RICHARDSON.   By AUSTIN DOBSON.

ROSSETTI.   By A. C. BENSON.

RUSKIN.   By FREDERIC HARRISON.

SHAKESPEARE.   By Sir WALTER RALEIGH.

ADAM SMITH.   By FRANCIS W. HIRST.

SYDNEY SMITH.   By the Rt. Hon. G. W. E. RUSSELL.

JEREMY TAYLOR.   By EDMUND GOSSE.

TENNYSON.   By Sir ALFRED LYALL.

JAMES THOMSON.   By G. C. MACAULAY.

LONDON: MACMILLAN AND CO., LTD.